Samuel Beckett and the Terror of Literature

Other Becketts
Edited by S. E. Gontarski

Published
Creative Involution: Bergson, Beckett, Deleuze
S. E. Gontarski

Beckett's Thing: Painting and Theatre
David Lloyd

Samuel Beckett and the Terror of Literature
Christopher Langlois

Samuel Beckett and the Terror of Literature

Christopher Langlois

EDINBURGH
University Press

Per Valeria

Edinburgh University Press is one of the leading university presses in the UK. We publish academic books and journals in our selected subject areas across the humanities and social sciences, combining cutting-edge scholarship with high editorial and production values to produce academic works of lasting importance. For more information visit our website: edinburghuniversitypress.com

© Christopher Langlois, 2017

Edinburgh University Press Ltd
The Tun – Holyrood Road
12(2f) Jackson's Entry
Edinburgh EH8 8PJ

Typeset in 11/13 Adobe Sabon by
Servis Filmsetting Ltd, Stockport, Cheshire,

A CIP record for this book is available from the British Library

ISBN 978 1 4744 1900 0 (hardback)
ISBN 978 1 4744 4437 8 (pbk.)
ISBN 978 1 4744 1901 7 (webready PDF)
ISBN 978 1 4744 1902 4 (epub)

The right of Christopher Langlois to be identified as the author of this work has been asserted in accordance with the Copyright, Designs and Patents Act 1988, and the Copyright and Related Rights Regulations 2003 (SI No. 2498).

Contents

Acknowledgements	vi
Series Editor's Preface	viii
Abbreviations	ix
Introduction: Terror in Philosophy, Politics and Literature	1
1 The Terror of Thinking in *The Unnamable*	41
2 The Beginning (Again) and Ending (Again) of Terror in *Texts for Nothing*	96
3 The Writing of *How It Is* in the Paratactic Delay of Terror	139
4 The Terror of Passivity in *Company*, *Ill Seen Ill Said* and *Worstward Ho*	184
Coda: Literature at the Turning Point of Terror	240
References	244
Index	254

Acknowledgements

This book began its life as a doctoral dissertation under the supervision of Jonathan Boulter. I cannot overstate how instrumental he has been to the development of this book, particularly through the example of his own scholarship on Samuel Beckett. Other colleagues and mentors have contributed to and read parts of this book along the way, and they are all deserving of my sincerest thanks, but I want to especially thank Martin Kreiswirth and Andre Furlani for the time and care they have taken to read and comment on various aspects of this book ahead of its completion. It is also my pleasure to thank Stanley Gontarski for his enthusiastic support for this book.

I want also to thank Jonathan Fardy and Cosmin Toma for their company, conversation and above all their friendship. Cosmin has also read several sections of this book, and his erudite criticisms were instrumental in helping me get through some of its more intractable conceptual problems.

My warmest and deepest thanks go out to my mother, Mary Ann Langlois-Smith, for her sacrifices, her selflessness and her encouragement.

I have dedicated this book to Valeria Puntorieri, my partner and my love. Her hard work, devotion and intelligence are a daily inspiration for me, and I am simply better for having her in my life.

The time needed to research and write this book was made possible by the Social Sciences and Humanities Research Council of Canada, which funded me through Doctoral and Postdoctoral Fellowships at the University of Western Ontario and McGill University, respectively. Parts of the book have appeared in modified form in the journals *Twentieth-Century Literature* (Duke University Press) and *College Literature* (Johns Hopkins University Press), as well as in the essay collection *Immanent Encounters:*

Literature and the Encounter with Immanence (Brill), edited by Brynnar Swenson. I thank these publishers for their permission to reprint some of this material.

Series Editor's Preface

In 1997 Apple computers launched an advertising campaign (in print and on television) that entreated us to 'Think Different', and Samuel Beckett was one of Apple's icons. Avoiding Apple's solecism, we might modify the appeal to say that *Other Becketts* is a call to think differently as well, in this case about Beckett's work, to question, that is, even the questions we ask about it. *Other Becketts*, then, is a series of monographs focused on alternative, unexplored or under-explored approaches to the work of Samuel Beckett, not a call for novelty *per se*, but a call to examine afresh those of Beckett's interests that were more arcane than mainstream, interests that might be deemed quirky or strange, and those of his works less thoroughly explored critically and theoretically, the late prose and drama, say, or even the poetry or criticism. Volumes might cover (but are not restricted to) any of the following: unusual illnesses or neurological disorders (the 'duck foot, goose foot' of *First Love*, akathisia or the invented duck's disease or panpygoptosis of Miss Dew in *Murphy*, proprioception, or its disturbance, in *Not I*, perhaps, or other unusual neurological lapses among Beckett's creatures, from Watt to the Listener of *That Time*); mathematical peculiarities (irrational numbers, factorials, Fibonacci numbers or sequences, or non-Euclidian approaches to geometry); linguistic failures (from Nominalism to Mauthner, say); citations of or allusions to contrarian aesthetic philosophers working in a more or less irrationalist tradition (Nietzsche, Bergson or Deleuze, among others), or in general 'the simple games that time plays with space'. Alternative approaches would be of interest as well, with foci on objects, animals, cognitive or memory issues and the like.

S. E. Gontarski, Florida State University

Abbreviations

Works by Samuel Beckett

CP	*Collected Shorter Plays*, New York: Grove Press, 1984.
CSP	*The Complete Short Prose: 1929–1989*, ed. S. E. Gontarski, New York: Grove Press, 1995.
D	*Disjecta*, ed. Ruby Cohn, New York: Grove Press, 1984.
HII	*How It Is*, New York: Grove Press, 1964.
Letters II	*The Letters of Samuel Beckett: 1941–1956*, ed. Lois More Overbeck et al., Cambridge: Cambridge University Press, 2011.
Letters III	*The Letters of Samuel Beckett: 1957–1965*, ed. Lois More Overbeck et al., Cambridge: Cambridge University Press, 2014.
NO	*Nohow On: Company, Ill Seen Ill Said, Worstward Ho*, New York: Grove Press, 1996.
TN	*Three Novels: Molloy, Malone Dies, The Unnamable*, New York: Grove Press, 2009.

Works by Maurice Blanchot

BC	*The Book to Come*, trans. Charlotte Mandell, Stanford: Stanford University Press, 2003.
FP	*Faux Pas*, trans. Susan Hanson, Minneapolis: University of Minnesota Press, 1993.
F	*Friendship*, trans. Elizabeth Rottenberg, Stanford: Stanford University Press, 1997.
IC	*The Infinite Conversation*, trans. Susan Hanson, Minneapolis: University of Minnesota Press, 1993.

GO	*The Gaze of Orpheus and Other Literary Essays*, ed. P. Adams Sitney, trans. Lydia Davis, Barrytown: Station Hill Press, 1981.
SNB	*The Step/Not Beyond*, trans. Lycette Nelson, Albany: SUNY Press, 1992.
'RI'	'Responses and Interventions', trans. Michael Holland, *Paragraph*, 30:3 (2007), 5–45.
WD	*The Writing of the Disaster*, trans. Ann Smock, Lincoln: University of Nebraska Press, 1986.

Introduction: Terror in Philosophy, Politics and Literature

> The impulse to think, to inquire, to reweave oneself ever more thoroughly, is not wonder but terror.
>
> (Richard Rorty)

I

In 1991 Don DeLillo gave an interview with the *New York Times* where he vigorously, if not scandalously, defends what he regards as the terroristic dimensions of literature and fiction. 'In a society that's filled with glut and repetition and endless consumption', DeLillo speculates, it is imperative 'to connect novelists and terrorists', for 'true terror is a language and a vision. There is a deep narrative structure to terrorist acts, and they infiltrate and alter consciousness in ways that writers used to aspire to' (cited in Passaro 1991). Casting acts of literature as acts of terror is DeLillo's provocative way of reinvesting the contemporary republic of letters with the shocks and transformations of consciousness that a distinctly modernist ideology of art and literature is so notoriously remembered for perpetrating. DeLillo stops just short of naming which writers in particular aspired to the infiltrations and alterations of consciousness that literature and terror are singularly positioned to accomplish. He also leaves as an open question just what it is that binds literature so inextricably to terror (and vice versa). What exactly is the language and vision that terror shares with literature? How does terror alter consciousness such that it recalls what literature and fiction once aspired to achieve? Does the relation between terror and literature truly exist, and if so, which writers of the past might it be apropos to label as terrorists? Since 2001, DeLillo's fiction has not only become synonymous with literature in the aftermath of terror, but also inseparable from assessing the limits of redemption from historical catastrophe in the contemporary world that violence and the threat of violence, and more specifically terrorism and the war on terror, continue to overshadow and darken.[1] If there are to be any redemptive consequences of acts of literature and fiction, consequences aimed at waking us not least from the ideological slumber of 'glut', 'repetition' and 'endless consumption', then according to DeLillo's logic they will be predicated on the subversive dimension inherent to acts of terror as well. Literature and fiction are therefore supposed to be training grounds for acts of ideological and phenomenological terror.

DeLillo concludes on a note of disappointment in what he sees as literature's contemporary forfeiture of its sacred, terroristic promises.[2] Nevertheless, he unwittingly joins the illustrious intellectual company of Alain Badiou and Maurice Blanchot in theorising literature *as* terror, but whereas DeLillo provides only fleeting commentary on how acts of literature double as acts of terror – both communicate through a 'deep narrative structure' – both Badiou and Blanchot pursue this problematic conjunction to the point of systematically interrogating what literature *is* when it is overtaken by terror, and of questioning what is the contribution of terror, if any, to committing acts of literature. While in several of Blanchot's theoretical writings on literature he emphatically subscribes to the poetics of terror as literature's lifeblood and salvation – 'the name of Terror is not any aesthetic or critical concept whatsoever; *it is literature, or at least its soul*' (FP 80; my italics) – Badiou, on the contrary, sees in terror the signature of literature's self-annihilating pact with nihilism and destruction. Blanchot and Badiou, in other words, diverge on the desire to advance protocols of terror in the space of literature. This book is about mediating this disagreement through a series of close readings of Samuel Beckett's major post-1945 writings – *The Unnamable, Texts for Nothing, How It Is, Company, Ill Seen Ill Said* and *Worstward Ho* – and if it comes down predominantly on the side of Blanchot, then this is because it is Blanchot's articulation of literature's constitutive dependence on terror that most effectively exposes Beckett's writing to the limits of language, the limits of thinking, and the limits of narrative and fiction that few writers other than Beckett, to paraphrase DeLillo, have ever targeted so incisively for transgression.

Although Blanchot does not cite Beckett directly as exemplary of the terror of literature, Badiou, in fact, does. In the essay 'The

Writing of the Generic: Samuel Beckett', Badiou provides a comprehensive reading of Beckett's post-1945 oeuvre, and in the process disparages precisely the imperative of terror that he sees overdetermining Beckett's composition of *L'Innommable/The Unnamable* and *Textes pour rien/Texts for Nothing*. Badiou indicts such an imperative for its responsibility in compelling Beckett to confess to Barney Rosset in 1954 that 'I think my writing days are over. L'Innommable finished me or expressed my finishedness' (*Letters II* 497). *Texts for Nothing* provoked in Beckett a similar feeling of resignation. As he indicates in the 1956 interview with Israel Shenker, 'the very last thing I wrote – "Textes pour rien" – was an attempt to get out of the attitude of disintegration, but it failed' (cited in Shenker 1999: 148). Needless to say, Beckett's writing days were not over. Badiou of course recognises this, and while he is certainly correct that we should not 'understand Beckett's continuation as a mere obsession, or as some servility to an imperative of acknowledged vacuity', he nevertheless overplays his hand in insisting that when Beckett finally did return to writing in prose with *Comment c'est/How It Is*, he 'passed, I am convinced, through a veritable intellectual and artistic mutation, and more precisely through a modification in his *orientation of thought*' (2008: 264; italics in original). On the contrary, and it is this that Blanchot is instrumental in helping us consider, perhaps Beckett's continuation was predicated on modifications of the language and poetics of terror, and not on a redirection, a radical eventual interruption, as Badiou would have us believe, of his entire modality of thinking in literature. The position that this book defends is that Beckett does not give up on the situation of his writing at the end of the 1950s by giving up on a literature of terror. The indispensable lesson of Blanchot is that literature *is* terror, and thus to give up on terror is tantamount to giving up on literature. Beckett does neither.

II

Before discussing Badiou's criticism of the phenomenon of terror in Beckett's writing of *The Unnamable* and *Texts for Nothing*, it is worthwhile addressing the status of terror in Badiou's philosophical reflections on revolutionary politics and the political disasters of the twentieth century. Badiou maintains that terror represents a category of political concepts that are *unthinkable* from a strictly philosophical (and phenomenological) perspective. The reason terror is unthinkable, however, has less to do with the epistemological limits of philosophical thinking and virtually everything to do with the historical (particularly historiographical) status of 'the Terror' that political modernity inherited from the French Revolution. Badiou is careful to pinpoint two valences of terror immanent to the French Revolution. On the one hand, terror designates the 'Reign of Terror' that was officially instituted in 1793[3] as the tactical avant-garde of the revolutionary government of Robespierre (and Saint-Just), who presented it as necessary for accomplishing the sequence of emancipation and purgation that delivered France from the sociopolitical tyranny of monarchical sovereignty. On the other hand, terror designates precisely that part of the French Revolution that the post-revolutionary government of the Thermidorians (responsible for sentencing Robespierre and other high-profile Jacobins to death by guillotine) actively embarked on expunging from the historiographical archive of the political modernity that the Revolution played no small part in inaugurating.[4] Importantly, and perhaps surprisingly, Badiou defers to the historiographical success of the Thermidorians in presenting terror as an unworkable philosophical concept. It is worth quoting at length the explanation he gives in *Metapolitics* for why terror cannot be sequestered as a philosophical object of critique independently of its post-revolutionary exposure to the conservative historiographical discourse of Thermidor:

> When all is said and done, 'Thermidorian' is the name for that which, whenever a truth procedure terminates, renders that procedure unthinkable. We have just seen how this constitution of the unthinkable can have a long-lasting power. It provides the historical matrix for a destitution of thought. Bearing this in mind, let us return to the Terror. In reality, when considered in isolation, 'terror' functions as one of the disarticulated terms of the unthinkable. The attempt to 'think terror' is impractical as such, because the isolation of the category of terror is precisely a Thermidorian operation (as is the attempt to think the socialist States solely on the basis of their terroristic dimension). It is an operation designed to produce something unintelligible and unthinkable. Considered in isolation, terror becomes an infra-political datum, one that is politically unthinkable, thereby leaving the terrain wide open for moralistic preaching against acts of violence. [. . .] What is subtracted from the Thermidorian operation is

something other than a clumsy attempt at justifying or elucidating the nature of terror considered 'in itself'. To proceed in this way would be to accept the unthinkable realm inhabited by the Thermidorian. We must examine the revolutionary work as a homogeneous multiplicity wherein terror functions as an *inseparable* category, and specifically as one that is inseparable from virtue. (Badiou 2005b: 138)

Badiou presents two analytically incompatible representations of terror. Because the Thermidorians tasked themselves with saving the historiographical archive of the French Revolution from the morally distasteful obligation of lionising Robespierre and valorising the Reign of Terror as the indispensable juridico-political mechanism responsible for steering the revolutionary sequence towards its success, they vigorously set to work in 1795 presenting the Terror as solely the illegitimate progeny of Robespierre's bloodthirsty paranoia and fanaticism, and thus as a regrettable anomaly to what would otherwise still have been a successful revolutionary sequence.[5] The Thermidorian operation consists in separating revolutionary virtue from revolutionary terror,[6] the Terror from the Revolution, and advocating for a post-Robespierre republican government freed from the illusion that 'the Terror' was the only efficacious juridico-political means available for achieving the state's revolutionary ends. Although Badiou is no doubt critical of the Thermidorian operation on the grounds that it sacrifices the revolutionary core of the revolutionary sequence, he concedes that the Thermidorian historiographical machine succeeded in nothing less than yoking revolutionary terror to totalitarian terror, terror to terrorism. Any subsequent attempt to think terror 'in-itself' is therefore subject to this historical and historiographical legacy. Accordingly, when Badiou confronts revolutionary terror in the context of the French Revolution, he does so not by thinking terror 'in-itself', which would play all too easily into the conservative hands of the Thermidorians, but by thinking it as reciprocally complementary of revolutionary virtue.

Readers of Badiou will remember that in *Manifesto for Philosophy* he nevertheless does not shy away from trying to understand 'the essence of terror' (1999: 131), though here he is referring to what happened under the governments of Stalin and Hitler (as nihilism and destruction), and not under the Jacobins and Robespierre (as subtraction and virtue). Badiou risks donning the cap of the Thermidorian in attempting to think the essence of terror philosophically through the destructive forms of violence and the widespread distributions of anxiety and fear with which terror is associated in today's political discourse. Here Badiou is accounting for what happens when philosophy is seduced by political promises rooted in terror. Badiou writes:

> The essence of terror is to pronounce the must-not-be of what is. Philosophy, when it is driven out of its operation by the temptation wielded upon it by the idea that Truth as substance produces terror, just as it produces ecstasy of the place and the sacred of the name. It is exactly this triple knotted effect, of ecstasy, the sacred and terror, which I name *disaster*. It is a matter of *thought's* own disaster. Every disaster has at its root a substantialization of Truth, that is, the 'illegal' passage of Truth as an empty operation to truth as the befalling-to-presence of the void itself [...]. There are potent and identified forms of such philosophemes. Stalinian Marxism's new Proletarian Man, National Socialism's historically destined German people are philosophemes, taken to unheard-of effects of terror against what does not have the right to be (the traitor to the cause, the Jew, the Communist ...), and pronouncing the ecstasy of the place (the German Land, Socialism's Homeland) and the sacred of the Name (the Fuhrer, the Father of the peoples). (1999: 131–2)

The philosophemes that take as their proper name the signatures of Stalinism and National Socialism are situated in Badiou's lexicon as exclusivist structures of thinking that are dogmatically sutured to their politico-historical embodiments (Marx hijacked by Soviet Communism; Nietzsche enlisted posthumously, and Heidegger voluntarily if not enthusiastically, in the ranks of National Socialism). When terror is clustered together with ecstasy of place and sacredness of the name, Badiou argues, it participates in constituting a disaster such as these 'philosophemes' have come to represent. Terror operates in this particular constellation as the imperative for the absolute negation – the liquidation – of persons and communities excluded by the restrictive criteria of belonging either to soil and blood or party and history. Terror, in other words, counts in this twentieth-century context as the *active* ingredient, the energising core of the deadly imperative of the performance of an unthinkable disaster (a disaster of thought). Ecstasy of place and sacredness of the name would be impotent ideologies if they were not invigorated by the terroristic imperative for unrestrained negativity and negation.[7] When this happens – i.e. when a political sequence goes horribly awry and does truly engender madness and destruction – terror no longer has anything to do with political virtue or revolutionary enthusiasm, but is instead complicit in an unthinkable political disaster against which the Thermidorians cautioned.

Badiou asks that we 'understand by terror, here, not the political concept of Terror, linked (in a universalizable couple) to the concept of Virtue by the Immortals of the Jacobin Committee of Public Safety, but the pure and simple reduction of all to their being-for-death. Terror thus conceived really postulates that in order to let substance be, *nothing* must be' (2001: 77; italics in original). All of this is to say that when Badiou approaches the politico-philosophical experience of terror *independently* of either Robespierre's insistence on terror's inextricable relation, as a 'universalizable couple', to revolutionary virtue, or the role that a politics of terror played in the nihilist destitution of thought perpetrated under Soviet totalitarianism and National Socialist fascism, i.e. when Badiou risks thinking the *essence of terror*, he does so firmly within a discursive space legislated over by the historiographical dictate of Thermidor: that the 'in-itself' of terror is unthinkable. Terror is politically amorphous in Badiou's hands, and its political value can only be properly measured and assessed in conjunction with supplementary political traits. In the case of twentieth-century totalitarian and fascist experiences of terror, such traits include 'the sacred' and 'ecstasy' (1999: 131), and their conjunction with terror resulted in political and philosophical disaster. In the case of revolutionary terror, Badiou cites 'revolutionary virtue' as essential for thinking terror. In both cases, and regardless of whether or not terror participates in a revolutionary political sequence productive of an eventual truth (under Robespierre and Saint-Just), or a nihilist political sequence productive of disaster (under Stalin and Hitler), terror cannot be isolated as a philosophical category 'in-itself'. Badiou is nothing if not consistent in his handling of terror and in his resistance to thinking terror 'in-itself'. And this is really the crucial point. The question with which this book begins is whether or not Badiou is right to think about terror in the space of literature, and specifically in the context of reading Beckett, *in the same way* that he thinks about terror in the space of politics. Thinking terror 'in-itself' in the space of politics might very well be either epistemologically ill-warranted or ethically ill-advised (or both), but must the same be said about the encounter with terror in the space of literature?

Badiou implicitly draws the conclusion not only that the 'in-itself' of terror is philosophically unthinkable in the space of politics, but also that it is hermeneutically unworkable in the space of literature, which is an argument that he articulates in his critical survey of the Beckettian oeuvre in 'The Writing of the Generic: Samuel Beckett'. Badiou's argument with respect to Beckett is that the reason why Beckett's aesthetic vision for literature undergoes a noticeable overhaul after *The Unnamable* and *Texts for Nothing*, and beginning with *How It Is*, is that Beckett somehow musters the strength to divorce the protocol of his thinking in literature from the imperative of terror, i.e. with what Badiou associates with the torture of the post-Cartesian and post-metaphysical cogito of Beckett's narrative voices. To attain the blessed gift of silence that Beckett's narrator-protagonists so valiantly yet tragically desire, Badiou explains, would require 'an internal violence', 'a superego fury that is capable of submitting, in the proper sense, the subject of the *cogito* to the question, to torture. That would necessitate that the avowal of its silence be *extorted*. Beckett stressed that if the "I think" comes to mark its own thinking-being, if thinking wants to grasp itself as the thinking of thought, then a reign of terror begins' (2008: 261; italics in original).

Beckettian terror is understood in Badiou's analysis as the operator of a disaster of thinking, particularly the type of thinking that is exemplified in modern philosophy by the work of the Cartesian cogito. Intrinsic to the Cartesian birthplace of modern philosophical subjectivity, Badiou suggests, is a complementary affinity with the self-reflexive imperative of terror. Beckett exposes this complementary relation by pushing the Cartesian mode of subjectivity to the absolute limit of its reflexive extension. If the absolute limit of the Cartesian subject is to think the self-same subject that thinks – the act whereby thinking grasps 'itself as the thinking of thought' – then the consequence of reaching this limit can be nothing less than the substitution of the transcendental 'I think' with the immanence of the suicidal and terror-driven subject of solipsistic self-reflexivity.

What first enables this consequence, however, is a distinctly Beckettian devastation of the operability of conceptual mediation between the narrating voice of a textual subject and the narrative space of the fictional world of its phenomenological inhabitancy. The arrival of terror onto the scene of Beckett's prose is not simply a spontaneous event. It is predicated on a tightly constructed 'fictional apparatus' that stages the necessary conditions for witnessing 'the closure of the *cogito*' (2008: 259). Representing 'the best-known part of Beckett's work', according to Badiou, 'this apparatus is that of the motionless voice, of the voice that is *assigned to residence* by a body. This body is mutilated and captive, reduced to being no more than the fixed localization of the voice' (2008: 259–60; italics in original). *The Unnamable* reads in Badiou's interpretation as a precisely controlled experiment set on investigating the resiliency of the cogito when it is isolated not only from the world outside the confines of its hermetic phenomenological perspective, but even more painfully from the *knowledge* that it has been hermetically sequestered accordingly within the finite limits of its bodily extension. Beckett gives the cogito only one avenue of escape from the inhuman conditions of its imprisonment: to capture in speech the cogito's very own primordial 'point of enunciation' (2008: 260). The cruelty of this hope inheres in the naked truth that what is thus being searched for is the inaccessible enunciation of silence.

Badiou is by no means the only reader to articulate this relation between silence and speech in Beckett's writing, but what saves his reading from being critically anachronistic and facile is the presentation of the idea that the inaccessibility of silence by speech cannot be explained away simply as a 'formal paradox, that is, from a necessity according to which the condition of being of all naming is itself unnameable' (Badiou 2008: 260). Beckett exploits literature's singular tools of signification to masterful effect by submitting this paradox of enunciation to a narrative representation of the life of the voice that must enact it. Not only does Beckett frame the conditions of a passive existence in language as the impossible desire to exist *outside* speech and language, but the voice that speaks from this desire is simultaneously tasked with ensuring that the only existence inhabitable is irreducibly inscribed *inside* speech and language. Beckett narrates a voice, in other words, that is trapped in the double bind of attaining what it knows to be impossible: 'I'll speak of me when I speak no more' (*TN* 385).

Rejecting that what we are dealing with in *The Unnamable* on the subject of silence and speech counts for nothing more than just a 'formal paradox', Badiou enjoins us 'to see that the situation of the cogito is far more complex' (2008: 260). Having the solipsistic voice of the Beckettian cogito confront the impasse of silence does not automatically divest this cogito of its power to speak and think, and therefore also divest it of the horizon of its power to exist as the subject of a narrative world. Only where Beckett subjects the voice to the imperative of bombarding this impasse again and again with the demand for its transcendence does a 'reign of terror' commence. As the voice of the unnamable is self-inundated by an 'insistence without hope' that drives it to violently and relentlessly penetrate 'the silent being of all speech' (2008: 260), it becomes increasingly apparent that the unnamable is only present in the 'fictional apparatus' of *The Unnamable* so that the 'terrorist commandment' of the cogito can be given an outlet of expression (2008: 261). By uncovering the unthinkable and perhaps unspeakable presupposition of the solipsistic voice of the cogito, namely the presupposition of terror as an 'imperative without concept' (2008: 261) and an 'insistence without hope' (2008: 260), Badiou believes he has discovered the underlying cause for 'the truth of a situation, namely Beckett's at the end of the 1950s: what he had written until this point could not *go on any further*' (2008: 263–4; italics in original). The conclusion Badiou draws from witnessing in *The Unnamable* the intolerable existence of a cogito locked into the repetition of its failure to seize the silence on which its existence is tragically predicated is that if literature cannot rise above this predicament of ontological immanence (thinking in the immanence of thought, speaking in the immanent silence of speech) then it too is ineluctably driven to disaster by submitting its existence to the tyrannical epistemological weight of imperatives without concepts and insistences without hope.

Because Beckett's orientation of thinking in literature is enthralled to an *eternal return of terror*, as this book argues variously throughout, his writing is precluded from breaking with this repetition and chancing upon the shores of interruption and the revolutionary truths that terror 'in-itself' violently, insidiously suppresses. The terror that we find operative in *The Unnamable* and *Texts for Nothing* is the terror of disaster, destruction and nihilism, argues Badiou, and so it is a terror that will need to be disavowed and surpassed (in Thermidorian fashion, we might be tempted to add) if Beckett's writing is to avoid suffering the same unworkable fate as the voice of the unnamable. What Beckett's writing sorely needs to do, Badiou suggests, is to be introduced to the aleatory world of the event, of the 'hazardous supplement', precisely the kind of supplement that Badiou locates in Mallarmé, the poetic supplement that 'interrupts repetition' (2008: 123). Fortunately for Beckett, Badiou posits, with *How It Is*, the text that signalled Beckett's return to prose in the late 1950s after the impasse of *The Unnamable* and *Texts for Nothing*, his writing began to demonstrate the ability to 'set out from entirely different categories, namely, that of the "what happens" (which was present in his work from the beginning but is reworked here), and that, above all, of alterity, of the encounter, of the figure of the Other, which fissures and displaces solipsistic imprisonment' (2008: 264). The secret behind the rejuvenation of Beckett's writing after *The Unnamable* and *Texts for Nothing* thus turns out to be its rupture with the imperative-without-concept of terror. Perhaps. This book thinks otherwise.

III

As Robert J. C. Young remarks, 'terror repulses', and as such 'discussions of terror move quickly away from terror to its cause. "Terror" gets conflated with "acts of terrorism", which produce the effect of terror or fear, or with "terrorists" who carry out acts of terrorism. This leaves terror itself unchallenged and unexamined' (2010: 308). Young's observation about the conceptual misprision that plagues the majority of analyses of terror demands that terror no longer be regarded as the exclusive critical reserve of political and historical research. Because 'terror moves you into a state of producing fiction', i.e. 'it makes you live imaginatively on the borderlines of the real', pursuing a critique of terror must of necessity take recourse to a critique of literature (the discourse of fiction *par excellence*) in order to measure terror's relation to the real (psychological, political, historical, aesthetic, etc.) that terror traumatically, disastrously disrupts, the real that terror reproduces contingently, repetitively and indecisively anew whenever it takes firm hold of a situation and of the psyche(s) that populate it (Young 2010: 309). Young therefore argues that 'literature is, unexpectedly, one of the best places to learn about the war on terror. It has been anticipating the condition of the twenty-first century for centuries: ever since, indeed, the French invented Terror in 1793. Fiction has the unique ability not only to represent terror, to mediate it through narration, but also to produce it' (2010: 310).

True terror does not intervene from the outside as an external threat breaching or obliterating either a material or psychic threshold; rather, terror is truly terrifying only when it is internalised as the means by which victims become their own victimisers, the tormented are metamorphosed into their tormenters, the tortured wield the weapons of their torture, and, perhaps less dramatically but formally no less apropos, conscious subjects never cease interrogating what their consciousness knows, how it knows it, and what the limits are to the words and concepts it uses in communicating the narratives and fictions that it endlessly produces (especially about itself). The questions 'Where now? Who now? When now?' that open *The Unnamable* trigger not the wonder of self-(re)discovery, but the fragmentary ordeal of interminable self-reflexivity (*TN* 285). To inquire into a symptomology of terror is thus to inquire into what is singularly literary in the language and space of literature. Young asks, 'can fiction also show us how to move out of terror, how to refuse its effects? Which is as much as to say: can literature tell us how to escape its own effects?' (2010: 310). Because such an interrogation of literature *by* literature reached its climax through the writing of Samuel Beckett, it can very easily be argued, the critique of literature that this book is interested in performing in dialogue with Blanchot is in some sense automatically drawn to both of these writers whose work embodied so many of the crises and contradictions arising out of the (eternal) return of terror in twentieth-century literary and political modernity.

From within the context of philosophical readings of Beckett, one of the more polemical contributions that this book makes by reading Beckett with Blanchot through the concept of the terror of literature is to put pressure on the fascination with ethical transcendence that captures so many philosophical readings of Beckett's work. That several of the more prominent philosophical readings of Beckett (which we will encounter variously throughout this book) conclude with appeals to ethical transcendence is taken by this book as evidence that Beckett studies is too often complicit in what Gilles Deleuze and Félix Guattari disparage as the pervasive ideological manoeuver of 'making us think that immanence is a prison (solipsism) from which the Transcendent will save us' (1994: 47). It would not be surprising if readers looking at this book's study of Beckett and terror did not immediately assume that its thesis is that Beckett's writing represents an ethical antidote to the violences and traumas of terror. Faced implicitly with the choice between immanence and transcendence, virtually all works of Beckett criticism choose transcendence, and they do so by dressing themselves up in the garb of ethical and political commitments. The polemical payoff behind saying that Beckett's writing occurs in the immanence of terror is that we expose ourselves to the unnerving possibility that the obligation to the singular exigencies of literature that Beckett's writing internalises forecloses any opening through which an event of ethical transcendence (of salvation or redemption) would enter into the space of literature.[8]

Admittedly, there have been notable instances of resistance to the demand for an 'ethicalised' Beckett. Beginning from the perspective of Blanchot's phenomenological conceptualisation of the imperatives of literature, Jeff Fort insists that what Beckett, no less than Kafka or Blanchot, 'encounters in attempting to strip writing of everything but its own most essential compulsion – in a movement that systematically confounds the difference between elevation and depth, between exaltation and baseness – is an empty necessity that insists all the more brutally for being voided of its contents' (2014: 2). The imperative to which Fort sees Kafka, Blanchot and Beckett singularly responding is the one that in *Heidegger and the Politics of Poetry* Philippe Lacoue-Labarthe identifies as 'an imperative without content',[9] and in so far as the imperative that constitutes the literary vocation of writers committed to such a radical degree to their profession is devoid of content, it is not an imperative that can be easily conceptualised outside the textual parameters of its symptomatic implementation in the uncanny depths of literature and of literature exclusively (cited in Fort 2014: 2).

Lacoue-Labarthe's 'imperative without content' is a concise distillation of Beckett's oft-cited description of literature's chiastic responsibility to the negativity of expression and the expression of negativity. What does literature's obligation to negativity express?: 'the expression that there is nothing to express, nothing with which to express, nothing from which to express, no power to express, no desire to express, together with the obligation to express' (D 139). Blanchot had drafted this formula almost verbatim in the introductory essay to the 1943 (French) publication of *Faux Pas*, 'From Anguish to Language'. Whenever the writer takes writing seriously, Blanchot writes, he 'finds himself in the increasingly ludicrous condition of having nothing to write, of having no means with which to write it, and of being constrained by the utter necessity of always writing it' (*FP* 3). If the only legitimate reason behind a commitment to literature is an imperative stripped of all content and responsibility to the world outside literature, if the writer's only answer to the question *why write?*, Fort posits, is reducible to 'a mode of helpless compulsion', then there is every reason to conclude that the situation of literature eschews 'any pretensions to an ethical, much less a sublime, dimension in the task of writing. [. . .] The important point to begin with', in considering Beckett and Blanchot (and Kafka), 'is that the irreducibility of writing's imperative is itself subject to disturbing vacilations that remove it from the sphere of ethics, and that reduce its echoes of sublimity to the varied and empty figures of its failure – figures of a law in default' (Fort 2014: 4).

The labour of literature becomes in this situation an all-consuming task for figures like Beckett and Blanchot. Literature is here fundamentally separated from the content-saturated context of 'life' where ethical discourse is essentially and practically situated. If there is to be an ethical call of literature it would thus have to derive from nowhere else but literature itself, and so whatever ethical discourse of literature is discoverable in the Beckettian world will by definition be confined to that world alone and to no other. What Fort identifies as the 'imperative to write' in the work of Beckett and Blanchot (and Kafka) translates as writing's imperative to reflect the sovereign law of its immanent ontological alterity. A sovereign imperative like the one that oversees the space of literature, because evacuated of all concept and content and abjected into a world of sovereign self-regulation, cannot be an ethical imperative. Ethics begins in relation to the world and in communion with and hospitality towards the alterity of the other; it is thereby subsumed with economies of content, concept and relation. In contrast, the imperative to which literature is beholden is precisely an imperative that interrupts economies of relation and sanctions the possibility of community and communication with any content or concept outside of the singular idiom of the literary imperative itself. Closer to the concerns of this book is the analogous conclusion that Badiou draws regarding the possibility of conceptualising terror. As noted above, Badiou regards terror as philosophically unthinkable in so far as terror, like literature, answers to 'an imperative without concept' (2008: 261). One of the aims of this book is to articulate terror precisely in this non-ethical and non-philosophical language of an imperative without content or concept, which is an imperative, moreover, that dovetails with the fragmentary imperative of writing formulated by Blanchot.

No sooner does Fort acknowledge the non-ethical imperatives of literature, however, than he pivots his argument towards defending a theory of ethical negativity buried deep within the aesthetic and historical unconsciousness of literature and writing. There would appear to be in Beckett criticism, and here Fort is no exception, a pervasive hesitation to refusing Beckett's writing an ethical commitment that does not force its way into its space from out of Beckett's autobiographical existence and memory. From the ethical viewpoint of Beckett criticism, Beckett's weaknesses and failures to adhere to the fragmentary imperative of writing convert almost automatically into the strengths and successes of the ethical imperatives that his writing upholds. If Beckett 'is "good for nothing but" writing', Fort speculates,

> it may also be that nothing is quite so good as writing, that writing is the last holdout against the good's corrosion and dispersion, the one thing that has managed, after all, to resist elimination in the all-devouring process of rejecting everything on offer [. . .]. In other words, the minimal and minimised vindication of writing actually harbors an extreme and hyperbolic affirmation, or even a receding and residual version of transcendence, that holds out the hope (and the persistent demand) of unparalleled satisfactions, not to say ecstasy, even in the midst of the extreme attenuations already noted. (2014: 6)

It is curious to see an ethical imperative weave its way into Fort's reading so insidiously and with so much promise of salvaging Fort's preliminary encounter with the hermeneutically unworkable hypothesis of literature's sovereign imperative outside ethics.

As it turns out, and this is Fort's culminating insight, occupying the space of an absolute commitment to literature proves to be an impossible task as history and memory, as 'life' forcibly penetrates across even the most heavily guarded thresholds (between life and literature[10]) as those that demarcate the sovereign ontological spaces of literature and writing. While the thesis of literature's failure to shut out history and memory is indisputable, it does not necessarily mean that literature is ethical by default of this failure. Fort's argument is that in so far as there is an ethical remainder in Beckett, or for that matter in Kafka, Blanchot, or whomever, it is a consequence of the sovereign imperative of writing having failed in its uncompromising demand for totalisation, and in inadequately living up to the ideal of the absolute subtraction of the literary subject from non-literary spheres of experience and existence. The ethics of literature would therefore have to be conceptualised as an accident of the inevitable failure of literature's sovereign imperative. Rather than call into question the desire for ethics *as such*, however, Fort is able to reconceptualise ethics on the basis of literature's intrinsic failure not to be ethical. Through this manoeuver, Fort advances the trend in Beckett criticism of always arriving at an ethical conclusion that redeems the anxieties, paradoxes, indecisions and scepticisms of the readings preceding it.

In the introduction to his *Beckett, Literature, and the Ethics of Alterity*, Shane Weller provides a somewhat more subversive response to the hegemony of ethical commitment predicated of the Beckettian space of literature. He counters the theoretical trend in Beckett criticism of attributing an ethical commitment to Beckett's writing by proposing the neologism of the 'anethical'[11] as a more precise concept for capturing the ambivalence that Beckett expresses towards the question of ethics and of ethical possibility. Weller begins his novel conceptualisation of the 'anethical' from the perspective of accepting that the ethical posturing of Beckett's writing tends to share a close affinity with the Levinasian notion of the *il y a*, the 'there is' that emanates (not without horror) out of the pure presence of being before existence:[12] 'the murmur of the *il y a* does indeed seem to be present in *The Unnamable* and the *Texts for Nothing*, which ends with an "it murmurs," a "voice murmuring a trace." In Beckett, though, there is no acceptance of the *il y a*, no living with it, but rather, as in Levinas, an unremitting attempt to escape it' (Weller 2006: 12–13). Successfully extricating his narrative voices from the solipsistic prison of the *il y a* is the first step Beckett's writing would have to take in order to avoid continually being drowned out by the 'voice murmuring a trace' that concludes and indeed swallows up the preceding narrative sequence of *The Unnamable* and *Texts for Nothing*.

Later in his introduction, however, Weller revises this Levinasian interpretation of Beckettian ethics and the interpretive applicability of the *il y a* to Beckett's writing, claiming that

> while, for Levinas, it is precisely the ethical relation with the Other that constitutes an escape from the horror of the *il y a*, in Beckett the *il y a* certainly appears to be irreducible and inescapable in a way that it is not for Levinas, blocking the path to the ethical. In *Texts for Nothing*, for instance, this persistence that is not an event of being is figured as a 'voice murmuring a trace' which appears to resist all efforts to silence it with 'no's knife.' The Beckettian *il y a* appears, then, to be the most radical form of unmasterable alterity. (2006: 29)

As Weller explains it elsewhere, the 'anethical' aims to capture 'the conjunction' in Beckett's writing of 'two, antithetical imperatives' that have thus far been responsible for cleaving the ethical discourse on Beckett in two between 'an ethics of negation or an ethics of affirmation' (2010: 128). Weller's 'anethical Beckett' is one for whom the imperatives 'to end and to go on, at once negation and affirmation', are not mutually exclusive (2010: 128). This is a Beckett who would therefore be incompatible with the Levinasian stand against dwelling interminably in confrontation with the philosophically unworkable exigencies of the *il y a*.

Through the conceptual lens of the 'anethical', Weller leverages his reading of *The Unnamable* and *Texts for Nothing* to take aim at Levinas's premature ethicalisation of the category of alterity and of literature's (failed) responsibility towards it in its most radical manifestation (as the incessantly murmuring voice of the *il y a*). In so far as Weller insists that the *il y a* is a productive concept for interpreting the ethical horizon of Beckett's writing, however, it will have to be the *il y a* as it is explicated in Blanchot as the non-ethical provenance where the absolute work of literature is disclosed: 'whereas Levinas's thought of the ethical relation to the Other is the escape from this irreducible *il y a*, Blanchot thinks literature itself in terms of this voice, and, far from attempting to silence it, he attempts to identify it, disclose it – in Kafka and Beckett, among others' (2006: 12). Weller does not pursue the close relation between Beckett and Blanchot's ontological as well as ethical priorities in the context of literature's encounter with the *il y a* much further than this. Nevertheless, his insistence that Beckett's writing is intimately connected with the space of the *il y a* as it is circumscribed in Blanchot's thinking as an *other than* ethical space of existence, language and human relation (more on this in Chapter 3 on *How It Is*) does provide a useful point of departure for taking up the question of precisely where and how

Beckett and Blanchot converge vis-à-vis what this book is naming the terror of literature.

IV

In her essay '"In Love with Hiding": Samuel Beckett's War', Marjorie Perloff investigates the ways that Beckett's wartime and post-war experience in France, first in Paris as part of the Resistance to Nazi Occupation and then in perilous exile once Beckett's underground cell (codenamed 'Gloria SMH') had been exposed, came to exert a profound influence over shaping the ascetic literary form that typified Beckett's writing immediately after the Second World War (from the 'Nouvelles' to *En attendant Godot*). Forced into hiding and exile in order to elude the German and French-Collaborationist patrols along the route to the Unoccupied Zone in the south of France, Perloff explains, Beckett underwent 'an elaborate war nightmare – a nightmare Beckett never wrote about directly, although allusions to it are [...] everywhere in the texts of the postwar decade' (2005: 77). Unable to differentiate 'between friend and enemy', Beckett and Suzanne Deschevaux-Dumesnil, his soon-to-be wife, lived in constant danger of being discovered and exposed (2005: 81). Beckett and Deschevaux-Dumesnil lived out the remainder of the war in a 'claustrophobic' environment, 'indeed a kind of prison' (2005: 82).

While there is no question that Beckett's wartime experience simply did not compare to what befell countless millions during what the world would soon come to know as the Holocaust, or *Shoah* (in Hebrew), this does not mean that he was not deeply and personally affected by what Hitler's Germany was planning at the onset of war and what it in fact carried out once war truly and brutally commenced. Anthony Cronin attributes Beckett's relationship with Alfred Péron, 'Beckett's oldest friend among French people', as one of the influences behind Beckett's decision to join the Resistance in 1941. Péron, 'a daily associate at this time even apart from their joint resistance activities, and a Jew who saw – and had reason to see – more clearly than most French people what the Nazis were up to, what their intentions regarding the new order really were and what future awaited Jews should they triumph' (Cronin 1997: 326), would eventually be interned in the Mauthausen concentration camp, and like 'Robert Desnos',

Beckett notifies Thomas MacGreevy in a letter dated 19 August 1945, he died 'on his way home from deportation' (*Letters II* 19). Cronin helps fill in some of the details surrounding the death of Péron:

> While in Ireland Beckett heard the news of the death of Alfred Péron. Apart from the grief it caused him, the news emphasized the difference between the complacencies of Foxrock and the life-and-death nature of the war years for so many people in Europe. Arrested in August 1942, Péron had been taken in February of the following year to Mauthausen, a camp where many who had been involved in resistance activities were kept. He had managed to survive there until liberation and had then been transferred to a Red Cross camp in Switzerland. Here, as a result of his ill treatment in Mauthausen, he died in June 1945. (1997: 346)

So although Beckett was luckily not counted amongst the victims of the Nazi Terror, he was not entirely spared from mourning the deaths of people he called his friends and from witnessing first-hand the suffering and violence that humanity was capable of inflicting on itself during times of pervasive paranoia, anxiety and aggression. After a brief sojourn in Ireland, Beckett managed to return to 'French soil, if not [immediately] to Paris and some semblance of normal life there' (Cronin 1997: 347). When Beckett finally did return to Paris in January 1946 (following his work with the Irish Red Cross at Saint-Lô, the so-called 'capital of the ruins' of France) for what would later be dubbed the 'siege in the room' period where he composed his most famous writings, he soon discovered that it was a Paris he no longer recognised. In the post-war aftermath of the Vichy collaboration with the *Wehrmacht*, the government of de Gaulle embarked on a Robespierresque 'Purge' of confirmed and suspected collaborationists and various other elements of France's now disgraced national heritage.

This 'period of political *épuration* (purging)', writes Weller, had 'immediate consequences for the literary world, not least the suicide on 15 March 1945 of the novelist Pierre Drieu La Rochelle, who during the German occupation had taken on the editorship of France's most influential pre-war journal, *La Nouvelle Revue Française*. On account of its collaborationist stance, the *NRF* was closed down after the Liberation and did not reappear until 1953, when it was relaunched under the title *La Nouvelle Nouvelle*

Revue Française' (2013: 161). If it was the case, as Beckett is said to have put it in the interview with Israel Shenker, that 'I preferred France in war to Ireland at peace', the same could not be said about the France, and Paris specifically, that Beckett inhabited now that the war had nominally been concluded (cited in Shenker 1999: 147). The Nazi collaboration left France morally humiliated and economically eviscerated once the Occupation came to an end with the dissolution of the Vichy regime, but with the conclusion of France's collaboration came the revival of an unmistakable recourse to the sociopolitical tactics of the Reign of Terror taken by the Vichy Purges under the government of de Gaulle. Andrew Gibson makes much of a letter Beckett wrote to Thomas MacGreevy dated 4 January 1948: 'The news of France is very depressing, depresses me anyhow. All the wrong things, all the wrong way. It is hard sometimes to feel the France that one clung to, that I still cling to' (*Letters II* 72). Gibson takes these remarks on 'the culture immediately around him' as 'central' to 'Beckett's work in the mid- and late 40s' (2010a: 1). Beckett 'returned to Paris at a time when, in the words of the historian Herbert Lottman, because of the Purge, *the atmosphere was one of terror*' (Gibson 2010a: 3; my italics).[13]

One of the reasons why Beckett's writing is exemplary of a literature of terror is not only that the writing of the 'siege in the room' period occurred under the historical auspices of the return of terror in France in the aftermath of the violence and brutality of the Second World War, but more fundamentally that it began to internalise a form of speech that expresses the dread of continuing to tell stories and to desire death despite its speakers, its voices, having been abjected into a world where the ontological supports of subjectivity, memory and finitude are no longer readily available.[14] In works like *The Unnamable*, *Texts for Nothing*, *How It Is*, *Company*, *Ill Seen Ill Said* and *Worstward Ho*, Beckett gives us the desolation of speech in a world where death has lost the power to function as the ultimate horizon of metaphysical value and experience. 'This is a speech', Blanchot writes in *The Infinite Conversation*, 'of which we are not directly aware and, it must be said again, a speech that is infinitely hazardous, *for it is encompassed by terror*' (*IC* 187; my italics). Blanchot signals our attention in this section of *The Infinite Conversation*, provocatively subtitled 'You can kill that man', to an argument that had already been intuited in some of his previous writings. Not only is the concept and historical experience of terror instrumental to Blanchot's argument in the 1947 essay 'Literature and the Right to Death', which can be read as tracing the genealogy of the Levinasian *il y a*[15] all the way back to the Reign of Terror as it was seen through the eyes of the Marquis de Sade and G. W. F. Hegel, but also in the critical review essay of Jean Paulhan's *Les Fleurs de Tarbes*, 'How Is Literature Possible?', that was part of the essays collected in 1943 in *Faux Pas*.

The links that Blanchot sees between literature and terror therefore go much deeper than merely supplying Blanchot with anything as banal as a remorseful alibi for his pre-war political activity with right-wing publications like *Le Rempart*, *L'Insurgé* and *Combat*. Rodolphe Gasché correctly insists that 'to suspect that Blanchot's discussion of revolutionary terror refers covertly to his own association with right-wing movements in prewar France and that it is a late attempt to come to grips with it misreads completely' Blanchot's post-Hegelian appropriation of the exigencies of terror as a constitutive condition of literature. 'If indeed the theme of terror enjoys a special privilege over all other themes', Gasché continues, 'this is not because it stands in for a personal past of guilt but because [...] it becomes the place *par excellence* for exemplifying all the paradoxes that make up literature and literary activity' (1999: 372). Heeding Gasché's caution (as a critical riposte to Jeffrey Mehlman) against reading Blanchot's post-1941 invocation of terror as a way for Blanchot to continue his pre-war, supposedly proto-fascist political commitments in less recognisably political publications – like 'Terror in Literature',[16] 'How is Literature Possible?' and 'Literature and the Right to Death' – enables us to focus on the far more interesting task of investigating whether or not terror *as such*, i.e. terror 'in-itself', has anything to teach us about the work of literature. One of the theses this book articulates is that the fragmentary imperative of writing that Blanchot theorises after the Second World War operates as a translation into the language of literature of the fragmentary imperative of terror. If this is the case, then perhaps it is true, as Young also suspects, that a better understanding of what terror is and how terror works at the limits of political and historical discourse will facilitate a concomitantly better understanding of what literature is and how literature works at the limits of speaking, thinking and writing, i.e. precisely at the limits where Beckett's writing so uncompromisingly dwells.

As Christopher Fynsk's reading of Blanchot's 'Literature and the Right to Death' points out, 'the Terror represents for literature that specular, speculative moment where literature "contemplates itself," "recognizes itself," and "justifies itself" in the realisation of absolute freedom. In the Terror, literature passes into the world' (1996a: 71). Taking as his point of reference Blanchot's essay on Paulhan, 'How Is Literature Possible?', Leslie Hill similarly observes that for Blanchot, in the process of radicalising the central argument of Paulhan, 'Terror is in fact the essence of literature as such' rather than 'a simple romantic aberration' (1997: 74). It would thus be fair to say that for Blanchot terror, particularly as it originates with the Reign of Terror in the French Revolution and is then transmitted all the way down through modernity (via Hegel, Jena Romanticism and Sade) to the aesthetic and political projects of the twentieth century, is both a privileged philosophical concept and a radicalising condition of historical experience that is far from irrelevant not only to explicating the formation of the modern political state, but perhaps more provocatively to engaging as incisively as does Blanchot with the literary history of post-revolutionary modernity.

In the twentieth-century context of modernity, terror is far from being an antiquated historical and political phenomenon associable only with the revolutionary turbulence of 1793. Blanchot's pre-1939 endorsement of the political tactics of terror in an article he published in the July 1936 issue of the journal *Combat*, 'Le Terrorisme, method de salut public', made it clear, in no uncertain terms, that a strategic and measured recourse to violence is sometimes necessary in order to reinvigorate the historical and political passions of a nation that has slipped into a state of what Hill calls 'parliamentary complacency' (1997: 39):

> It is important to note that the purpose of such violence was self-evidently not to install fascist dictatorship in France nor to impose a small nationalist clique in government, but rather to interrupt a specific type of oppressive parliamentary politics and thus to allow the possibility of a different political future. So if Blanchot endorsed acts of terror in the piece, it was solely in order to deliver, as he put it, to the very people who might be ready to condemn them – the French electorate at large – the benefits of such an interruption. [. . .] [I]t was no doubt a calculated move on the writer's part that the acts of terror he advocated in the article were justified – at least in Blanchot's presen-

tation – by an unmistakable reference back to the memory of Danton, Robespierre, and St-Just, those earlier revolutionaries of 1793, who, in similar times of national crisis, set up a more famous Comité du Salut Public, or Committee of Public Safety, to defend the nation against the challenge from within and aggression from without, and eventually embarked on a campaign of terror whose purpose was the saving of the Jacobin revolution. If Blanchot's article espouses terrorism, it was in order to effect a political hiatus; indeed, such a hiatus was indispensable if politics was to be refashioned anew. (1997: 39–40)

The event of historical and political hiatus would indeed arrive in Europe and France, but it was not the progressive revolutionary hiatus that Blanchot envisioned. The hiatus – the interruption, the suspension – that occurred originated in Germany, not France, and its political provenance was the increasingly sprawling epicentre of twentieth-century fascism and not a repetition of France's revolutionary inheritance. Blanchot's watershed pivot away from politics and political journalism and towards literature and literary criticism on or around 1941 (he would return to the political arena in solidarity against the Algerian War and with the protests of May 1968) was neither spontaneous nor opportunistic; rather, it was a strategic decision reflective of the new historical and political exigencies that the fascist appropriation of the tactics of terror imposed. From Blanchot's perspective as a writer, critic and intellectual, literature had a responsibility to preserve at least one last space of resistance to the fascist destruction not least of thought, imagination and creative expression. As Blanchot explains in 1977 in a letter to Maurice Nadeau, 'I have always considered Nazism and anti-semitism to be pure evil, against which we were ill defended. [. . .] Come what may, our duty was to keep alive centres of resistance in France, intellectual ones if nothing else. [. . .] That was how I met Georges Bataille, and also became involved in clandestine activity which I have never spoken about, and shall not speak here. But the feeling of horror never left me' ('RI' 19).

Turning to literature as the space where such 'centres of resistance' might still be kept alive was a far from straightforward proposition in the context of French cultural politics during the Occupation and after. According to Gisèle Sapiro, the political boundaries of the cultural landscape under the Occupation were bookmarked by two contradictory ideologies that would remain unreconciled during the Gaullist years of the Vichy Purge. On the one side was the position of many of the contributors to *La Nouvelle Revue Française* while it was under the editorship of Drieu La Rochelle, which provided 'the option of "art for art's sake" as a mode of political detachment from political and social constraints, and thus an affirmation of the writer's autonomy' (Sapiro 2014: 45). On the other side was the position of 'writers of refusal' like Jean Guéhenno, Michel Leiris and Simone de Beauvoir that continuing to publish literary work that did not explicitly acknowledge and unequivocally denounce the Occupation was to tacitly support 'German cultural politics that aimed to normalize the situation under occupation' (Sapiro 2014: 46). This position was articulated most decisively in a February 1941 issue of *La Pensée libre*, which declared that only '"one lone thought can be expressed legally in France: *propaganda* in favor of submission"' (cited in Sapiro 2014: 582; italics in original). Under the Occupation, 'legal literature means literature of treason' (Sapiro 2014: 46).

It is within this cultural climate that Michael Holland pinpoints the problematic that Blanchot faced in deciding to write about the relation between literature and terror, specifically, during the Second World War without explicit reference to the murderous brutality of Nazism or the disgraceful complicity of Vichy France. 'In the harsh light' of the disaster of France's capitulation to the brutish, genocidal ideology of Nazism, 'the fact that Blanchot's weekly chronicles appear to take no account' of this disaster 'becomes glaringly apparent' (Holland 2014: 2). Holland continues:

> However clear it is by 1942 that something called *literature* is providing his only preoccupation and the sole measure of human affairs, it is hard to see what *value* that literary ideal could lay claim to, let alone the writing in which Blanchot so resolutely defends it. What interest could the situation of the nineteenth-century poet Lamartine possibly hold, when the situation of so many living people had become an unimaginable horror simply because they were Jewish? Could 'Terror in Literature' be of any import when terror and counterterror were pitting French patriots against the German occupiers in a viciously unequal struggle? (2014: 2)

These are serious, difficult questions, and the answers that Blanchot's writing and thinking give to the aesthetic, political, historical and of course ethical problematics they propose were anything but evasive. Only by submitting literature to the imperative of terror whereby the work of literature is suspended in a state of restless ambiguity, indecision and suspicion vis-à-vis its relation to its language and to the language of the outside world would it be possible to ensure that literature continue to represent a language of absolute freedom, a space of absolute refusal to being pacified or silenced through collaboration with the ideology of normalisation. Literature must be sacrificed, in other words, in order that the world have recourse to a space of refusal where the forces of censorship, oppression and destruction (of memory, community and life) would be continually subject to the promise of transgression. This was not a temporary, emergency measure of literature in the context of the Second World War, but rather the new condition of literature that the disasters of the war precipitated.[17]

Hill explains the significance of Blanchot's intellectual itinerary continuing to pivot around the language of terror after the war:

> For if it is true that literature, like death, seizes paroxystically within the immediacy of a paramount moment of absolute freedom, as the rhetoric of terror would suggest, it is also the case that literature, like death, is an encounter with the limitless impossibility of that moment, and with the lack of power that leaves writing forever suspended as an absent event that can never properly come to be, since the only domain it occupies is the domain of worklessness, impotence, and disaster. (1997: 47–8)

Blanchot's 'Literature and the Right to Death' is the place where terror's ongoing migration into the space of literature (commencing with revolutionary terror and accelerating with the disasters of the Second World War) is most conspicuously and comprehensively excavated, but it is in his critical review essay of Paulhan's *Flowers for Tarbes* where Blanchot elevates Terror (the concept as it relates to literature is Paulhan's before it is Blanchot's) to the status of something like a new absolute of literature that will have become singularly responsive to the post-1945 imperatives of writing should literature survive the war as a viable centre of resistance (i.e. through its responsiveness to the fragmentary imperatives of worklessness, impotence and disaster, as Hill emphasises, that the migration of terror into the space of literature compels).

Blanchot, commenting on Paulhan, associates terror with an

approach to language that intends to dissolve both its intermediary status as a vehicle of representation as well as its symbolist status as directly productive, and thus not merely representative, of the images, values and meanings it calls into reality. The terrorists of language are those who desire it purified of its everyday banalities, vulgar commonplaces, worn out clichés and unmediated romantic idealisms. They intend to 'rid language', explains Blanchot, 'of the words, symbols, and turns of phrase that made it resemble a means of exchange or a precise system of substitution' (*FP* 80). To approach language as a destructive and alien space that nevertheless contains within it the secret of what has not yet been thought or expressed is to similarly demand a newly inventive means capable of approaching it in this way, 'but this demand', worries Blanchot, 'could be nothing but all-consuming' (*FP* 80). Literature intervenes into language as the means of unveiling the metaphysical secrets that language hides, but it cannot perform its duty if all that it has at its disposal are the techniques and forms that the aesthetic and literary tradition has already devised and subsequently over-used. Literature implies, like language, its own commonplaces and clichés, and so literature, if it is to truly *be* literature, must also disrupt the aesthetic language that it knows and practises all too comfortably. 'The writer', this 'terrorist' of language and literature alike, 'thus has the duty to break with these conventions, a kind of ready-made language [of literature], more impure than the other [ordinary language]. If he can, he must free himself from all intermediaries that custom has fashioned and, delighting the reader, place him in direct relationship with the veiled world that he wishes him to discover, with the metaphysical secret, the pure religion whose pursuit is his true fate' (*FP* 80). The hostility that the writer shows to language and to literary forms presents a number of difficulties for maintaining the belief that literature is at all practicable. Blanchot's enumeration, via Paulhan, of all the presuppositions literature must negate if it is to begin approaching the secret of refusal embedded in language succeeds in rendering literature *inconceivable* as a concept and as a practice. Literature is saturated here by a suspicion and hostility towards its material (language and words), its tradition, its purpose, and its very existence during (and after) the time of the world at war.

It is at the point of realising literature's essential inoperability that Blanchot advances 'two rather serious remarks' about the relation that links literature indissolubly with the language and *logos* of terror:

> The first is that the concept that we have just learned to know under the name of Terror is not any aesthetic or critical concept whatsoever; it covers the entire field of letters; *it is literature, or at least its soul.* The result of this is that when we call Terror into question in order to refute it or to show the consequences of its logic, it is literature itself that we question and drive towards nothingness. Moreover, we are forced to state that aside from a few famous exceptions, writers of one or the other kind, even the most severe ones, the ones most attached to their ambition, have not renounced either language or the form of their art. It is a fact; literature exists. It continues to exist despite the inherent absurdity that lives in it, divides it, and makes it actually inconceivable. (*FP* 80–1; my italics)

That literature exists at all immediately strikes Blanchot as a counter-intuitive proposition. If literature is sustained by a dual internal movement of self-revelation and self-destruction, which together secure its continual disappearance from the world of knowledge, communication and discourse, then the indisputable fact of its existence suggests that where literature does begin to exist, it is because it has ceased its agreement with the ideals of its conceptualisation: 'literature begins at the moment when literature becomes a question' (*GO* 21). Literature inherits the relentless, inquisitorial drive of suspicion and purgation – the drive towards nothingness – that had likewise rendered the Reign of Terror inconceivable (and ultimately impracticable because unsustainable) from the perspective of its historical and political commencement and continuation. Just as the revolutionary perpetuation of the Reign of Terror, writes Rebecca Comay, 'can elaborate itself only as the repetitive production of nothing – the empty negativity of an unworked death' (2011: 76), so too does literature, *pace* Blanchot, arise only in a movement that 'brings death to the inhuman', for it is literature that comes to be, via 'the writer *par excellence*' (*GO* 40), the Marquis de Sade, 'in possession of nothingness and destruction' (*IC* 182).

Articulating literature's responsibilities before the fragmentary imperative of terror would be an incomplete exercise if the indomitable presence of Sade were left out of account. Georges Bataille, Pierre Klossowski, Roland Barthes, Jean Paulhan, Jean-Paul Sartre, Simone de Beauvoir, Michel Foucault and Jacques Lacan (to name only some of the more notable French thinkers) have all produced substantive essays on the literary value and continuing aesthetic and political relevance of that notorious and notoriously lettered prisoner of the Bastille prison and Charenton asylum, the Marquis de Sade. Blanchot is no outlier when it comes to the responsibility of confronting Sade and the impact his writing has exerted over the trajectory and genesis of modern (and above all modernist) literature. That Sade is a contemporary of the Terror is an essential observation for Blanchot's assessment of Sade's mastery at surpassing the formal limitations and aesthetic good taste of the literature and politics of his time. The influence of Sade's contemporaneity with Terror swings both ways: 'Something of Sade belongs to the Terror, as something of the Terror belongs to Sade' (*IC* 227).

What is this 'something' of the Terror that belongs to Sade? Caroline Weber, commenting on Sade's privileged perspective on the political realities of revolutionary France before and during the implementation of the Terror right outside the window of his cell at the Bastille (where he was perched right above a guillotine), has argued that

> whereas the monarchy at least made no bones about its arbitrary judicial practices – shamelessly reveling, as the Montagnards themselves argued at Louis's trial, in despotism and bloodlust – the revolutionaries justified their killings in the abstract, joyless language of public interest. To witness countless scenes of death and suffering: not a problem. But to watch these slayings carried out, in Mantel's phrase, 'with no passion at all' and in the name of a polity that construed passion itself as a threat to liberty: this, perhaps, was to Sade the Terror's ultimate outrage. (2003: 173)

When parcelling out what it is of the Terror that for Blanchot belongs to Sade we need to be careful not to conclude prematurely that just because Sade's literature is riddled with extreme (and extremely boring) scenes of violence and torture (sexual or otherwise), exhaustive recitations of libertinage and debauchery, and blasphemies of all stripes and persuasions, it is straightforwardly predisposed to the revolutionary discourse and brutality of the Terror.

If Sade's relation with the Terror is beset by an aversion to and distrust of its dispassionate spectacularisation of death and desire on the public platform of the guillotine – as is the case with most spectacles, the purges quickly lapsed into the banality of their daily repetition – then in order to salvage Blanchot's interpretation of Sade we will have to consider what the spectacle of the Terror occludes such that what is *not* banal and *not* dispassionately repetitive in the experience of terror is destined for migration to the literary space of Sade's (and eventually Beckett's) writing. If 'something' of the Terror belongs to Sade, in other words, then surely it is not its exhausting spectacles or the passionless bureaucratic sterility of the discourse of Robespierre. As Blanchot reads him, Sade is perhaps one of the first major representatives of modern literature (alongside Jena Romanticism) to deterritorialise the political imperative of terror as an essential ingredient of fragmentary writing.

Blanchot's most sustained reflections on Sade in *The Infinite Conversation* culminate with the intriguing suggestion that with the 'instant of prodigious suspense for which Sade reserves the title revolutionary' (*IC* 226), a suspense in which 'all laws are silent', the true significance of Sade's writing is most powerfully illuminated. Sade's writing delivers us to the limits of the reason of literature and history alike: 'this reason is certainly dangerous, terrible, and, properly speaking, terror itself, but nothing ill-fated is to be expected from it – on condition, however, that one "*never lack the force necessary to go beyond the furthermost limits*"' (*IC* 227; italics in original). Blanchot can easily be accused of administering a theoretical sleight of hand in this passage. Two pairings, two pairings that double as two disjunctions – the terror of literature and the terror of the political – are immediately apparent as the ingredients called upon by Blanchot to communicate what, in the literature of Sade as much as in the historical operability of revolutionary politics, circulates around a central concept and trope – *terror itself*. What Blanchot is (in part) after in *The Infinite Conversation* is an account of what makes violence and terror destructive in the space of politics, as Badiou argues, but imperatives for the creative, aleatory repetition of suspension, interruption and discontinuity in the space of literature.

This seemingly incommensurable pairing of disjunctions becomes less intransigent, however, once Blanchot proceeds to supplement the first stage of its formulation with the added caveat – 'on condition' – that what is responsible for the danger and the sterility of this reason – the reason of *terror itself* – derives its force from somewhere other than what the already established limits of historical and aesthetic judgement declare. Inside history, inside the literary tradition as any historical moment knows and understands it, this power to persist in the fragmentary excess of the furthermost limits is strictly speaking an impossibility, i.e. it is simply not pragmatic or practicable to advance the imperative of terror as the answer to the question of literature. A limit only exists as a limit in so far as what it demarcates precludes precisely the prospect of going beyond its borders (and therefore there is no such thing as a limit *per se*). To speak about a reason that is somehow dangerous in a paradoxically sterile kind of way – terror nevertheless *is* the answer to the question of literature in so far as it is the imperative of the ceaselessness of the question itself – is to speak about the possibility of an *outside* of history and of an *outside* of literature. These two outsides are in no way alien to one another either; rather, their interdependence, dependent, that is to say, on *terror itself*, means that to begin navigating the reason of literature as it is personified in the oeuvre of Sade is to already be engaged in mapping out the reason of history in terms of how it is reincarnated in literature as the revolution personified in writing.

Without terror there cannot be a suspension of, or a rupture with, the temporal tyranny of a past that overwhelms a present which itself hijacks the coming realities of the future. This is indeed one side of the thesis that Blanchot is attempting to communicate with respect to the historical and literary significance of Sade's incomparable acts of writing and commitments to desire, and it is a significance that extends far beyond just the biographical Sade and migrates all the way into the essential conditions of historical and literary possibility that, from *Faux Pas* all the way up to *The Writing of the Disaster*, Blanchot is unceasingly labouring to coordinate. Precisely because it is terror that is responsible for the most radical suspension that history has perhaps ever experienced, a suspension that cut the secular world from its theological moorings (enacted symbolically and perhaps even literally in the decapitation of the divine institution of monarchy), it is terror as well that is enlisted whenever literature glimpses the opportunity to suspend the laws of its continuing possibility and existence:

> With Sade – and in a very high form of paradoxical truth – we have the first example (but is there a second?) of the way in which writing, the freedom to write, can coincide with the movement of true freedom, when the latter enters into crisis and gives rise to a vacancy in history. A coincidence that is not an identification. For Sade's motives are not

those that had set the forces of revolution into motion; they even contradict them. And yet without them, without the mad excess that the name, the life, and the truth of Sade have represented, the revolution would have been deprived of a part of its Reason. (*IC* 222)

If we can refer to Sade as the subject of a revolution in literature, this writer who put to himself the impossible task to speak the unspeakable, incessantly, and to think the unthinkable, perversely, then it is because in the flashing instant of the historical disruption that Sade witnessed and in which he participated, his writing demonstrates for literature that it too can have its revolution, though only if it never lacks the courage to enter into a quasi-Faustian bargain that it knows from the beginning that it cannot outwit. Literature must continuously reinforce the terror of its repetitive self-interrogation if it is to have a relevant existence as the rightful historical heir to the radical suspension, the radical affirmation of refusal, through which modernity originally commenced.

According to Blanchot, 'Sade's major impropriety resides in the simply repetitive force of a narration that encounters no interdict (the whole of this limit-work recounting the interdict by way of the monotony of its terrifying murmur) because there is no other time than that of the interval of speaking: the pure arrest that can be reached only by never stopping speaking' (*IC* 221). No dialectical dialogue is permitted with Sade because his writing accords no respect or recognition of the logics and the authorities that exist outside his writing. Blanchot is insistent that 'the books of the Marquis de Sade are unreadable – capable of putting into question the honest act of reading' (*IC* 328). But,

> nevertheless they are read, read outside reading. Let us say, perhaps, that works such as these, *and first of all Beckett's*, come closer than is customary to the movement of writing and to the movement of reading, seeking to combine them in an experience that, if not common to both, is at least scarcely differentiated – and here we meet up again with the idea of indifference, of a neutral affirmation, equal-unequal, eluding all that would give it value or even affirm it. (*IC* 329; my italics)

The idea that Sade gives to modern literature, *and first of all to Beckett*, is the idea of the fragmentary imperative that Sade's witnessing of the Terror demonstrated how to harness as a constitutive principle of writing's insurrectionary commitment to refusal.

Blanchot's decision to trace a genealogy of the literature of refusal that begins with Sade and continues through Beckett is an association that Beckett would not necessarily have gone out of his way to dispute.

V

Responding to a letter from Georges Duthuit dated 28 October 1948, Beckett thanks Duthuit for his 'kind letter with the Blanchot article' (*Letters II* 107). It is not entirely certain which of Blanchot's articles Beckett had read (the editors of Beckett's *Letters* point out that Blanchot published five articles in 1948 alone), but in another letter to Duthuit, dated 3 January 1951, it is clear that it is Blanchot's essay 'Sade's Reason', which originally appeared as the second part of *Lautréamont et Sade* (later retitled *Sade et Lautréamont*), that has piqued Beckett's interest, so much so in fact that he started translating passages from it into English: 'I have finished with the Blanchot. [. . .] What emerges from it is a truly gigantic Sade, jealous of Satan and of his eternal torments, and confronting nature more than humankind' (*Letters II* 219). By the time Blanchot published his review essay of *The Unnamable*, 'Where Now? Who Now?', it is clear that Beckett was already favourably predisposed to the way that Blanchot approached the problematic of thinking about literature. Indeed, Blanchot's essay, 'Where Now? Who Now?', 'which was', according to Bruno Clément, 'to provide the tonality of Beckettian studies for a long time' (2006: 120), elicited enthusiastic approval from Beckett that would show little sign of diminishing over the next decade: 'On *Molloy* Maurice Nadeau and Georges Bataille[18] seem to me the best. I also liked Nadeau's general critique (I forget what in). But the big thing, for me, is the recent piece by Maurice Blanchot on *L'Innommable*' (*Letters II* 442).

On 21 April 1960, Robert Mallet, writing in the capacity as editor of Gallimard's La Bibliothèque Idéale series, wrote to Beckett requesting his approval for the commission of a critical study of his work. In this letter Mallet also requested of Beckett, if he 'would be kind enough, when replying, to tell me which critic (or critics) you would recommend' for taking on this project (*Letters III* 332). Beckett graciously agreed 'on the principle of a study of my work, to appear in your Bibliothèque Idéale series', adding that 'if Maurice Blanchot were willing to take on this study

I would be delighted' (*Letters III* 332). When asked by Mallet to take on this project, Blanchot regrettably declined, explaining that he was simply too busy at the time to pursue a project of such undeniable importance and depth. *Samuel Beckett and the Terror of Literature* does not presume to speculate on what Blanchot would have said in the event of acquiescing to Beckett's recommendation, but it does regard Beckett's recommendation as evidence that perhaps the contribution of Blanchot to thinking through the Beckettian corpus, contrary to what critics like Pascale Casanova have recently argued, has not yet been exhausted.[19]

Chapter 1 will develop this contribution further through its consideration of what Blanchot's notion of radical suffering, derived through his reading of Robert Antelme in *The Infinite Conversation*, has to teach us about how the interrelated ordeals of suffering, thinking and terror are circumscribed in Beckett's writing of *The Unnamable*. This chapter is concerned with seeing what happens to the question of thinking in Beckett's writing when it is submitted to the terror that its eponymous narrative voice experiences by being inscribed so indelibly in the space and time of radical suffering. Chapter 2 looks closely at how *Texts for Nothing* negotiates the imperative of getting beyond the terrifying disintegration of narrative and narrative voice that Beckett enacted in *The Unnamable*. In doing so, it renders Beckett's writing of *Texts for Nothing* symptomatic of the twentieth-century experience of deciphering when and where a new historical and political sequence begins and ends. Can there be an authentic, radical beginning or ending if it must be predicated on nothing more ontologically stable than fictions of endings and beginnings that the twentieth century, particularly its politics, worked so obsessively (and oftentimes violently) to construct? This chapter asks, through Beckett, what happens to subjectivity precisely when it is suspended precariously, indeed threateningly, in the space where such fictions reign?

Chapter 3 on *How It Is* assesses the limits to the ethics of language precisely in so far as it is through language, or rather through the *place* of language, that dialogue between self and other is always first, before a word is spoken, the disquieting uncertainty over whether or not the other is to be met with violence or speech. Blanchot's disagreement with Levinas over the ethics of language is instrumental to the thesis of this chapter, which is that *How It Is* is fundamentally about exposing (and indeed performing) how the economy of human relation *qua* economy of dialogue must be orchestrated by the imperative that there be the possibility of violence, that the memory, the archive of suffering and pain, opened in and through dialogue with the other and through which the other *qua* other speaks, never be forgotten or closed. It is through *How It Is* that we see nothing more but also nothing less than the 'meremost minimum' of a difference between the terror associated by Hannah Arendt with totalitarian terror, and the terror that this book is associating with the terror of literature (*NO* 90).

The focus of Chapter 4 is on Beckett's late trilogy of novels, *Company*, *Ill Seen Ill Said* and *Worstward Ho*, and particularly on how the fragmentary aesthetic Beckett uses for the composition of these works is responsive to the distress of what we can call, through Blanchot and also through Judith Butler, the figures of passivity that dwell within Beckett's writing. Its argument is that through the fragmentary aesthetic responsible for the compositional structures of these works, Beckett's writing exhibits compassion towards but also complicity in the experience of suffering, pain and distress that the textual figures of these novels are condemned by Beckett's writing to always communicate and endure. The wager of *Samuel Beckett and the Terror of Literature*, finally, is that reading Beckett through the language of terror on which Blanchot enables us to reflect is to give new significance and erect new obstacles to how we read and think through the violence, the suffering and the pain that speaks in and through Beckett's texts.

Notes

1. In the Epilogue to his *Miracle and Machine*, Michael Naas writes that DeLillo's magnum opus, *Underworld*, is, 'like all literature, [...] related to the experience of the miracle, to the experience of a testimony that is equivalent to asking someone to believe in you as they would believe in a miracle' (2012: 277). The faith to which DeLillo's fiction struggles so desperately to attest, however, is always at risk of succumbing to its nightmarish double, a 'second faith [...] that feels like terror, abandonment, and hopelessness' (2012: 279).
2. Terry Eagleton is aware that 'the affinity between terror and the sacred may sound peculiarly, even offensively irrelevant to the terrorism of our own time. There is nothing especially saintly about tearing someone's head from their shoulders in the name of Allah the All-Merciful, or burning Arab children to death in the cause of

democracy. Yet it is not wholly possible to understand the notion of terror without also grasping this curious double-edgedness. Terror begins as a religious idea, as indeed much terrorism is still today; and religion is all about deeply ambivalent powers which both enrapture and annihilate' (2005: 2).

3. Candidates for the *de facto* historical birthplace of the Terror include the 1789 Constitution of the Rights of Man (François Furet's candidate), the September Massacre of 1792 (this is Sophie Wahnich's preferred candidate), the inauguration of the Revolutionary Tribunal, the Law of Suspects, and also the Law of 22 Prairial (which granted the Revolutionary Tribunal the ability to expedite the trials and executions previously administered by the National Convention). All of these options were floated during the Thermidorian reaction to the Terror, and the purpose of sifting through all available candidates was so that the Thermidorians could begin the arduous work of cleansing the Revolution and the Republic of any superfluous uses of violence that the Terror had implemented and systematised.

4. As Andrew Gibson writes in *Beckett and Badiou*, 'modernity begins with the French Revolution, the first great historical experience of the void underlying established structures, and therefore of the possibility of the tabula rasa and radical transformation' (2006: 257). The question arises, however, of the precise role played by the Terror in positioning the French Revolution at the foundation of the political history of modernity. Here we might recall Jürgen Habermas's stern condemnation of 'those who link the project of modernity with the conscious attitudes and spectacular public deeds of individual terrorists' (1987: 50).

5. Wahnich's *In Defence of the Terror* represents the most recent and perhaps most forceful repudiation of this post-Thermidorian obfuscation of 'the Terror', which she sees as largely responsible for the anti-revolutionary political ideology that dominates the politically conservative horizon of late modernity. She counters the Thermidorian narrative of 'the Terror' by insisting that 'establishing the Terror had the aim of preventing emotion from giving rise to dissolution or massacre, symbolizing what had not been done in September 1792 and thus reintroducing a regulatory function for the Assembly. [. . .] Contrary to the prevailing interpretations today, then, the Terror was thus aimed at establishing limits to the sovereign exception, putting a brake on the legitimate violence of the people and giving a public and institutionalized form to vengeance' (2012: 64–5).

6. Robespierre's terror saved the virtue of the Revolution, and it is for this reason that terror as such cannot be submitted as an object of philosophical conceptualisation independently of the revolutionary principle of virtue. Robespierre puts the matter succinctly and pointedly in a speech on political morality in February 1794: 'virtue, without which terror is disastrous; terror, without which virtue is powerless' (2006: 115).
7. There is nothing in *Manifesto for Philosophy* to suggest that Badiou intends to privilege terror over ecstasy of place and sacredness of the name. However, if we widen our focus to Badiou's oeuvre as a whole, we see terror appearing with much greater regularity, suggesting that Badiou never succeeds in figuring out how, exactly, terror is to be subjected to philosophical analysis.
8. Accordingly, David Kleinberg-Levin is right to stress that in so far as the 'light of [. . .] redemption, weak though it is, can occasionally be glimpsed' in Beckett's writing (2015: 2), it is only through Beckett's emphasis on its 'haunting *absence*' in the historical and political context of late modernity (2015: 6; italics in original).
9. The full quote from Lacoue-Labarthe begins with reference to Blanchot and ends with a reference to Beckett. Lacoue-Labarthe: '"To write, the exigency to write": The formulation is from Maurice Blanchot. Such a formulation, and one can hear this immediately, touches on the very essentiality of what we can no longer have the nerve to name "literature" [*la littérature*]. And it does so without any commotion, almost modestly, but in a way that is altogether decisive. By means of this imperative without content, what was known as "literature" – a term that has authorised so many immense pretensions and inspired poses – is given over to its own naked existence as a fact and as a sort of duty without reason, much as the Rimbaud of a Season in Hell says that he is given over to the earth and to a harsh reality. In a register that is quite close to this (despite appearances), when Beckett was asked by a newspaper survey "Why do you write?" he gave this lapidary response: 'Bon qu'à ça' ('It's all I'm good for')' (2007: 38).
10. Deleuze characterises this relation in terms of literature's singular expressions of the immanence of lived experience, but given Deleuze's non-phenomenological conception of living-in-immanence, the emphasis falls on literature's *non*-relation with what is liveable: 'writing is a question of becoming, always incomplete, always in the midst of being formed, and goes beyond the matter of any livable or lived experience. It is a process, that is, a passage of Life that trav-

erses both the livable and the lived. [...] The shame of being a man – is there any better reason to write?' (1997: 1).

11. Weller's insistence on deploying what he terms 'the anethical' derives from his interest in analysing 'the works of Beckett and others in a manner that is less polarized by the nihilist/anti-nihilist model, but that does not assume either the possibility of an analysis of literature that would be clearly distinguishable from the ethical, or the possibility of a literary practice that would have, as Blanchot argues in his 1963 preface to *Lautréamont and Sade* (1949), a power of affirmation wholly liberated from the notion of value. [...] [W]hat I have termed the anethical [...] is to be distinguished from, although not necessarily to be thought as either prior or posterior to, the "ethics of alterity" or the "ethics of difference" that has come to dominate what is generally termed "postmodern" thought' (2006: viii). Weller deploys his notion of the 'anethical' in a way that is designed to highlight the failure inherent in any attempt to distinguish, in the context of Beckett, between ethical and unethical discourses. Weller's aversion to discourses of relation, then, repeats what Blanchot had already argued vis-à-vis the *il y a*, or the neutered speech that speaks through Beckett's writing.

12. Levinas uses the term '*il y a*' to describe 'the impersonal, anonymous, yet inextinguishable "consummation" of being, which murmurs in the depths of nothingness itself' (2001: 57).

13. 'The political plans and conflicts of the period initiated by 9 Thermidor', explains Bronisław Baczko, 'cluster around a central issue: that of emerging from the Terror. The overthrow of Robespierre on that date was a seminal event that gave a name to a political period and plan, as well as to its instigators. We might say then that the Thermidorians were those who accepted emergence from the Terror as a crucial, urgently necessary, political imperative. Within a few weeks of 9 Thermidor, it became clear that the "happy revolution" could not end with the execution of Robespierre and his accomplices. It had to go further; it had to dismantle an entire system of power' (1994: 19). The representatives of Thermidor immediately recognised that only by purging the political scene of any and all traces of Robespierre would it be possible to dissipate the remnants of the Terror that was implemented in his name.

14. That the publication of Beckett's writing during this time could not evade being implicated in the post-war constellation of historical, political and cultural crisis in France, accordingly, is to concede the legitimacy of the first premise of Jean-Paul Sartre's thesis on

the commitment of literature as it was articulated for the inaugural issue of the journal *Les temps modernes*. 'The writer', according to Sartre, 'is *situated* in his time; every word he writes has reverberations. As does his silence' (1988: 252; italics in original). Writing in the essay 'Situation of the Writer in 1947', Sartre elaborates further on what the politics of silence means for post-war culture in France, particularly as it owed much of its ethical capital to the men and women, Beckett and Deschevaux-Dumesnil not excluded, of the Resistance to the Nazi Occupation: 'most of the resisters, though beaten, burned, blinded, and broken, did not speak. [. . .] Everything concurred in making them believe that they were only insects, that man is the impossible dream of spies and squealers, and that they would awaken as vermin like everybody else. [. . .] But they remained silent and man was born of their silence' (1988: 180).
15. Blanchot follows Levinas's argument in *Existence and Existents* that literature induces the 'horror' of the *il y a*. 'The rustling of the *there is [il y a]* . . . is horror. [. . .] To be conscious is to be torn away from the there is, since the existence of a consciousness constitutes a subjectivity, a subject of existence, that is, to some extent a master of being, already a name in the anonymity of the night. Horror is somehow a movement which will strip consciousness of its very "subjectivity." Not in lulling it into unconsciousness, but in throwing it into an *impersonal vigilance*, a *participation*' (GO 55).
16. Newly translated into English by Michael Holland and collected in *Into Disaster: Chronicles of Intellectual Life, 1941* (Blanchot 2014).
17. In the essay 'War and Literature', which Blanchot wrote in response to a Polish magazine asking what influence the war had on literature after 1945, Blanchot explains that 'the change undergone by the concept of literature [. . .] is not in immediate relation to the "Second World War," having been in the process of becoming long before; however, it found the accelerated confirmation of the fundamental crisis in the war, the change of an era that we do not yet know how to measure for lack of a language. Which amounts to saying, in the crisis that keeps getting deeper and that literature also conveys according to its mode, war is always present and, in some ways, pursued. Which also amounts to saying, the war (the Second World War) was not only a war, a historical event like any other, circumscribed and limited with its causes, its turns, and its results. It was an *absolute*. This absolute is named when one utters the names of Auschwitz, Warsaw (the ghetto and the struggle for liberation of the city), Treblinka, Dachau, Buchenwald, Neuengamme, Oranienburg,

Belsen, Mauthausen, Ravensbrück, and so many others' (*F* 109; italics in original).

18. Jean-Michel Rabaté has recently commented on Bataille's appraisal of Beckett, particularly in his review essay of *Molloy*, 'The Silence of Molloy', and also their subsequent meeting and friendly exchange of letters. He writes: 'From the start, Bataille felt that he had found in Beckett an artist close to his heart: here was someone, who, like him, found himself alone after having belonged to a group (*transition* for Beckett, the Surrealist dissidence of *Documents* for Bataille), they both had escaped from the horrors of the war, and their tentative groping in the dark had generated an experimental prose that debunked all values. Both were attempting to think at the limit of the human' (2012: 56).

19. Casanova accuses Blanchot's short review essay of *The Unnamable*, 'Where Now? Who Now?' of 'helping to "fabricate" a tailor-made Beckett, hero of "pure" criticism', who was thereby made to serve 'the obscurantist designs of Blanchot-style criticism' (2006: 11). Terry Eagleton is perhaps even more dismissive of Blanchot's contemporary value for reading Beckett when he endorses Casanova's *Samuel Beckett: Anatomy of a Literary Revolution* on the basis of her portrayal of 'Maurice Blanchot [...] more or less as the villain of this book' (2006a: 1). Shane Weller provides a useful explanation of why critics like Casanova and Eagleton might want to be so hostile towards Blanchot's reading of Beckett: 'when Foucault, Deleuze, Barthes, Simon Critchley, Christophe Bident, and [Curt] Willits analyse Beckett's texts', it is the anonymous voice of Blanchot's 'the neuter' that 'they hear, and in so doing they are, in fact, countersigning Blanchot's reading of Beckett' (2007: 29). The result of such readings tends to be 'a reduction of being to language', as Weller writes elsewhere with Dirk Van Hulle, and consequently 'the disappearance of any referential function' operative in Beckett's writing (Hulle and Weller 2014: 27). What Blanchot seems committed to saying in his reading of Beckett, and it is this with which Casanova and Eagleton take issue, is that there is no place in the Beckettian oeuvre for history and politics, and above all literary history and the politics of literature. If reading Beckett through Blanchot has tended to produce ahistorical readings of his novels, short stories and plays, however, then this is perhaps as a consequence of the criticism of Blanchot within Beckett studies being similarly blind to the historical horizon pressuring Blanchot's own thinking. Accordingly, it is by excavating the interpretive resources buried in the conceptual

archive of the historical phenomenon of terror that this book eludes repeating a so-called 'tailor-made Beckett' fabricated by an equally 'tailor-made Blanchot'.

I

The Terror of Thinking in
The Unnamable

Suffering – why, this is the sole cause of consciousness.
(Fyodor Dostoevsky)

I

From the very first pages of *The Unnamable* the reader is made aware that the work's narrative voice[1] is immersed in a radically sceptical and unforgiving reflexive encounter with virtually all the prerequisites of its narrative existence: 'Where now? Who now? When now? Unquestioning. I, say I. Unbelieving. Questions, hypotheses, call them that. Keep going, going on, call that going, call that on' (*TN* 286). The difficulty of these opening lines, as readers of Beckett's work have long since recognised, is that the narrative voice that speaks them has, from the start, hijacked the labour of interpreting the work's formal and thematic components that readers standing outside of the fictional world of *The Unnamable* require if they are to productively engage in a critical intervention into the text. *The Unnamable* immediately presents itself, in other words, as a self-hermeneutic enterprise committed to articulating the limits and measuring the conditions of the life of its voice in narrative. One of the drawbacks of these opening lines is that they preclude the possibility of authenticating (unquestioning, unbelieving) that the voice is or was present as the author or witness of the testimonial fictions that the inhospitable architecture of its subsequent narrative goes on to compel it ceaselessly to give. The rhetorical status of these three questions, which is underscored as quickly as it is undermined by the (ironic) assertion, 'Unquestioning', leaves the reader virtually paralysed with having to consent to the implication that there is no definite 'where' situating the narrative voice, there is no identifiable 'who' grounding the voice's narrative subjectivity (and thus also authorising the veracity of its speech), and, perhaps most damagingly to the coherence of the entire narrative structure, there is no trace, no archival evidence of 'when' the stories and events of which the voice speaks, 'knowing that it lies', could be said ever to have occurred precisely and paradoxically in the midst of its very occurrence (*TN* 301).

Blanchot was one of the first serious readers of *The Unnamable* to address the significance that these questions have on the work as a whole: 'Who is speaking in the books of Samuel Beckett? What is this tireless "I" that seemingly always says the same thing? Where does it hope to come? What does the author, who must be somewhere, hope for? What do we hope for, when we read?' (*BC* 210). Blanchot is right to pause on these opening questions and to risk proposing an answer to what they ask. Noting the threatening position *The Unnamable* assumes in reducing the methods and aims of literary critique to little more than exercises in meta-hermeneutical redundancy, Blanchot nevertheless goes on to propose that 'what speaks' in *The Unnamable* is a form of neutral (or neutered) speech that is as radically disintegrative as it is constitutively productive of what and how language and literary forms of representation seek to communicate. In *The Unnamable*, 'language does not speak, it is; in it nothing begins, nothing is said, but it is always new and always begins again' (*BC* 216).

Accordingly, with *The Unnamable* we are privy to a work of literature that contains within its textual structure the beginning and end of narrative speech. *The Unnamable* opens itself onto 'the pure approach of the impulse from which all books come, of that original point where the work is lost, which always ruins the work, which restores the endless pointlessness in it, but with which it must also maintain a relationship that is always beginning again, under the risk of being nothing' (*BC* 213). Blanchot's analysis of the fragility of the speaking presence that grounds the narrative discourse of *The Unnamable* as it enters into a tenuous, radically unworkable literary existence is indispensable for subsequent critical encounters with this voice that dwells so disastrously in Beckett's writing. Blanchot's attention is not only on the question of how *The Unnamable* functions as a work of literature, or on the necessity that the author behind this work (i.e. Beckett) efface himself before the anonymous event of the narrative that outlives him, but also on how the narrative voice inside

The Unnamable speaks and exists in this place in narrative where there should be no possibility of speech or existence. Dividing his analysis between the work (of writing) and the voice (of narrative speech) of *The Unnamable* enables Blanchot to operate at two levels of reading simultaneously, and to do so precisely because *The Unnamable* itself unfolds according to the illusion that there is no distance separating these two dimensions of the work's compositional architecture. Blanchot interrogates the voice and the void of language into which the voice is plunged, and out of which the voice speaks: 'what is this void that becomes the voice of the man disappearing into it? Where has he fallen?' (BC 210).

Blanchot's investigation is therefore an investigation into this space where speaking subjectivity is silenced, effaced and essentially destroyed, but where it somehow (coerced of its own volition) goes on speaking (and goes on suffering) nevertheless. The emphasis of Blanchot's reading, in other words, is not solely on language and the language of literature and narrative, but rather on the voice that shoulders the unbearable responsibility of continuing speaking where speech itself articulates as the purest modality of torture and torment. Accordingly, one of the consequences of Blanchot's critique of *The Unnamable* is that by zeroing in on the figure of the narrative voice tasked with surviving the unending (because etiologically indeterminate) trauma of its textual imprisonment, it indicts the desire to read *The Unnamable* simply as an ethical or rhetorical testament to perseverance: 'there is nothing admirable in an ordeal from which one cannot extricate oneself, nothing that deserves admiration in the fact of being trapped and turning in circles in a space one can't leave, even by death, since to be in this space in the first place, one had precisely to have fallen outside of life. Aesthetic feelings are no longer appropriate here' (BC 213). This is not to deny that the figure of the unnamable is not a subject predicated, at least partially, by its ethic of perseverance, or that Beckett's (ironic) use of the rhetorical device of aporia, as Amanda Dennis reminds us, is designed and deployed in the textual space of *The Unnamable* in order to 'spur a creative endurance that entails an aesthetic of survival – a going *on* (if not forward)' (2015: 181; italics in original); rather, Blanchot is expressing a sensitivity to the suffering figure of *The Unnamable*, but in the process of doing so will have to concede that whatever modality of suffering the unnamable is obliged to endure will be a modality of suffering that the unnamable itself has been rendered complicit in orchestrating. Implicit in Blanchot's analysis of *The Unnamable* is the cautionary demand that subsequent encounters with *The Unnamable* avoid the temptation of revisionist readings of its textual ethics as an ethics of aesthetic perseverance. To properly understand the unnamable's conditions of narrative survival would require a critique of how it is that the unnamable is circumscribed, and circumscribes itself in turn, in the terror of dying interminably, speaking interminably, and thinking interminably in the space of Beckett's writing.

The purpose of this chapter is to begin the task of mobilising the conceptual resources of Blanchot precisely for understanding how it is that *The Unnamable* stages the limits and establishes the preconditions for its narrative voice to become embroiled in the terrifying convergence of radical protocols of suffering with radical protocols of thinking. The phenomenon of suffering in *The Unnamable* is not reducible to an experience or an image that the work's narrative voice is in a position to communicate analytically or internalise phenomenologically. What is required on behalf of the figure of the unnamable, accordingly, is a way not only of traversing the disquieting link between suffering and thinking, but also, to borrow from Gilles Deleuze, of learning how to think by way of 'trespass and violence', whereby thinking is severed from its paralysing convergence with such unthinkable modalities of existence as radical suffering reflected in *The Unnamable* (Deleuze 1994: 139). What readers of *The Unnamable* have to contend with is the analytical impasse that the narrative voice erects to thinking through the 'how' and the 'why' of this 'labyrinthine torment that can't be grasped, or limited, or felt, or suffered, no, not even suffered' (*TN* 308). This phenomenon in *The Unnamable* of a torment that cannot be conceptually grasped, of a suffering that cannot be phenomenologically suffered, demands that we reimagine what suffering *is*, or rather what suffering *becomes*, precisely when it is experienced according to these epistemological, phenomenological and ontological deficits and restrictions.

Things would be altogether easier if Beckett had made *The Unnamable* adhere to the generic requirements of a personal narrative or a testimonial account of a traumatic experience, a survivor's recollection of an event that is separated temporally by the distance that ordinarily obtains between the traumatic event that happened then, and the memory, the testimonial event of narrative as it is happening now. This erasure of epistemo-phenomenological distance between event of suffering and narrative of suffering sets up a situation where the *failure* to narrate suffering doubles as the suffering that instigates the event of narrative in the first place. It remains to be determined just why it is that this erasure operates so pervasively and incessantly in the narrative world of the unnamable, and also just why the unnamable is so riveted to the tragic position of overseeing and experiencing – as tormentor and tormented simultaneously – this unendingly repetitive metamorphosis of narrative into suffering and suffering into narrative. In other words, what is the nature of the suffering that the unnamable can neither remember nor communicate, the suffering, it comes to pass, of the failure to remember (or forget) and the impossibility to communicate (or be silent)? The emphasis on the unnamable's (ontologically inscrutable) identification with a subjectivity predicated on suffering is ubiquitous in the text, so much so that a close reading of *The Unnamable* would be ethically, epistemologically and hermeneutically irresponsible if it did not attempt to address the questions of how and why the unnamable suffers in the disconcerting way that it does.

II

In *The Infinite Conversation* Blanchot posits the existence of 'a suffering that has lost time altogether. It is the horror of a suffering without end, a suffering time can no longer redeem, that has escaped time and for which there is no longer recourse; it is irremediable' (*IC* 172). As with so many other notions in Blanchot's work, 'suffering' becomes a relevant category for understanding the work of literature when literature too is divested of access to a conscious, nameable subjectivity that would experience and contemplate its suffering in the space and time of suffering's phenomenological apprehension. What Blanchot describes as the (non-)experience of 'suffering without end' is not a worldly or corporeal experience of suffering. It is not derivative of physical suffering and does not have bodily or psychological afflictions as either its cause or manifestation. Accordingly, it is imperative that we distinguish between two forms of suffering that inform Blanchot's reflections on suffering, particularly as it is the more radical experience of suffering, of a suffering that is not vulnerable to phenomenological capture, that for Blanchot represents a site that it is the singular responsibility of literature and narrative to interrogate (and perhaps, terrifyingly, reproduce).

The radical experience of suffering that occupies Blanchot's reflections on voices of narrative and spaces of literature is not detached altogether from the suffering that remains experientially and conceptually accessible to historical and philosophical consciousness; they are not 'worlds apart', as it were. 'The horror of a suffering without end' does not substitute or negate, and it certainly does not minimise or discredit the stakes involved in the imperative to investigate, articulate and ultimately alleviate the finite experiences of corporeal and psychic suffering experienced daily all over the world. The point that Blanchot emphasises in juxtaposing these two forms of suffering – radical suffering and finite suffering – is that the radical modality of suffering without end, the suffering essentially bereft of temporality and detached from all hope of redemption or expiration, only becomes operational where its migration from the ontological context of finitude goes unnoticed precisely by the subject whose suffering has hit such an extreme pitch of weariness and affliction that this self-same subject 'is no longer there to undergo' its suffering 'in the first person' (*IC* 173).

Radical suffering is circumscribed, for Blanchot, according to a fragmentary logic whereby it is subtracted from ontological oversight in the space-time of the present, and in this modality of subtraction it deconstructs the phenomenology of diachronic experience that is at the root of linking before with after and the subject with its subjectivity.[2] Radical suffering signals for Blanchot an epistemological disaster of thinking no less than an ontological disaster of subjectivity:

> if I had recourse to the thought of such suffering, it was so that in this un-power, the I excluded from mastery and from its status as subject (as first person) – the I destitute even of obligation – could lose itself as a self capable of undergoing suffering. There is suffering, there would be suffering, but no longer any 'I' suffering, and this suffering does not make itself known in the present; it is not borne into the present (still less is it experienced in the present). It is without present, just as it is without beginning or end; time has radically changed its meaning and its flow. Time without present, I without I: this is not anything of which one could say that experience – a form of knowledge – would either reveal or conceal it. (*WD* 14–15)

So long as the act of philosophical thinking is constrained by seizing conceptually on its objects of analysis, radical suffering is by definition an unthinkable concept. Thinking philosophically through the dialectical logic (and language) of negativity on which concepts are constitutively predicated requires that a phenomenon like radical suffering somehow be divested of its resistance to philosophical conceptualisation. However, because Blanchot does not desire to think suffering other than in its most radical, that is to say, unthinkable form, he decides to turn to alternative modes of thinking that are not necessarily beholden to the conceptual laws of negativity as are ways of thinking philosophically.

Radical suffering is an object of critique and a modality of experience accessible only to the perspective of literature and literary writing. This becomes clearer still through Blanchot's encounter in *The Infinite Conversation* with Robert Antelme's concentration camp memoir *L'Espéce humaine*/*The Human Race*.[3] Looking at Blanchot's critique of radical suffering in the context of Antelme's concentrationary internment necessitates a discussion of how radical suffering is a real-world phenomenon that paradoxically demands expression only through the language and perspective of literature and fiction. Because radical suffering dispossesses the subject of suffering of its consciousness and subjectivity, of its power to say 'I', Blanchot tells us, any recollection or memory of suffering will have to be translated as though it was lived through vicariously outside of historical and phenomenological reality. Like the disaster, Blanchot writes in *The Writing of the Disaster*, radical suffering 'is outside history, but historically so' (*WD* 40).

It is through Blanchot's notion of radical suffering that we can begin to understand Antelme when he struggles to explain that 'in those first days' of liberation from the camps, 'we saw that it was impossible to bridge the gap we discovered opening up between the words at our disposal and that experience which, in the case of most of us, was still going on within our bodies. [. . .] No sooner would we begin to tell our story than we would be choking over it. And then, even to us, what we had to tell would start to seem *unimaginable*' (Antelme 1998: 3; italics in original). The experience of surviving the targeted destruction of his humanity places Antelme at an infinite distance from the narrative of destruction still playing itself out in his body and in his consciousness, and so despite his intimate proximity to this narrative of destruction, Antelme cannot straightforwardly translate it through the language of autobiographical recollection. Antelme's *The Human Race* is a work of autobiographical fiction, and the reason why it must be a work of autobiographical *fiction* is that Antelme can only write from the ontologically foreign vantage point, paradoxically, of posthumous survival, and not from the vantage point of the one who was there, targeted for destruction by the profoundly unimaginable events and experiences that Antelme has knowingly tasked himself with only ever vicariously recounting.

Through his assessment of the post-war significance of Antelme, Blanchot considers that Antelme's is a lesson that was not possible to teach or anticipate prior to the ontological crisis of suffering brought on by the catastrophic events of the Second World War. The enigmatic lesson that Blanchot draws from Antelme's autobiographical reflections of his internment in Dachau and Buchenwald is that 'man is the indestructible. And this means there is no limit to the destruction of man' (*IC* 135). Put more aphoristically, the lesson is that 'man is the indestructible that can be destroyed' (*IC* 130). Far from asserting that humanity is invulnerable to all human attempts at annihilating the human, Blanchot's emphasis falls disconcertingly on humankind's infinite vulnerability to (and propensity for) destruction and violence. This reserve of vulnerability is only exposed in rare (but not rare enough), unimaginable situations like the one endured by Antelme. When it is exposed, however, it reveals something not only about the vulnerable fragility of being human, but also about humankind's infinite capacity for perpetrating violence, extortion and torture against others. It is this other capacity – the capacity of humankind for perpetrating violence, extortion and torture without end by feeding so insatiability and indeed creatively on humankind's essential indestructability – that Blanchot is concerned primarily if not impossibly with investigating through the encounter with Antelme.

Can suffering this radical be inscribed in the texture and language of narrative (autobiographical or fictional)? What are the demands on composing (recounting) narratives of radical suffering in order not to violate the law of the disempowerment of subjectivity that modalities of suffering such as this always already induce in the suffering subject? In 'the neutral space' that writing circumscribes through the voice of narrative, Blanchot writes, 'the bearers of speech [. . .] fall into a relation of self-nonidentification. Something happens to them that they can only recapture by relinquishing their power to say "I." And what happens has always already happened: they can only indirectly account for it as a sort of self-forgetting, the forgetting that introduces them into the present without memory that is the present of narrating speech' (*IC* 384–5). The subjectivity of radical suffering and the voice of narrative *as such* converge at the point where they expose us to the abyssal recesses of times we can neither imagine nor recount, and therefore experiences we can neither remember nor forget. In suffering and in narrative we are withdrawn from the world, but denied the gift of death. How are we to predicate the narrative voice in its convergence with the subjectivity of radical suffering, particularly as this would be an existence demanding of predication precisely through its resistance to predication? Blanchot hazards an answer for what this existence would be if predicated through the work of literature:

> Let us (on a whim) call it spectral, ghostlike. Not that it comes from beyond the grave, or even because it would once and for all represent some essential absence, but because it always tends to absent itself in its bearer and also efface him as the center: it is thus neutral in the decisive sense that it cannot be central, does not create a center, does not speak from out of a center, but, on the contrary, at the limit would prevent the work from having one; withdrawing from it every privileged point of interest (even afocal), and also not allowing it to exist as a completed whole, once and forever achieved. (*IC* 386)

Radical suffering introduces us to a relation, not with the exuberant affirmation of Heideggerian finitude nor with the unstoppable productivity of Hegelian negativity, but with the outside of all ontological or metaphysical possibility. This is a relation with the impossibility of dying that captive existences like Antelme's, like the unnamable's, like the spectral, narrative voice's that have been displaced into *death itself* open up. Before seeing how the Beckettian figure of the unnamable negotiates its inscription in its narrative of suffering, we need to accompany Blanchot through his reading of Antelme in order to appreciate just how ontologically as well as hermeneutically severe the narrative situation of *The Unnamable* might be.

III

Blanchot's reading of Antelme develops according to three interpretive movements before concluding (provisionally) with the disquieting, utterly inhuman revelation that 'man is the indestructible that can be destroyed' (*IC* 130). The first movement involves tracing the descent of a subjectivity, of an '*ego cogito* (understood as the inalienable foundation of every possibility of being alienated)', into the phenomenological darkness of radical suffering experienced by Antelme, a movement which passes in its first account as a straightforward critique of finite affliction (*IC* 130). Blanchot cites Antelme as a biographical index of the subjectivity – the person and prisoner named Robert Antelme – reduced at the hands of the SS to this subject of the narrative of suffering that remains when all remnants of Antelme's pre-war subjectivity have been eviscerated by the gradual intensification of what he was forced to experience in the camps. This first movement begins with (the strategic ideological illusion of) admitting the relative ontological stability of Antelme's pre-war subjectivity as a productive citizen of France and ends with Antelme's arrival at an existence of utterly abject inhumanity. 'In affliction – and in our society affliction is *always first* the loss of social status – the one who suffers at the hands of men is radically altered' (*IC* 131; my italics). Names are reduced to numbers, faces are deprived of personality, and humans are denied their belonging to humanity. In this regard Antelme, who was imprisoned not as a Jew (Antelme was French Catholic), but as a member of the Resistance to the Nazi Occupation of France, was no exception to what subsistence in the camps entailed. Indeed, the nightmarish transformation that the SS sought to perform was of persons deported from their homes and communities in cities and societies all across Europe (and perhaps eventually the world) to what Blanchot reads as 'essentially deported' persons. The 'essentially deported person', Blanchot explains, is 'the one who no longer has either a face or speech, the work he is forced to do is designed to exhaust his power to live and to deliver him over to the boundless insecurity of the elements. Nowhere any recourse: outside the cold, inside hunger; everywhere an indeterminate violence. "*The cold, SS*", Antelme says profoundly' (*IC* 131).

Once the 'essentially deported person' arrives where there is no longer any reason or prospect to seek shelter from the harshness of the natural elements, when the violence of the elements is indistinguishable in its irrationality and relentlessness from the physical violence and murderous neglect meted out daily by the SS, 'at this moment when he becomes the unknown and the foreign, when, that is, he becomes a fate for himself, his last recourse is to know that he has been struck not by the elements, but by men, and to give the name *man* to everything that assails him. So when everything ceases to be true, "anthropomorphism" would be truth's ultimate echo' (*IC* 131). At the bottom of Antelme's degradation, which relates inversely to the apex of the violence and inhumanity of the SS, all that remains is this presence of 'man' in which coheres the penchant of humanity for executing radical violence, and the vulnerability that humanity represents and confronts as the victim of this very same violence. The common denominator between Antelme and the SS is simply this category called 'man' that can suffer as much as it can cause to suffer. While, we need hardly point out, there is a vast ethical divide between Antelme and the SS, ontologically speaking they are indistinguishable. The first movement of Blanchot's reading of Antelme, then, concludes with the confirmation of anthropomorphism that neither the SS nor Antelme can evade: the SS, the violence of anthropomorphism; Antelme, the anthropomorphism that cannot be stripped away in the suffering imposed by the violence of the SS.

In the experience of radical suffering that Antelme's autobiographical narrative circumscribes, the one afflicted so radically that he cannot remember what the experience of this suffering truly involved is faced with the phenomenologically unworkable realisation that it is 'man alone who kills him' and 'man' alone that he irreducibly remains: 'the nature of affliction is such that there is no longer anyone either to cause it or to suffer it; at the limit, there are never any afflicted – no one who is afflicted ever really appears. The one afflicted no longer has any identity other than the situation with which he merges and that never allows him to be himself; for as a situation of affliction, it tends incessantly to de-situate itself, to dissolve in the void of a nowhere without foundation' (*IC* 131–2). This is the end-point of the first movement that guides Blanchot's reading of Antelme, and which of course signals the transition of his reading into the second movement. There is no doubting that 'man' can be destroyed and that there is no finite limit to either the quality or quantity of suffering that 'man' can be made to undergo. '*But, there is no ambiguity*', and here Blanchot turns things over to Antelme, that '*we remain men and will end only as men . . . It is because we are men as they are that the SS will finally be powerless before us . . . [the executioner] can kill a man, but he cannot change him into something else*' (*IC* 130; italics in original). Antelme's disquieting revelation here is that the anthropomorphic facticity of humankind that neither prisoner nor SS can disavow is precisely what is responsible for humankind's vulnerability and attraction to the dehumanising use of violence, extortion and torture.

While there is no dialectical transfer of power from the torturer (master) to the victim (slave) in the universe of the camps, nevertheless in the 'situation of affliction' where torturer and victim congregate through the inhumanity of their interrelatedness, the limitless application of violence cannot altogether negate 'the simplicity of a presence that is the infinite of human presence' (*IC* 132). It is in this, the second movement of Blanchot's reading of Antelme, that we are exposed to a non-anthropomorphic conception of human presence to which the ontologically exiled situation of radical suffering gives voice. What violence and torture cannot annihilate is the indestructability of what makes humankind so vulnerable to destruction in the first place. Humankind can always be made to speak and to scream. This is humankind's fundamental right, Adorno tells us in *Negative Dialectics*, but it is a right and a basic physiological fact that is forever positioned as grist for the mill of a violence that capitalises on the inexhaustibility of humankind's ontological susceptibility to destruction. As we will see at length in later paragraphs, the Beckettian unnamable is doubly instantiated in the positions of victim and tormentor through the relation its narrative orchestrates of an extorted subjectivity and an imperative of inquisition that tirelessly extorts speech on the basis of its indestructible alterity. One of the more dominant thematic concerns of *The Unnamable* is indeed this thematic of limitless destruction and unending extortion that exposes the narrative existence of the unnamable to the terror of its indestructibility.

The victim that is forced by extreme acts of violence to speak and to suffer can be made to speak and to suffer *again and again* so long as it continues to occupy the place of its victimisation:

> Hence the furious movement of the inquisitor who wants by force to obtain a scrap of language in order to bring all speech down to the level of force. To make speak, and through torture, is to attempt to master infinite distance by reducing expression to this language of power through which the one who speaks would once again lay himself open to force's hold; and the one who is being tortured refuses to speak in order not to enter through the extorted words into this game of opposing violence, but also, at the same time, in order to preserve the true

speech that he very well knows is at this instant merged with his silent presence – which is the very presence of *autrui* himself. (*IC* 132)

The inviolable trace of indestructibility in the self having become other (of having become *autrui*) through the execution of torture articulates as the 'silent presence' of the 'true speech' that merges with the subjectivity of the one who is thereby reduced (broken down) to nothing but its refusal to speak (and therefore no longer there to undergo the experience of its suffering). The subjectivity that remains of radical suffering gives voice to the 'silent presence' of this self become other, of the presence of *autrui*. Up to this point in *The Infinite Conversation* Blanchot is still in tacit agreement with Levinas on the value that *autrui* represents in an historical and philosophical context that continues to thrive on dehumanising, (self-) destructive metaphysical investments in logics of negation: the indestructible presence of the voice and trace of *autrui* 'bears in itself and as the last affirmation what Robert Antelme calls *the ultimate feeling of belonging to mankind*' (*IC* 132; italics in original). In this second movement of Blanchot's reading of Antelme we see how 'man' merges with the limit-experience of radical suffering, and in this experience is exposed to the affirmation of its ultimate indestructibility, which translates as the imperative that *autrui* not disappear without a murmur or a trace, as it were. This second movement, in other words, details the transformation of the biographical subject that says 'I', Robert Antelme, into the anonymous voice of *autrui* that has been exiled from Antelme's autobiographical narrative to the outside of the radical situation of its suffering, of its coerced refusal to speak over the voice of its silence.

Blanchot's diagnosis of the situation of *autrui* turns in this second movement on the recourse that the prisoner Antelme takes to an impersonal attachment with *need*. With this development in Blanchot's reading of Antelme we find ourselves in territory likely familiar to readers of *The Unnamable* and to Beckett's aesthetic programme as it is famously laid out in the 'Three Dialogues with Georges Duthuit'. Like *autrui*, the eponymous narrative voice of *The Unnamable* ceaselessly speaks in spite of all that would silence its speech because of the extreme and non-locatable obligation it is under simply and inexorably to speak (and to write and to think): 'you must go on, I can't go on, you must go on, I'll go on, you must say words, as long as there are any, until they find me, until they say me, strange pain, strange sin, you must go on' (*TN* 407). Blanchot confronts the phenomenon of obligation and need in the essay on Antelme by asking the very pragmatic question, 'what happens nonetheless to the one who is no longer a presence – a terrifying transformation – in the first person? Destroyed as a Subject, that is, in this sense, essentially destroyed, how can he respond to this exigency that is the exigency of the presence [of *autrui*] in him?' (*IC* 132). It is IC thing to speak coherently at the level of philosophical discourse about the convergence and substitution of one's identity with the anonymous (im)personality of *autrui*, but it is another thing entirely to return these considerations back into the historical and phenomenological (experiential) contexts where they in fact originated and are ceaselessly played out and negotiated. Blanchot tentatively holds that this can be accomplished through a second-order critique of obligation and need, since it appears that through its commitment to obligation and need, *autrui* keeps in contact with the world in order to discredit the totalising successes of the world's murderous recourse to violence and torture. The way that *autrui* does this, Blanchot learns from the life and writing of Antelme (and others), is through its presence as the indestructible remainder that murderous violence cannot absolutely negate.

'Here again', according to Blanchot, 'Antelme's book gives us the right response, and it is the book's most forceful truth. When man is reduced to the extreme destitution of need, when he becomes "someone who eats scraps," we see that he is reduced to himself, and reveals himself as one who has need of nothing other than need in order to maintain the human relation in its primacy, negating what negates him' (*IC* 132–4). This pure reduction of suffering subjectivity to the alterity inscribed in need manifests as an infinite obligation to reinforce need in its most radically irreducible form. Devoid of pleasure, devoid of the excesses of living that make of need a conduit to satisfaction and enjoyment, the need that Antelme recollects 'is immediately' and exclusively 'the need to live' (*IC* 133). Such a feeling of need becomes not 'my' need, but the abstracted need of all who participate in Antelme's ultimate feeling of belonging to humankind *via* precisely this indestructability of need. This need, stubbornly attached to '*an egoism without ego*', is a need that 'becomes the impersonal exigency that alone bears the future and the meaning of every value or, more precisely, of every human relation' (*IC* 133; italics in original).

When the desire to satisfy need can be manifested exclusively in the obligation to keep need alive, when need as such becomes the only end in sight, it is then not *I* that need sustains, but the *I*'s obligation and responsibility to this neutral need of *autrui* that the *I* has all of a sudden and without knowledge of its metamorphosis become. This affirmation of need, which coincides with the limit-situation of radical suffering, represents the second movement of Blanchot's reading of Antelme, and with the emphasis that it places on the indestructible exigency of obligation this interpretive movement alone would suffice to legitimate a comparative reading, via Blanchot, of Antelme and Beckett, all three of whom are writing in the midst and in the aftermath of the Nazi Terror (though Beckett, like Blanchot, was never personally present to the horror of the camps). The structural affinities between, on the one hand, the obligation that Antelme internalises to somehow continue existing through an (unwilled) act of convergence with the need of *autrui*, and, on the other, the obligation that keeps Beckett's the unnamable trapped in narrative, the unnamable 'I who am here, who cannot speak, cannot think, and who must speak, and therefore perhaps think a little', circulate interminably around the affirmation of this strange presence of *autrui* that simply subsists in the depersonalising situations of radical historical suffering and unredeemed narrative anonymity.

However, with Blanchot, and the same goes for Beckett, things are never as simple as submitting to Antelme's one 'last affirmation' of belonging to humankind through merging one's subjectivity with the spectral universality of the need to live and to speak – signatures of the indestructible presence of *autrui*. To Antelme's heroically depersonalised affirmation of belonging, in spite of all, to humankind, one of Blanchot's interlocutors in *The Infinite Conversation* again raises the objection that 'for such a movement to begin truly to be affirmed, there must be restored – beyond this self that I have ceased to be, and within this anonymous community – the instance of a Self-Subject: no longer as a dominating and oppressing power drawn up against the "other" that is autrui, but as what can receive the unknown and the foreign, receive them in the justice of a true *speech*' (IC 133–4). This reservation brings us to the third and final movement of Blanchot's encounter with Antelme, and in this movement Blanchot is hesitant to locate in radical suffering the grounds for one final affirmation of the true speech that would confirm once and for all the irreducibility of belonging to humankind. Blanchot's consistency as a thinker inheres in this uncompromising refusal not to enlist his thinking on the road to transcendence or redemption, however appealing such a road looks in the philosophically competent and historically wizened hands of Antelme. Where affirmation verges on the possibility of overcoming subjective destitution and suffering, Blanchot never tires of suspecting, is where nihilism begins and begins to make its metaphysical presence permanent.

Blanchot's interlocutor is therefore right to ask if, after all that has been said about radical suffering, it is now in a position to present radical suffering as a form of knowledge and as a phenomenological concept of experience. Blanchot concludes his reading of Antelme with the following indecisive exchange between the two fictional interlocutors through which Blanchot has been speaking:

> – That man is the indestructible that can be destroyed? I continue to be wary of this formulation.
> – How could it be otherwise? But even if we are to delete it, let us agree to keep what it has most plainly taught us. Yes, I believe we must say this, hold onto it for an instant: man is the indestructible. And this means there is no limit to the destruction of man.
> – Is this not to formulate a radical nihilism?
> – If so I should be quite willing, for to formulate it would also perhaps already be to overturn it. But I doubt that nihilism will allow itself to be taken so easily. (*IC* 135)

Nihilism is resurrected, if not at the genocidal endpoint of the destruction of humankind, then precisely where the indestructability of humankind is turned around as the point of commencement for the endlessness of humankind's vulnerability to destruction. We can neither endorse nor condemn this ambivalent condition of being human, for to endorse it would be to endorse destruction, and to condemn it would be to belittle what remains of humanity when the destruction of humankind nears completion. Nihilism persists precisely in this fragmentary space of detour, or turning, from one impossibility to the other, and that Blanchot, in the very next chapter on Nietzsche and fragmentary writing, describes as nihilism's 'final and rather grim truth: it tells of the impossibility of nihilism' (*IC* 149): 'nihilism is this very turning itself, the affirmation that, in passing from the No to the Yes, refutes nihilism, but does nothing other than affirm it, and henceforth extends it to every possible affirmation' (*IC* 150).

What is so epistemologically as well as ontologically disorienting about Blanchot's encounter with radical suffering in the autobiographical writing of Antelme is that positing it as an object of reflection, as a conduit of thinking, has to presuppose that the subjectivity of thinking, the *ego cogito* of Blanchot's reflections, has crossed the threshold of what is thinkable – the threshold of radical suffering – with its own subjectivity intact, in which case the unthinkable phenomenon of radical suffering is nihilistically effaced as the knowable, thinkable experience of finite affliction. However, because radical suffering, as we have already seen Blanchot insisting in *The Writing of the Disaster*, is strictly speaking as unthinkable as it is unspeakable (*unimaginable*, says Antelme), Blanchot is logically committed to searching out a new protocol of thinking that can encounter radical suffering without recourse to the dialectical knowledge of a concept that would thereby sacrifice radical suffering to radical nihilism, i.e. to the nihilism of negativity and transcendence. The problem first and foremost, then, is this: what is a non-philosophical protocol of thinking, a protocol that remains a protocol of *thinking* in the encounter with radical suffering? Only if Blanchot can uncover a non-philosophical protocol of thinking can the fragmentary detour (the fragmentary *qua* detour) of radical nihilism be deferred (but never decisively blocked) in the analytic encounter with radical suffering.

In *The Book to Come*, Blanchot uses the occasion of commenting on Antonin Artaud's fascinating epistolary exchange with Jacques Rivière to suggest that what the writing of Artaud says, which places his work in the literary constellation that is formed around Blanchot's pantheon of writers that includes Sade, Hölderlin, Mallarmé, Kafka, Joubert, Char, Celan and of course Beckett, 'is of an intensity that we could not bear. Here speaks a pain that refuses all profundity, all illusion, and all hope, but that, in this refusal, offers to thought "the ether of a new space"' (*BC* 40). Blanchot continues teasing out the broader implications that Artaud's writing has on its encounter with the act of thinking, which desires to encounter in this writing something other than the impossibility of reading and thinking, something other than the anguish that these activities provoke the instant that they confront, as they do in Antelme (and Beckett) no less than in Artaud, 'what one is forbidden to read' (*WD* 10):

the act of thinking can only be deeply shocking; what is to be thought about is in thought that which turns away from it and inexhaustibly exhausts itself in it; suffering and thinking are secretly linked, for if suffering, when it becomes extreme, is such that it destroys the capacity to suffer, always destroying ahead of itself, in time, the time when suffering could be grasped and ended, it is perhaps the same with thought. Strange connections. Might it be that extreme thought and extreme suffering open onto the same horizon? Might suffering be, finally, thinking? (*BC* 40)

Without simply conflating the difference that obtains to the relation of thinking and suffering, which even if thinking and suffering are synonymous, is a relation of veiled symmetry that is maintained by the dissymmetry of a repetition (thinking *becomes* suffering in the act of thinking), Blanchot is nevertheless committed to respecting the limit that radical suffering imposes on the analytical approach of thinking. The intermediary status of writing in the dissymmetrical repetition of thinking *as* suffering is absolutely indispensable. Artaud demands that thinking be suffocated by its encounter with writing, and in this suffocating encounter it becomes inextricably linked to radical suffering.

Even before Blanchot comes up against the experience of suffering that mobilises the indestructible ontological surplus of *autrui* in Antelme's autobiographical text, it is *perhaps* the case that without this more intrinsic encounter with radical suffering that Artaud's writing exposes, the act of thinking could not possibly commence as an approach onto the literary space of fiction and into the outside of historical disaster that Antelme's memoir bridges. Perhaps the threat of radical nihilism that works to undo all of the advancements Blanchot makes into his reading of Antelme is predicated on Blanchot failing to reconsider in the essay on Antelme in *The Infinite Conversation* the lesson he learned from reading Artaud in *The Book to Come*, namely that suffering and thinking perhaps converge around 'the same horizon' (*BC* 40). Perhaps, in other words, it is not so much the case that radical suffering is unthinkable and unspeakable, so much as it is that thinking *is* the exigency of radical suffering where thinking is overtaken by the fragmentary imperative of writing. In the same way that Antelme's narrative of suffering reveals anthropomorphism as 'truth's ultimate echo' (*IC* 131), so too is the act of thinking obliged by the fragmentary imperative of writing to merge with the exigency of radical suffering, thereby *always destroying ahead of itself, in time, the time when THINKING could be grasped and ended.*

IV

Whereas Blanchot's reading of suffering in Antelme develops according to successive logical movements that culminate in the philosophical impasse of thinking in its convergence with the phenomenon of radical suffering, the reading of Beckett's *The Unnamable* developed here unfolds first by juxtaposing two contradictory modalities of suffering – Mahood's and Worm's – and then, second, by suggesting that the reason why the suffering experienced by the narrative voice of *The Unnamable* is so intractable in its resistance to conceptualisation is that it unveils precisely this strange link between suffering and thinking that Blanchot first diagnosed in the poetics of Artaud. *The Unnamable* stages the terrifying convergence of the imperative of suffering with the imperative of thinking, which implicates the hermeneutical encounter with Beckett's writing in this disconcerting constellation as well.[4] Leslie Hill worries that too 'much published criticism' about Beckett 'makes little claim upon the reader, not because commentators are insufficiently discriminating or because they discriminate too much, but because they necessarily always run the risk of falling victim to the infantile disorder of all literary criticism – which may be the fate of all criticism in general – which, in the guise of enabling access to the text, is to domesticate and normalise it, to reduce it to the horizon of expectation of the already known' (2010: 12). This chapter's strategy for avoiding precisely this disorder of criticism is to focus on the convergence of suffering and thinking in *The Unnamable*, and specifically on the terror that arises when the act of thinking converges with and precipitates the ordeal of radical suffering. What this chapter is naming the *terror* of thinking in *The Unnamable*, in other words, is a reflection of the narrative circumscription of this convergence through the fragmentary protocols of Beckett's writing.

Accepting the argument that thinking and suffering are 'secretly linked' through a relation of terror and advancing through our reading of Beckett with the hypothesis that this link accounts for much that is going on in *The Unnamable* entails that in the critical encounter with this narrative and its narrative voice, hermeneutical subjectivity is obliged to negotiate with the demand that it too undergo an ordeal of metamorphosis through the suffering of thinking. It is not just that thinking is linked to suffering, but that through this link with suffering, thinking is subject to the imperative of its own unending withdrawal from its established epistemological securities. *The Unnamable*, as a site of narrative disorientation and ontological disintegration, instantiates what Deleuze identifies as the '*terra incognita*' of thinking (1994: 136). When thinking is circumscribed in spaces like *The Unnamable* where the laws of thinking as well as the laws of reading are suspended, it faces up to the disquieting truth, continues Deleuze, that 'the conditions of a true critique and a true creation are the same: the destruction of an image of thought which presupposes itself and the genesis of the act of thinking itself. Something in the world forces us to think. This something is an object not of recognition but of a fundamental *encounter*' (1994: 139; italics in original).[5]

Deleuze is substituting the dialectical relation of destruction and creation with an event of thinking that fundamentally dislocates or exiles the act of thinking from the enlightenment narrative of its accumulating knowledge. Thinking begins, accordingly, only by subtracting itself from all the hard-won logics, laws and knowledges that thinking suddenly, unpredictably renounces as it is made by a 'fundamental encounter' to trespass into the aleatory future of thought. When this trespass is staged in the space of literature, however, thinking is precluded from subtracting itself absolutely from the archives (the indelible memories, the dialectical narratives) of these logics, laws and knowledges. As it stages an encounter between thinking and suffering, *The Unnamable* precipitates an experience of the suffering *of* thinking that is no less severe in its ontological consequences than the ordeal of radical suffering that Blanchot encounters through Antelme. This experience is one that links the inquisitorial imperatives for memory, speech and existence that drive the narrative discourse of *The Unnamable* with the desperate desire of the work's narrative voice to end its condemnation to the ontological nightmare of always failing and of therefore always returning to the place before this imperative. When the vicious economy of this relation is accepted as the *a priori* of how the unnamable is condemned to make its way through the torturous narrative passageway of *The Unnamable*, we finally begin to approximate what it perhaps means when the unnamable explicitly states that the act of thinking in *The Unnamable* begins only by crossing the incomprehensible threshold of terror: '*I only think,* if that is the name for this vertiginous panic as of hornets smoked out of their nest, *once a certain degree of terror has been exceeded*' (*TN* 344; my italics). Thinking is trespass and violence, but so too is it ineluctably traversed by the impossibility of transcending the words, memories and responsibilities that keep thinking riveted to the logics, laws and knowledges that precede and legislate the event of its commencement and the narrative of its continuation. The terror of thinking inheres in this space of incommensurability between what thinking demands of itself as the demand for a rupture with itself, and what, in compelling the act of thinking in the space of literature, precludes this demand's fulfilment as a project that would inaugurate (and with the promise of redeeming) the future of thinking: the eternal return of language, memory and history through the fragmentary imperative of writing.

V

Beckett approaches the exigency of radical suffering primarily from a literary perspective, rather than from an autobiographical (Antelme) or philosophical (Blanchot) perspective. Consequently, the problematic of radical suffering that this perspective negotiates is positioned so as to take the insight that radical suffering dispossesses subjectivity of its power to say 'I' as its *a priori* point of narrative departure, rather than as an autobiographical or philosophical endpoint of disastrous revelation. Radical suffering and the narrative voice of literature, Blanchot suggests in *The Infinite Conversation*, converge precisely around the ontological site of the subject being dispossessed of its subjectivity. Assuming that what Blanchot calls 'radical suffering' is indeed an apt characterisation of the peculiar modality of existence of the Beckettian unnamable, then perhaps a productive way to begin an interpretive critique of the image of thinking operative in *The Unnamable* is to ask what is, in the context of *The Unnamable*, a patently unanswerable question: *after 'radical suffering', what comes next?* One of the signatures of radical suffering is that it throws the metaphysics of diachronic temporality into irredeemable confusion. Accordingly, framing the question of what comes after radical suffering must be done outside of the metaphysical prerequisites of a beginning and end paradigm of narrative development: 'One can be before beginning, they have set their hearts on that' (*TN* 346). This is where Blanchot's hypothesis of a secret link between suffering and thinking becomes relevant for a reading of Beckett's *The Unnamable*, where there is indeed a subtle and perhaps even untraceable narrative transition from out of the unnamable's immersion in its situation of radical suffering and into its sudden appearance before the problematic of what it means to be continuing speaking and thinking amidst the ongoing ontological disaster of its indestructible subjectivity (and therefore vulnerability to limitless destruction).

The endgame of *The Unnamable* is not one of playing out or giving testimony to the experience of suffering at its most radically traumatic or post-traumatic historical and psychological extreme. With very little historical or geographical points of reference in his writing of this work, the suffering, trauma and above all the terror that Beckett's writing reflects is negotiated using a literary perspective that is not reducible to the task of recording or communicating 'real' historical configurations of disaster, catastrophe and ruin. The contribution that *The Unnamable* makes to the analytical discourse on radical suffering inheres in its experimentation with the unnerving possibility that in the exigency of radical suffering there can be no return to the time of non-radical or 'worldly' forms of suffering. Radical suffering represents the ontological condition *par excellence* of the existence that a life lived exclusively in the non-historical margins of literature and narrative retroactively exposes.[6] Behind the endlessly aporetic repetitions and disavowals of discourse and words, through the incessant affirmation and negation of images and concepts in the imagination of the unnamable, there stands a narrative existence that is forever chained to the inhospitable space of literature where memory and logic have no ontological or epistemological purchase over the trial of suffering subjectivity. The subjectivity to which the narrative voice of *The Unnamable* desperately yet reluctantly clings is predicated on the imperative of continuing speaking and thinking in a time and a place where speaking is reduced to sounds signifying little more than babble, and where encounters with the blind spots of reflection and reflexivity trigger the unnamable's submission to exhaustive, extortionist regimes of rote regurgitation and memory: 'I shall submit, more corpse-obliging than ever' (*TN* 343).

This situation leads the unnamable to describe itself as a caged beast whose existence is predicated solely on its unthinkable instantiation of a life interminably lived in the ongoing disintegration of its subjectivity. Without ever coming into phenomenological proximity with the exigency of its suffering – 'where I am there is no one but me, who am not' (*TN* 348) – the unnamable is nevertheless left to conclude, and it is a conclusion that serves only to perpetuate its suffering indefinitely, that its life in suffering is intertwined with the words and images it uses to fumble its way through understanding how it suffers in the way that it suffers:

> I'm all these words, all these strangers, this dust of words, with no ground for their settling, no sky for their dispersing, coming together to say, fleeing one another to say, that I am they, all of them, those that merge, those that part, those that never meet, and nothing else, yes, something else, that I'm something quite different, a quite different thing, a wordless thing in an empty place, a hard shut dry cold black place, where nothing stirs, nothing speaks, and that I listen, and that I seek, like a caged beast born of caged beasts born of caged beasts born of caged beasts born in a cage and dead in a cage, born and then dead, born in a cage and then dead in a cage, in a word like a beast, in one of their words, like such a beast, and that I seek, like such a beast, with my little strength, such a beast, with nothing of its species left but fear and fury, no, the fury is past, nothing but fear, nothing of all its due but fear centupled, fear of its shadow, no, blind from birth, of sound then, if you like, we'll have that, one must have something, it's a pity, but there it is, fear of sound, fear of sounds, the sounds of beasts, the sounds of men, sounds in the daytime and sounds at night, that's enough [. . .] (*TN* 380)

The terror imposed onto the narrative world of *The Unnamable* is succinctly captured in these lines. What this excerpt entails, by forcing into view the image of this caged beast, the progeny of caged beasts no sooner dead than born, is that the suffering experienced by the unnamable does not begin prior to the brute fact of an existence in suffering, nor does its coincidence with suffering end once this suffering has run its murderous course. By dying, the caged beast is born, 'born in a cage and then dead in a cage, born and then dead' (*TN* 380). Its cage is made up of words, but it is a cage that is not any the less claustrophobically constructed as a result. With nothing but the fear of what it might be, if it could be, what it might say, if it could speak, and what it might think, if it could think, the unnamable can do little else except pace back and forth between the words circumscribing its existence until its existence, circumscribed by words, is eroded down to nothing but words, at which point (a turn of the fragmentary) its pacing, its incremental disintegration, begins *again* anew: 'it all boils down to a question of words, I must not forget this, I have not forgotten it. But I must have said this before, since I say it now. I have to speak in a certain way, with warmth perhaps, all is possible, first of the creature I am not, as if I were he, and then, as if I were he, of the creature I am' (*TN* 329). This is not a figure that has entered, in time, the space of suffering; rather, this is a figure that has never been anywhere other than in the space of suffering. The implication of this revelation is that the figure of the unnamable is obliged to pursue its narrative trajectory as a being displaced from temporality and devoid of a narrative subjectivity empowered with the capacity of imagining what an existence lived outside of suffering was, is, or would be like if the unnamable were anywhere but here in the imprisoning words of *The Unnamable*.

The Unnamable does not hide the fact that the figure of its narrative voice, the figure of the unnamable, is in perpetual contact with suffering: 'No one asks him to think, simply to suffer, always in the same way, without hope of diminution, without hope of dissolution, it's no more complicated than that' (*TN* 361). Suffering speaks through the unnamable's speech with the pain of the one who is compelled to speak by an unidentified and indeed unidentifiable spirit of violence that demands nothing less of the unnamable than the torturous continuation of its unliveable narrative existence. It is important that we not misunderstand or devalue what is entailed by the Beckettian phenomenon of a voice that cannot go silent. Having lost the capacity to go silent, yet still being enlisted in the act of speaking the words that fiercely demand that speech become silence, the unnamable's very existence is predicated on the ceaseless reminder that there is no recourse to death as the limit to the suffering through which its life in narrative is orchestrated.

According to Blanchot, Socrates was the first to invest the enlightened use of speech with the civilising power to 'get the better of violence: that is the certainty he calmly represents, and his death is heroic but calm, because the violence that interrupts his life cannot interrupt the reasonable language that is his true life and at the end of which we find harmony, and violence disarmed' (*BC* 152). If civilised humanity commences with the philosophical speech of Socrates, it hits its climax and aggressively begins to degenerate in the radical suffering of the Beckettian unnamable.

In the inhuman world of the unnamable, where the ontological barrier that divides the within from the without, life from death, signified from signifier, speech from torment, torturer from tortured, is as 'thin as foil', and where, as a consequence, the unnamable thinks and speaks from 'neither one side nor the other, I'm in the middle, I'm the partition, I've two surfaces and no thickness', there is implanted in each and every word that the unnamable is compelled to speak a constituting violence the force of which is exponentially redoubled by the intractably repetitive movement of the work's narrative inertia (*TN* 376).

Suffering in *The Unnamable* is not, therefore, an ethical or epistemological anomaly that arises because its speaker has not yet 'let them put into my mouth at last the words that will save me, damn me' (*TN* 362). Suffering is not a transitional pathway to silence, salvation and civilisation here, nor is it the refuge of the damned who at least have the knowledge, and thus do not threaten the ethical order of judgement, guilt, reason and hope, that their punishment is the etiological consequence of their crimes: 'my crime is my punishment, that's what they judge me for' (*TN* 362). Rather, the unnamable contends with the truly unimaginable reality of a situation that balks at the very metaphysics of a causality of suffering. The unnamable's is a situation that 'reasonable language' cannot recuperate, a situation wherein 'reasonable language' cannot overpower the suffering of the unnamable because the unnamable itself is that which eludes the dialectics of salvation that since Socrates has been the promise made by negativity and death, speech and death.

In the space of literature that the unnamable stoically inhabits, then, what speaks is a narrative voice whose fictional reality precludes predication by the metaphysical and phenomenological modes of existence requisite for a reconciliatory critique of suffering. To suggest otherwise would be to commit a fundamental misreading of the unnamable's subjection to the exigency of radical suffering. Evidence of the sorts of misreading that an inadequate critique of suffering produces can be found in the work of such eminent Beckett scholars as Mary Bryden. Bryden claims that there is the possibility of salvation for Beckett's suffering voices from the radical modality of their suffering, thus enabling us to see in what way Beckett's writing is ceaselessly able 'to generate a kind of recursive energy', an energy capable of implementing 'a switch of focus which brings sufficient relief' from suffering and pain

(2012: 211). The alleviation of suffering via what Bryden describes as a 'continuance despite all odds' is, unfortunately, not an equation that *The Unnamable* can unproblematically endorse given the extreme modality of suffering that plagues its narrative voice. While there undoubtedly is a thematic of continuation operative throughout the narrative discourse of the unnamable – 'there is silence, from the moment the messenger departs until he returns with his orders, namely, Continue' (*TN* 363) – there is little evidence in definitive support of the claim that the path on which the unnamable's discourse continues is one that is any way traversable as a teleological route to the alleviation or redemption of suffering and pain by the narrative's end. Seeing the Beckettian negotiation of suffering as a problematic immanent to the space of literature precludes joining Paul Sheehan as well in believing that from the 'therapeutic heroism' of Beckettian humour, for instance, 'it is but a small step to an ethic of redemption' (2002: 153).

Against Bryden and Sheehan, Garin Dowd and Sam Slote are more on track in arguing, as Dowd puts it, that although 'in many respects Beckett's oeuvre is an appropriate candidate for inclusion in [Elaine] Scarry's category of literary works adding to the sum of a *shared* examination of pain and suffering', nevertheless 'one does not find in it the utopian opening which Scarry believes resides in the redemptive power of literature' (2012: 87). Similarly for Slote, 'if narration might be a palliative', as Scarry optimistically suggests, 'it is also an exacerbator. [. . .] Thus the unnamable continues on, perhaps even when it does not need to. [. . .] It exists in a state that conjoins compulsion with powerlessness, a state that cannot be rendered into language, which is to say, it exists in pain' (2014: 57). The closer we get to penetrating conceptually into the inscrutability of radical suffering, however, the more radical suffering causes the act of conceptualisation, the act of thinking, to asphyxiate on what it is about radical suffering that conceptual thinking cannot digest: 'I've got nowhere, in their affair, that's what galls them, they want me there somewhere, anywhere, if only they'd stop committing reason, on them, on me, on the purpose to be achieved, and simply go on, with no illusion about having begun one day or ever being able to conclude, but it's too difficult, too difficult, for one bereft of purpose, not to look forward to his end, and bereft of all reason to exist, back to a time he did not' (*TN* 378). Narrative immobility and the permanence of suffering are what the unnamable is made 'to make the best of', but if the narrative goes nowhere, if it circles back endlessly to the melancholic site of its departure from the world of reason, memory and speech, and if the measure of suffering is as infinite and unthinkable today as it was yesterday and as it will be tomorrow, then the image of the existence that the unnamable projects becomes unworkable as a subject of analytic dissemination.

Bryden mistakenly presumes that from one end of the narrative structure of *The Unnamable* to the other, the suffering of its eponymous voice will either get worse or (hopefully) get better. The problematic so central to the narrative architecture of *The Unnamable*, the problematic that eludes Bryden, it would appear, is that the measure of suffering that the unnamable endures is not commensurable with suffering experienced in the historical and empirical world outside of literature (hence the recourse Bryden takes to Scarry's *The Body in Pain*). This would be the suffering that commences, Blanchot explains, with 'the loss of social status' and the onset of physical and psychological pain (*IC* 131). This is not to say that *The Unnamable* permits of no recognition of finite suffering; on the contrary, the problematic of narrative as it articulates through *The Unnamable* is precisely that it is historical and finite suffering that the unnamable struggles so desperately and futilely to experience. The ontological catch in all of this is that it is only radical suffering that the unnamable, *qua* narrative voice dispossessed of the power to say 'I', experiences and knows, and such an experience of radical suffering, as we have already cited Blanchot defining it in *The Writing of the Disaster*, is 'suffering such that I could not suffer it. [. . .] There is suffering, there would be suffering, but no longer any "I" suffering, and this suffering does not make itself known in the present; it is not borne in the present (still less is it experienced in the present)' (*WD* 14–15). The problematic of radical suffering, in other words, is such that it not only precludes the 'epistemological verification of pain by the nonsufferer', as Ato Quayson writes in *Aesthetic Nervousness* (and he too cites Scarry for these insights into Beckett), but that it also interrupts 'the epistemological certainty of the bearer of pain', the bearer of radical suffering (2007: 80).

We can perhaps approach an understanding of the phenomenon of suffering in *The Unnamable* through Blanchot's conception of the two slopes of literature in 'Literature and the Right to Death', such that Antelme and Beckett would represent two slopes of the pathway to and from radical suffering. Blanchot's reading of Antelme maps out for us the first of these slopes, the one that begins in the painful light of affliction, the 'loss of social status' that elicits falling 'not only below the individual, but also below every real collective relation' (*IC* 131), and ends in the nocturnal darkness without end of radical suffering where 'the person no longer exists in his or her personal identity. In this sense the one afflicted is already outside the world, a being without horizon' (*IC* 131). Beckett sketches the narrative outline of what we might call the second slope of suffering. This commences in the permanence of radical suffering and proceeds towards restoring the metaphysical, etiological integrity of diachronic temporality in order to reconstruct the subject of consciousness – the subjectivity of the subject that thinks, speaks and exists through its belonging to humanity – that radical suffering by definition destroyed and, again by definition, keeps on destroying.

Writing on this second slope is arguably more dangerous than writing on the first. Because radical suffering precludes the faith that a subject can traverse radical suffering with its subjectivity intact, once radical suffering has been activated in the time and space of writing there is, logically speaking, no place or time for the subject of suffering to go. The problematic of suffering on this second slope is an incredibly disorienting and therefore discouraging one to negotiate:

> suppose, instead of suffering less, as time flies, he continues to suffer as much, precisely, as the first day. That must be possible. And but suppose, instead of suffering less than the first day, or no less, he suffers more and more, as time flies, and the metamorphosis is accomplished, of unchanging future into unchangeable past. Eh? Another thing, but of a different order. The affair is thorny. Is not a uniform suffering preferable to one which, by its ups and downs, is liable at certain moments to encourage the view that perhaps after all it is not eternal? [...] Agreed then on monotony, it's more stimulating. (*TN* 360–1)

Although the unnamable foregrounds the possibility of distinguishing between two forms of suffering, of suffering 'less and less' on the way to an 'unchanging future', and suffering 'more and more' from an 'unchangeable past', its adoption of the third person pronoun to diagnose the temporality one way or the other of how 'he' suffers, automatically precludes that the unnamable's 'preference' for its modality of suffering will possess any transformative power over how the narrative situation of its suffering is in fact determined. The unnamable's suffering, in other words, cannot be subjectively mediated through any measure of volitional narrative preference. The phenomenon of the unnamable's pronominal splitting between first and third persons implicitly draws attention to an impersonal form of suffering that cannot be controlled, pacified or even intensified from either of these grammatical subject-positions – from the 'I' or from the 'he' – of the unnamable itself. The narrative exigency of its suffering is permanent and permanently inscrutable precisely because it dissolves the metaphysics of the subject and of the temporality of the subject that are otherwise required for attributing to suffering a definite beginning and a definite end in the life and in the time of the subject of suffering.

VI

The unnamable's attempted escape from radical suffering (by converting it into finite suffering) is instigated in response to the imperative that it tell stories, that it write fictions. These stories, if they are not to further entrench the unnamable in the suffering that it can neither experience nor properly communicate, must be about a narrative existence other than that of the unnamable itself (assuming that the unnamable can be referenced at all as a singular narrative entity). These stories, in other words, must stake out a measure of distance between the teller and the told of the fictions and stories that the unnamable is compelled to construct. The unnamable is driven in these efforts by an avowed (and therefore misleading) desire for survival, escape and redemption just as fervently as it is held back by the knowledge that survival, escape and redemption are not realities that the unnamable can generate *ex nihilo* in the solitude of its suffering. Where the unnamable precipitates the appearance of Mahood and Worm into its narrative confinement, it is confronted with two (mutually exclusive) avenues of escape from its existence in radical suffering. The problem is that in order to do this – to be birthed into the suffering of the living so that it can begin its salvation in the rush towards death – the unnamable is in need of another's judgement and gaze to be reflected back onto itself in confirmation that its punishment and its subjectivity are empirical and real, that however anonymous its identity remains in the spectral narrative space of radical suffering, however innocent it is of the infinitely punishable offence of its indestructible existence, its indestructible humanity, coming face-to-face with another unlike itself will engage it in the dialectics of recognition required for proclaiming the blessed gift of the death sentence that the work's narrative order otherwise refuses to finalise.

Mahood is the first 'vice-exister' that the unnamable foists into the pathway of the encounter with recognition that it so desperately desires:[7]

> Here, in my domain, what is Mahood doing in my domain, and how does he get here? There I am launched again on the same old hopeless business, there we are face to face, Mahood and I, if we are twain, as I say we are. I never saw him, I don't see him, he has told me what he is like, what I am like, they have all told me that, it must be one of their principal functions. It isn't enough that I should know what I'm doing, I must also know what I'm looking like. (*TN* 309)

The introduction of Mahood signals the ease with which the unnamable capitulates to an imaginary narrative authority in order to acquire independent recognition – from the perspective of knowing 'what I'm looking like' – of its narrative existence. Mahood enters the narrative and very quickly adopts the role of storyteller that interpellates the unnamable as the protagonist of his tale. Because all judgements of the unnamable's existence are left undetermined as to their ultimate veracity, the unnamable is perpetually left wondering if it has 'been in the places where [Mahood] says I have been, instead of having stayed on here, trying to take advantage of his absence to unravel my tangle' (*TN* 309).

The unknowability attached to what Mahood says about the unnamable, the unknowability that surrounds Mahood's existence as dependent or independent of the unnamable's imagination, means that what the unnamable does in fact know is that whatever enters its zone of narrative visibility through the voice of Mahood cannot be disregarded as false. So long as the possibility persists that what Mahood says of the unnamable is true, that Mahood's existence can be independently verified as being distinct from a creative projection of the unnamable, the unnamable has no choice except to subscribe wholeheartedly to the illusion that all is not false in the discourse of Mahood. This places the unnamable in the ontological position of being the object of Mahood's narrative experiment, 'the programme', which consists in dressing up the unnamable as a convincing character in the story of his life. So it is that the unnamable considers its situation of temporary subservience to 'Mahood and Co.' accordingly:

> The poor bastards. They could clap an artificial anus in the hollow of my hand and still I wouldn't be there, alive with their life, not far short of a man, just barely a man, sufficiently a man to have hopes one day of being one, my avatars behind me. And yet sometimes it seems to me I am there, among the incriminated scenes, tottering under the attributes peculiar to the lords of creation, dumb with howling to be put out of my misery, and all round me the spinach blue rustling with satisfaction. Yes, more than once I almost took myself for the other, all but suffered after his fashion, the space of an instant. (*TN* 309)

Like the 'dupe of every time and tense' that the narrative voice becomes in *Texts for Nothing*, here the unnamable expressly acknowledges the illusoriness of the existence that Mahood is in the throes of imputing to it (*CSP* 85). Upon denigrating Mahood and Co., the 'poor bastards', for the farcical faith they have in being able to weave for the unnamable a fiction in which it would truly believe, the unnamable nevertheless musters the requisite modicum of strength to go along with the narrative that Mahood produces – 'sometimes it seems to me I am there' (*TN* 309). Through the questionable though no doubt appealing storytelling powers of Mahood, then, the unnamable is suddenly transformed into the protagonist of a fiction that involves him in circling around a home and a family, which produces the added benefit of transposing the unnamable from the meta-narrative heights of its tortured soliloquy – like a caged beast, in one of their words – to the fictional discourse of Mahood's familial narrative.

Undertaking a close reading of the Mahood and Worm episodes is necessary if we are to responsibly investigate the possibility that the unnamable could begin accessing phenomenologically – vicariously through the (opposing) narrative perspectives of Mahood and Worm – the narrative ordeal of its suffering. Within the first site of the unnamable's attempted extrication from suffering – the site of Mahood – there is a concerted effort to convincingly make the unnamable resemble something more ontologically substantive than the empty cipher of the anonymous subjectivity that it otherwise ineluctably is throughout the narrative. In the first instance in the fairy-tale of Mahood, which ultimately leads to 'the panic of the moment' that triggers the introduction of Worm, the narrative orientation that the unnamable adopts figures as an erratic, inverted and horizontally distributed spiral closing laboriously around a traumatic space populated by the rotting corpses of the unnamable's family.[8]

The purpose of this movement is to get the unnamable to cross the threshold of the subjectivity that radical suffering denies it from possessing, i.e. the subjectivity that was always already destroyed by the unnamable being 'alone, in the unthinkable unspeakable' subjectivity of radical suffering, 'where I have not ceased to be, where they will not let me be' (*TN* 328). This movement adheres, we are told, to the promising teleological architecture of an 'inverted spiral':

> I had already advanced a good ten paces, if one may call them paces, not in a straight line I need hardly say, but in a sharp curve which, if I continued to follow it, seemed likely to restore me to my point of departure, or to one adjacent. I must have got embroiled in a kind of inverted spiral, I mean one the coils of which, instead of widening more and more, grew narrower and narrower and finally, given the kind of space in which I was supposed to evolve, would come to an end for lack of room. (*TN* 310)

The narrowing spiral projects the image of an ideal point of narrative subtraction that would permit the unnamable to come to that blessed 'end for lack of room' (*TN* 310). This story is remarkable in the overall narrative context of *The Unnamable* because it is guided by a teleological line of flight. The story would come to an end if only the unnamable, taking 'myself for Mahood' (*TN* 311), could join its family in the comfort of its home, that is to say, if only the unnamable could convincingly retrieve 'the historical existence' it ostensibly left behind upon its entry into the ontological desert of *The Unnamable* (*TN* 312).

The affinities with the epic journey of Odysseus are perhaps too obvious to rehearse here, but what bears underscoring is that with the guidance of Mahood, the unnamable is given the chance to account once and for all for the identity that its life in narrative has so far precluded it from (re-)possessing: 'without being quite sure I had seen it before, I had been so long from home, I kept saying to myself, Yonder is the nest you should never have left, there your dear absent ones are awaiting your return, patiently, and you too must be patient. It was swarming with them, grandpa, grandma, little mother and the eight or nine brats. With their eyes glued to the slits and their hearts going out to me they surveyed my efforts' (*TN* 311). This movement proves to have been undertaken in vain, because 'according to Mahood I never reached them, that is to say they all died first, the whole ten or eleven of them, carried off by sausage-poisoning, in great agony' (*TN* 312). What matters here are not the details of this story; rather, it is that Mahood is up to one of his 'favourite tricks, to produce ostensibly independent testimony in support of my historical existence' (*TN* 312). The unnamable is even willing to go along with the ruse, but only so far as nothing other than the imperative to 'keep going on' in the direction that leads irreversibly out of radical suffering is expected of it. Needless to say, there is no basis to conclude that Mahood is something other than just an avatar of the unnamable, the fictional representative of an existence that the unnamable has devised in order to temper the ontological distress of its suffering and solitude.

The story that Mahood tells of the unnamable consists in a journey of the unnamable returning home and being reunited with his wife, children and parents. This story begins by detailing the exhausting experience of the unnamable struggling to approach his (soon-to-be-dead) family: 'After each thrust of my crutches I stopped, to devour a narcotic and measure the distance gone, the distance yet to go' (*TN* 310). Hardly has the story progressed beyond the point of introducing its protagonist's struggles and desires than does it culminate in the untimely death of the unnamable's family. The unnamable wastes no time stepping outside of the fictional space of Mahood. This story is being told on the basis of Mahood swearing on its testimony of what the unnamable experienced, the report of which Mahood whispers into the ear of the unnamable so that the unnamable can repeat it as accurately as is within his powers to do. That Mahood is the sole author of this fiction, however, is something that the unnamable feels compelled to repeat and that we should therefore be cautioned not to trivialise as an insignificant detail of the narrative: 'According to Mahood' (*TN* 312); 'Still Mahood speaking' (*TN* 314); 'Mahood must have remarked' (*TN* 315); '(Mahood dixit)' (*TN* 315); etc. The unnamable is at the mercy of Mahood's fictional conjectures only up to the point where Mahood all of a sudden goes 'silent, that is to say his voice continues, but is no longer renewed' (*TN* 319). Here the unnamable breaks free from the influence of Mahood and expresses his contempt over the recognition that 'they consider me so plastered with their rubbish that I can never extricate myself, never make a gesture but their cast must come to life' (*TN* 319). No sooner is the unnamable transported into one of Mahood's family fairy-tales than does it find itself trying to get out and return back to the space of radical suffering from which it was speaking before Mahood crossed into the narrative territory of its essentially destroyed subjectivity.

Before this hostility towards Mahood asserts itself, however, the unnamable permits that Mahood's fiction exercises a powerful hold over the images and words it selects in constructing its memory and existence in the text. The unnamable is all too aware – as is Beckett – that the subjectivity of whatever existence it adopts in the narrative will have to be constructed using words, images, concepts and metaphors, there being nothing else with which to construct a life, particularly a life in narrative, and so whichever of these it inherits from Mahood will be just as convincing and meaningful as any that it may itself devise. Whether its memories are embedded in its consciousness and are merely awaiting their retrieval in the narrative present, or if it is Mahood that implants them in the unnamable's imagination and then violently brings them to the surface of their recollection, the conclusion is the same. Inducing and implanting memories and recollections is tantamount to the violence of manufacturing a consciousness and a subjectivity precisely where, in radical suffering, consciousness and subjectivity have been and, terrifyingly, are being targeted for destruction. The point, then, is not to attribute a distinct ontological presence to Mahood, one that either substitutes for the unnamable or demotes the unnamable to the position of protagonist. Mahood is a projection of the unnamable's imagination, a reflection of the unnamable's insatiable ontological desire to 'suffer like true thinking flesh' (*TN* 347). The unnamable even admits that while playing at being 'Mahood I felt a little, now and then', only to ask rhetorically, 'can that be called a life which vanishes when the subject is changed?' (*TN* 347).

Inventing Mahood as the teller to the unnamable's told gives the unnamable a momentary glimpse into what it would be like to experience suffering *like true thinking flesh*, as the proprietor of a subjectivity obliged to encounter, remember and mourn the violent and painful death of his entire kith and kin. Mahood is supposed to represent an existence ontologically substantive and solid enough to present the unnamable with the possibility of transcending radical suffering by adopting the subjectivity, in narrative, of a subject that suffers with the memory intact of what its suffering and affliction has cost it. All that the unnamable desires is simply to suffer in accordance with all who remember their suffering, and therefore with all who can have their suffering memorialised in historical and phenomenological consciousness. Mahood represents the possibility (but only the possibility) of achieving this in so far as he operates as the unnamable's only hope (so far) of transcending its existence and standing in as witness to the unnamable's suffering. The fictional testimony that Mahood promises to provide of the suffering that the unnamable experiences in encountering the death of its family, however, never materialises, and this because the unnamable is ontologically complicit in its failure to suffer 'like true thinking flesh' (*TN* 347).

At the instant in Mahood's family narrative where the unnamable is expected to be repelled by 'the misfortune experienced by my family and brought to my notice first by the noise of their agony, then by the smell of their corpses', i.e. where it is supposed to turn around and set out on another journey, the journey of mourning what it has just lost, is precisely where the unnamable refuses to cooperate any longer with the ontological conspiracy of Mahood: 'from that moment on I ceased to go along with him. I'll explain why, that will permit me to think of something else and in the first place of how to get back to me, back to where I am waiting for me, I'd just as soon not, but it's my only chance, at least I think so, the only chance I have of going silent, of saying something at last that is not false, if that is what they want, so as to have nothing more to say' (*TN* 315). The reasons that the unnamable subsequently gives for its momentary abandonment of the 'tricks' of Mahood have everything to do with its reluctant optimism that if it swallows the stories of Mahood lock, stock and barrel it will be assimilated into the historical existence that Mahood's very presence in the narrative suggests it is possible for the unnamable to possess.

Whatever historical existence the unnamable inherits from Mahood will be purely an illusion of ontological security. To be sure, in the ontologically inverted world of the unnamable the illusion of its real historical existence cannot last long. There is no second long enough that would make the unnamable forget, with a memory that, alas, it is denied from having, that 'in my life, since we must call it so, there were three things, the inability to speak, the inability to be silent, and solitude, that's what I've had to make the best of' (*TN* 389). The unnamable cannot therefore sincerely tolerate what it is that Mahood says it must acknowledge and internalise: 'that the bacillus botulinus should have exterminated my entire kith and kin, I shall never weary of repeating this, was something I could readily admit, but only on condition that my personal behaviour had not to suffer by it' (*TN* 316). There are two options for interpreting this 'condition' (*TN* 316). Either the unnamable refuses to admit the extermination of his 'entire kith and kin' because the act of narrating this traumatic event would entail its integration into the re-traumatising event of narrative itself, or the unnamable is ontologically incapable of suffering with the words and with the tears that the fiction of its historical existence expects it to suffer. The unnamable is incapable, according to this second interpretive option, of being devastated by the misfortune of his family in so far as the suffering that would interrupt his 'personal behaviour' arrives too late, arrives after the unnamable's 'personal behaviour' has always already been interrupted in the radical mode of suffering that neither Mahood's discourse nor, as it comes to pass, Worm's murmurings (obviously) can articulate. This tragic event cannot move the unnamable to commence a post-traumatic narrative of suffering because the type of existence that the unnamable possesses is disconnected so inexorably from the personality that its family, ostensibly independent proof of its historical existence, knows and remembers. The event of the death of the unnamable's family cannot cause the unnamable to pursue the ontological trajectory that Mahood has set it on towards reclaiming the subjectivity of a subject that experiences its suffering as a phenomenologically accessible phenomenon.

Becoming the subjectivity of a worldly form of suffering, rebuilding the ontological (and metaphysical) structures presupposed by the capacity for mourning the deaths of this sausage-induced atrocity, would be to fulfil the expectations of what the unnamable once learned about how to belong to humanity. The unnamable even begins to recall the instructions it was given about the particulars of this belonging, which directs our attention to an unspecified biographical moment in the unnamable's youth when the narrative shape of its existence may still have been that of an autobiographical *bildungsroman*: 'the lectures they gave me on men, before they even began trying to assimilate me to him' (*TN* 318). Earlier in the text the unnamable says that 'I remember little or nothing of these lectures. I cannot have understood a great deal. But I seem to have retained certain descriptions, in spite of myself. They gave me courses on love, on intelligence, most precious, most precious' (*TN* 292).

We may presume that in the context with Mahood the unnamable is being faced with one of those 'occasions' when 'some of this rubbish has come in handy [...], I don't deny it' (*TN* 292). Mahood gives to the unnamable not more lessons on humanity, but rather the pedagogically expedient occasion of having to put these lessons into practice in light of the demand for an emotional response through which the unnamable might express its humanity amidst the horror and trauma into which Mahood has placed it. This too fails. Instead, the unnamable invites us to 'consider what really occurred' once it retracted its consent to be the mouthpiece of Mahood's autobiographical fiction and the eternal pupil of its lessons on love, on intelligence, and on how best to belong to humanity:

> Finally I found myself, without surprise, within the building, circular in form as already stated, its ground floor consisting of a single room flush with the arena, and there completed my rounds, stamping under foot the unrecognized remains of my family, here a face, there a stomach, as the case might be, and sinking into them with the ends of my crutches, both coming and going. To say I did so with satisfaction would be stretching the truth. For my feeling was rather one of annoyance at having to flounder in such muck just at the moment when my closing contortions called for a firm and level surface. I like to fancy, even if it is not true, that it was in mother's entrails I spent the last days of my long voyage, and set out on the next. No, I have no preference, Isolde's breast would have done just as well, or papa's private parts, or the heart of one of the little bastards. But is it certain? Would I have not been more likely, in a sudden access of independence, to devour what remained of the fatal corned-beef? How often did I fall during these final stages, while the storms raged without? But enough of this nonsense. I was never anywhere but here, no one ever got me out of here. (*TN* 317–18)

Balking at Mahood's not-so-secret intention of initiating it as a loving and caring, indeed a mournful son, grandson, husband and father, the unnamable revels in its utter incapacity to suffer, think and feel as 'they' expect it to suffer, think and feel, as it is expected to suffer, think and feel by all those who wittingly or unwittingly consent to belonging to humanity: 'it's a poor trick that consists in ramming a set of words down your gullet on the principle that you can't bring them up without being branded as belonging to their breed. But I'll fix their gibberish for them' (*TN* 318), murmuring 'what it is their humanity stifles, the little gasp of the condemned to life, rotting in his dungeon garrotted and racked, to gasp what it is to have to celebrate banishment' (*TN* 319). With these remarks Mahood's humanising experiment comes to a close and the unnamable turns its attention elsewhere in pursuit of extrication from the ontological cage of radical suffering.

VII

Before turning to the unnamable's encounter with Worm, we should not overlook the degree to which Mahood comes tantalisingly close to succeeding in providing 'independent testimony' of the 'historical existence' that the unnamable, alas, cannot inscribe for itself from the narrative position of pupil and protagonist of its suffering. One of the 'tricks' of Beckett's writing, explicitly rendered through the figure of Mahood, is that the landscapes and contexts that it engenders and recalls in constructing its narrative and dramatic settings approximate so closely actually existing historical sites without ever permitting the imputation of a one-to-one mimetic correspondence between the literary and the historical. Perhaps the uncanniest of these is the 'vast yard or campus' that Mahood has the unnamable circle in the spiralling approach to the rotting corpses of his family. David Houston Jones takes this image as evidence that 'the dominant narrative mode [of *The Unnamable*] is once more one of concentrationary camp innuendo: the allusion to a yard of "dirt and ashes" suggests a camp or compound, but subsequently softens into the unverifiable "campus"'. Jones concludes that, 'once again, unlocalisable reference and indeterminate viewpoint combine the work's unsituated suggestions of atrocity with a distressed ontology' (2011: 32). The proximity of *The Unnamable* to historically determinate events of suffering and disaster, particularly the suffering associated with the concentration and extermination camps of the Nazi Terror, is justification for reading *The Unnamable* as a text that is very specifically historically inscribed even as it refuses any straightforward historical references and scoffs at the temptation of ascribing definite geographical locations to the narrative existence that the unnamable is ceaselessly (though futilely) at pangs to acquire. Jeff Fort is thus at risk of exaggerating the degree of attenuation of geographical historicity in *The Unnamable* when he writes that 'in *The Unnamable* we are finally *nowhere at all*, certainly not on earth or in the light of day, but in an indeterminate space that is both enclosed and limitless, all-encompassing and featureless' (2014: 321–2; italics in original).

The problem with Jones's reading of the Mahood section of *The Unnamable*, however, is that he takes the atrocity narrative that Mahood tells to the unnamable, and that the unnamable passively (if not self-consciously) dramatises in the role of its witness, too literally and too exclusively relative to what supersedes it in the unnamable's subsequent encounter with Worm. What Jones does not adequately consider is the fact that the material that comes out of the Mahood episode, and particularly its relevance for positioning the unnamable in the aporetic impossibility of bearing testimony to an unnamed trauma and atrocity that it was never ontologically present to witness in the first place, represents only a single stage in the overall narrative edifice of the text. This interpretive omission carries with it the consequence of regarding the unnamable only in its testimonial guise as a witnessing subjectivity forever struggling with the shame of desiring the recuperation of the presence of a past trauma: 'realising that his narration has achieved nothing but a perpetuation in the narrative present of the trauma of the past, the narrator angrily demands "give me back the pains I lent them and vanish, from my life, my memory, my terrors and shames." Shame, then, is the privileged figure of this deposition, associated with the desire "to witness it" and giving rise to an identification which is, in Agamben's terms, both "absolutely foreign and perfectly intimate"' (Jones 2011: 31). The image of the unnamable that Jones constructs is that of an archival machine or belated witness to an event that never makes its way definitively into the memory-text of the present. The unnamable's 'shame' projects its narrative consciousness irreversibly into the past, except that with the introduction of Worm into the narrative, the unnamable's backward-gazing attention is disrupted, and the thematic structure of witnessing and testifying to an event of the past is supplemented with the imperative of severing its relation to the past and of thinking its way into the future by way of an act of temporal trespass and transgression. In focusing exclusively on the phenomenon of shame as the dominant affective condition of the unnamable's testimony, Jones misses out on reading the terror of the imperative that the unnamable continue speaking, start thinking, and stop suffering.

By basing his interpretation of *The Unnamable* almost exclusively on what transpires throughout the unnamable's encounter with Mahood, Jones succeeds in providing a penetrating analysis of only one part of the unnamable's relation to the exigency of its suffering. Again, the consequence of this omission is that it compels ignoring the fertile philosophical and hermeneutical ground the unnamable sows in its encounter with Worm, which demands that we interrogate how it is that the question *what does it mean to think* from one discontinuous, fragmentary encounter (with Mahood, with Worm) to the next becomes heavily implicated in the overall narrative architecture of *The Unnamable*. Ultimately, Jones mobilises his reading of *The Unnamable* as a stepping stone to invoking the figure of the 'vanquished' in Beckett's *The Lost Ones* as a further illustration of how 'Beckett anticipates a key strand of Agamben's argument in *Remnants of Auschwitz*', particularly 'Agamben's account of the impossibility of testimony [which] refers not only to the inevitable betrayal of the dead, who can no longer bear witness and are "spoken for" by survivors, but, more specifically, to the figure who incarnates that impossibility. That figure is the "Muselmann," the concentration camp inmate who expresses death in life and the contamination of the human by the inhuman' (2011: 36). Surely with respect to *The Unnamable*, however, the subjectivity of suffering that Beckett's writing excavates is not as innocent in its responsibility for the ordeal of its suffering as Jones makes it out to be. It is with Worm that we will see how this is the case and what some of its consequences are for acquiring a more comprehensive idea of what is involved in the unnamable's terror-stricken contact with radical suffering.

VIII

The unnamable fails with Mahood in so far as it pursues a dialectics of recognition and a nostalgic retrieval of its historical existence as strategies for exiting radical suffering. The narrative significance of the introduction of Worm is that Worm represents for the unnamable the possibility of disavowing altogether his search for a strategy of exiting radical suffering, and in its place pursuing the knowing embrace of the non-historical and non-phenomenological existence that in Blanchot's diagnosis radical suffering constitutively prescribes. Worm is fundamentally unlike Mahood, and so we should be cautious in identifying the transition from Mahood to Worm as a linear or consecutive passage through what Paul Stewart calls the 'wretch-circuit' of the unnamable's failed series of identifications (2006: 142). According to Stewart, 'the Unnamable cannot entirely cohere with the identity of Mahood, as we have seen, and this gap in identification spurs him on to a further attempted identification with Worm in the hope that this will complete the project of being Mahood. The series is then fixed, with each new attempted identification set in motion by the failure of the last. The disjunction in identification between the Unnamable and his surrogates activates the necessity for yet further failed surrogates' (2006: 143). There is little point disputing that the unnamable's attempted identification with Worm does in fact lapse into yet another failed identification like the one with Mahood, which occasions the unnamable's admission that 'at no moment do I know what I'm talking about, nor of whom, nor of where, nor how, nor why, but I could employ fifty wretches for this sinister operation and still be short of a fifty-first, to close the circuit, that I know, without knowing what it means' (*TN* 332). Arguing that the unnamable fails at being Worm just as he failed at being Mahood, that failing to be Worm he fails to finally be Mahood, is stated explicitly and repeatedly enough in *The Unnamable* so as to be rendered a moot point of contention. What matters, then, is not the conclusion that the unnamable fails throughout the series of its attempted identifications (with Mahood, Worm, etc.). What matters is *how* it fails in each of these discrete instances of ontological noncorrespondence.

After the ontological debacle with Mahood, the unnamable comes into contact with this other unnamable not entirely unlike itself, but since there is apparently 'nothing doing without proper names', the unnamable decides to 'baptise him Worm' (*TN* 331):

> I don't like it, but I haven't much choice. It will be my name too, when the time comes, when I needn't be called Mahood any more, if that happy time ever comes. Before Mahood there were others like him, of

> the same breed and creed, armed with the same prong. But Worm is the first of his kind. That's soon said. I must not forget I don't know him. Perhaps he too will weary, renounce the task of forming me and make way for another, having laid the foundations. He has not yet been able to speak his mind, only murmur, I have not ceased to hear his murmur, all the while the other discoursed. He has survived them all, Mahood too, if Mahood is dead. (*TN* 331)

In a narrative that places so much emphasis on aporetic imperatives like being before beginning, dying after death, speaking the unspeakable, thinking the unthinkable, and suffering in the exigency of radical suffering, the relatively coherent distinction on which the unnamable insists in this excerpt between the murmuring of Worm and the discoursing of Mahood is worth bracketing off before the narrative continues on and threatens to elide the significance of this distinction in favour of Worm's eventual convergence on the circuit with Mahood. Worm represents a peculiarly singular existence that only needs to be conceived in order to be: 'Worm is, since we conceive him, as if there could be no being but being conceived' (*TN* 340). Accordingly, we are made to presume that when Worm speaks, it is from a pre-linguistic, pre-ontological space (the space of the *il y a* of being *before* existence) where the essence of persons and things that words and concepts invariably negate is still (inconceivably) intact, pristine in its non-existence. This is why Worm calmly, incessantly murmurs, and Mahood only clumsily, occasionally discourses. The instant Worm appears in the narrative, however, its singular non-existence, 'the first of his kind', risks being violated through enlistment in the ongoing dialectical desire for recognition, the satisfaction of which the unnamable had already tried to extort out of its encounter and convergence with Mahood.

Acting against the irrepressible impulse to speak and to name, the unnamable elicits the non-existence of Worm as an antidote to the failed convergence with the existence of one like Mahood. Even as he inadvertently engages in the dialectics of substituting Worm's non-existence with the existence of Mahood, an action that is once again initiated in the service of acquiring some form of conceptual or phenomenological mastery over its suffering subjectivity, the unnamable continues to optimistically insist that becoming Worm will lead it to glimpsing the horizon of transcendence on which the promise of Mahood failed to make good:

> Tears gush from [his eye] practically without ceasing, why is not known, nothing is known, whether it's with rage, or whether it's with grief, the fact is there, perhaps it's the voice that makes it weep, with rage, or some other passion, or at having to see, from time to time, some sight or other, perhaps that's it, perhaps he weeps in order not to see, though it seems difficult to credit him with an initiative of this complexity. The rascal, he's getting humanized, he's going to lose if he doesn't watch out, if he doesn't take care, and with what could he take care, with what could he form the faintest conception of the condition they are decoying him into, with their ears, their eyes, their tears and a brainpan where anything may happen. That's his strength, his only strength, that he understands nothing, can't take thought, doesn't know what they want, doesn't know they are there, feels nothing, ah but just a moment, he feels, he suffers, the noise makes him suffer, and he knows, he knows it's a voice, and he understands, a few expressions here and there, a few intonations, ah it looks bad, bad, no, perhaps not, for it's they describe him thus, without knowing, thus because they need him thus, perhaps he hears nothing, suffers nothing, and this eye, more mere imagination. (*TN* 353)

In this excerpt the unnamable goes through the motions of its hypothetical convergence with Worm, tracing the movement whereby the tears of Worm begin to flow towards any number of perceptions and conclusions about the particularity of Worm's suffering. We can say that Worm is on the threshold of vulnerability to the creatively destructive violence of ontological inauguration, of destructively creative thinking, on the basis that as of yet 'nothing is known' about why or from whence Worm will continue to suffer. His suffering, his tears, are an incomprehensible fact of his spectral existence, and it is this fact – 'the fact is there' – that is responsible for positioning Worm in the vulnerable position of being extorted into acquiring an existence outside of the timeless, pre-or post-ontological void of radical suffering. Terror's denegative capacity (according to the fragmentary imperative of writing) for turning thinking against thought and speaking against speech is activated in this excerpt precisely at the point where the unnamable's tone shifts around the exclamatory phrase *ah but just a moment*.

Worm's reduction to an existence in passive ontological vulnerability means that anything and everything can hypothetically be said about and attributed to him so long as Worm continues to occupy such an existence always already torn down to the indestructibility of its nothingness. Terror is activated at the apotheosis of Worm's measureless vulnerability in this state of ontological passivity where the unnamable begins to humanise 'the rascal' by 'decoying' him into the existence that he is expected to have, 'because they need him thus' (*TN* 353). Extorted speech, extorted thinking and extorted existence can only be extracted from a subject reduced by extreme acts of violence to the figure of a subjectivity permanently exiled from the context of the living. The unnamable, not knowing whether or not it is Worm in this scenario, or whether, through the power of its imagination, it is the one subjecting Worm to the (de)humanising violence that Worm's ontological vulnerability invites, is permitted to conclude that perhaps, after all, Worm 'hears nothing, suffers nothing', and therefore continues to murmur from a place that the discourse of Mahood has not yet failed at miscomprehending. It is on the basis of Worm's non-discursive murmurings (non-discursive in relation to Mahood), and not on Worm's susceptibility to, or reflection of the unnamable's terroristic methods of the extortion and extraction of speech and existence, that the unnamable does not regard Worm as the representative of 'another trap to snap me up among the living', a trap to 'make me believe I have an ego all my own, and can speak of it, as they of theirs' (*TN* 339).

On the contrary, according to the unnamable, it is through the murmuring presence of Worm that it acquires the perspective of one who does not need to feel or to think in the way that Mahood wants it to feel and to think as prerequisites of belonging to humanity. Worm's spectral existence is appealing because, in stark contrast to Mahood, as the unnamable explains, Worm has

> come into the world unborn, abiding there unliving, with no hope of death, epicentre of joys, of griefs, of calm. Who seems the truest possession, because the most unchanging. The one outside of life we always were in the end, all our long vain life long. Who is not spared by the mad need to speak, to think, to know where one is, where one was, during the wild dream, up above, under the skies, venturing forth at night. The one ignorant of himself and silent, ignorant of his silence and silent, who could not be and gave up trying. (*TN* 340)

As was the case for confirming that Antelme had slipped into radical suffering, here too the suffering of Worm is such that it predicates of Worm the anthropomorphically irreducible phenomenon of need. Just as Antelme experienced hunger as need, experienced the ubiquity of pain (the elements, the SS), so too is Worm suddenly predicated by the 'mad need to speak, to think' (*TN* 340). The mad need that overtakes Worm is not autonomously generated by Worm himself, but is the desire of the 'others', of the unnamable, who 'conceive him' thus and who, because of having to occupy with Worm so radical a state of ontological dispossession, need to see in Worm a reflection of the indestructible (because essentially destroyed) existence that they too possess.

The unnamable is the representative of these 'others' in this context, and what he needs to get out of Worm is simple: to acquire irrefutable proof, a neat formulation of the fact that an existence in radical suffering is not something that can be redeemed or transcended, but is simply suffered 'outside of [the] life we always were in the end' (*TN* 340). Although the anonymous voices that whisper into the ear of the unnamable the words that announce the presence of Worm are fixated on getting the unnamable 'to be he, the anti-Mahood' (340), the ontological project of inciting the unnamable to exist in the spirit of Worm that they are trying to coordinate on the unnamable's behalf stalls before it begins, not only because the project has nowhere to go, no telos to guide its forward narrative movement, but also because 'having no ear, no head, no memory', the unnamable is not in a position to broker the continuity of the murmuring of Worm with the discourse of Mahood: 'I'm Worm, no if I were Worm I wouldn't know it, I wouldn't say it, I wouldn't say anything, I'd be Worm. But I don't say anything, I don't know anything, these voices are not mine, nor these thoughts, but the voices and thoughts of the devils who beset me. Who make me say that [. . .] since I couldn't be Mahood, as I might have been, I must be Worm, as I cannot be. But is it still they who say that when I have failed to be Worm I'll be Mahood, automatically, on the rebound?' (*TN* 341).

With Worm, the unnamable reconfirms its earlier suspicion that its presence in the narrative context of *The Unnamable* is reducible 'solely [to] a question of voices, no other image is appropriate. Let it go through me at last, the last one, his who has none, by his own confession' (*TN* 340–1). So long as the unnamable's attention is focused (by the voices) on becoming Worm, it is Worm that the unnamable decidedly cannot be. The existence of Worm is predicated purely on its coerced materialisation through the words and in the mind of the unnamable as it speaks and thinks in the narrative space of the present:

> Yes, now that I've forgotten who Worm is, where he is, what he's like, I'll begin to be he. [...] Feeling nothing, knowing nothing, capable of nothing, wanting nothing. Until the instant he hears the sound that will never stop. Then it's the end. Worm no longer is. We know it, but we don't say it, we say it's the awakening, the beginning of Worm, for now we must speak, and speak of Worm. It's no longer he, but let us proceed as if it were still he, he at last, who hears, and trembles, and is delivered over, to affliction and the struggle to withstand it, the starting eye, the labouring mind. (*TN* 342)

What prevents the unnamable from becoming Worm, first and foremost, is that the unnamable is convinced of beginning to hear and understand the murmurings of Worm, murmurings 'that will never stop' (*TN* 342). To listen and above all to hear the constant droning of Worm's murmurs is to be implicitly convinced that such murmurings can be translated into a comprehensible discourse of recitation, and thus to hear Worm amounts to not being able to be Worm: 'I'm Worm, that is to say I am no longer he, since I hear' (*TN* 343). The pretension to existing precisely as Worm exists is symptomatic of the illusion that momentarily convinced the unnamable of its existence in the fictional world and in the fictional mode of that of Mahood. The virtue of Worm is that the peculiarity of his faceless, anonymous existence does not permit the unnamable to go along with the ruse of identification for such an extended length of time as it had under the authorial auspices of Mahood: 'let us call that thing Worm, so as to exclaim, the sleight of hand accomplished, Oh look, life again, life everywhere and always, the life that's on every tongue, the only possible! Poor Worm, who thought he was different, there he is in the madhouse for life' (*TN* 342). It is with the unnamable's confession, delivered in this ironic and sarcastic tone, that he can never converge with the non-existence of Worm, that ends the project of experiencing the suffering of Worm's incapacity to experience his suffering. Although the unnamable cannot pronounce this conclusion, nevertheless it is at this point certain that the unnamable, despite its desires and its capitulations, is very much in an analogous situation as Worm in so far as it too is not able to stave off the mad need to speak and to think amidst its seeming inability to do either outside of the painfully mute, ontologically inhospitable presence of its suffering.

According to Anthony Uhlmann's description of the ontological aporia of Mahood and Worm, 'Worm cannot properly speaking be said to exist until he comes to feel (and at this point he stops being Worm, who does not feel, who is only conceived). The opposite problem to that of Worm plagues Mahood. Mahood feels but, finally, he is no longer conceived, the others fail to believe in him and so he ceases to exist' (Uhlmann 1999: 159). The virtue of Uhlmann's reading of this section of *The Unnamable* is that it emphasises and therefore respects the ontological incompatibility of Worm with Mahood. The non-existence of Worm, Uhlmann insists, is not synonymous with the non-existence of Mahood (though Mahood, too, is 'more mere imagination'). Conversely, the *existence* of Worm, as a fictional construct in a narrative situation composed of nothing but fictional constructs, is fundamentally different from the fictional existence of Mahood. Were the unnamable to go on continuing believing in the fictions of Mahood, it would not end up existing in the way of Worm, passing from one fictional node on the circuit of non-existence to another. Conversely, were the unnamable to give up once and for all on the prospect of existing like Mahood, murmuring 'what it is their humanity stifles' in the idiom of Worm, it would not be able to reconcile this existence with the discourse authored by Mahood. The aporetic impasse manned by Mahood and Worm is unbreakable: the unnamable cannot fail at one project of identification without reviving the other in its absence, and it is this structure of passing back and forth from Mahood and Worm that opens up the space in the narrative for claiming that what the unnamable does not know, what it cannot possibly know, is that its narrative existence is synonymous with an event of ontological disintegration occurring continuously in a past that cannot ever be recalled from the vantage point of the narrative present.

What thus forces the conclusion that in *The Unnamable* there is no way of returning to a time before the unnamable's encounter with the event of its ontological disintegration is that what the unnamable is being compelled to search for is the beginning of an existence and the acquisition of a subjectivity that would betray no false illusions of resurrecting the existence and subjectivity that preceded its descent into radical suffering. The presence of Worm forecloses the desire to experience and recollect the subjectivity of a non-radical, finite experience of affliction instigated by the humanising fictions of Mahood. When reading *The Unnamable* it is therefore imperative to recognise that the movements the unnamable makes through the space of its narrative are evocative of its confrontation with new and contingently unpredictable problematics of suffering, subjectivity, speaking and thinking, i.e. problematics that, while advancing the discourse of the text in new directions, do not simply invalidate earlier problematics (like the episode with Mahood) that are nevertheless so quickly and easily forgotten: 'Mahood I couldn't die. Worm will I ever get born? It's the same problem. But perhaps not the same personage after all. The scytheman will tell, it's all one to him' (*TN* 345–6). Whether the unnamable can ever exist in continuity with Mahood or Worm remains thoroughly undecidable, but nevertheless the desire surely persists for a violent, unpredictable *shock* that will disengage it from the liminal non-existence that its submersion in radical suffering prescribes. Such a shock, however, cannot come from the unnamable itself: 'That's why there are all these little silences, to try and make me break them. They think I can't bear silence, that some day, somehow, my horror of silence will force me to break it. That's why they are always leaving off, to try and drive me to extremities' (*TN* 342).

To expect of the unnamable that it will say something that will unlock the aporetic impasses of the text, that buried somewhere within its murmuring and its discourse is the image or word that will fill in the blanks with which the unnamable began its narrative misery, is to abdicate a responsibility that has no business being transferred onto the figure of the narrative voice of *The Unnamable*: 'What doesn't come to me from me has come to the wrong address. Similarly my understanding is not yet sufficiently well-oiled to function without the pressure of some critical circumstance, such as a violent pain felt for the first time' (*TN* 343–4). The violent shock that the unnamable desires as the catalyst for it to commence thinking and suffering 'for the first time' is a shock that the unnamable is as yet powerless to induce by provoking the entrance of either Worm or Mahood into the narrative. The unnamable cannot begin thinking and suffering, 'like true thinking flesh', for the simple reason that only through the already established and already confirmed experience of thinking and suffering would it know and feel that what it is doing is what is called thinking and suffering: 'they say I suffer like true thinking flesh, but I'm sorry, I feel nothing' (*TN* 347).

Beckett ties a negative symptomology of suffering to a negative epistemology of thinking as the only conditions of the unnamable's existence that are visible inside the narrative architecture of the text, and so responsibility for overcoming the unsublatable negativity of these conditions falls irrevocably on the external perspective of criticism engaged in coming to terms with the fact and in overriding the hermeneutically paralysing grip, as Wolfgang Iser puts it apropos the experience of reading Beckett, of being 'locked *out of* the text' (1980: 208; italics in original). The event of literature, the event of thinking *in* literature, can only be instigated in the encounter with the 'critical circumstance' that would unhinge the unnamable from its essential incapacity to think and to suffer as it is expected to think and to suffer as one who belongs to humanity. At this point in our reading of the narrative there is little choice in moving forward except to take the unnamable at its word when it says, '*I only think [. . .] once a certain degree of terror has been exceeded*' (TN 344; my italics). The question that we must answer as we advance towards developing a critique of the terror of thinking is whether or not *The Unnamable*, *qua* unresolved narrative of radical suffering, represents, from a meta-narrative perspective, the maximal intensification of terror requisite for us to say that the unnamable is embroiled in the act of thinking. The wager here is that a critique of the experience of radical suffering in *The Unnamable* doubles as a critique of the terror of thinking.

The unnamable insists that its vigilance in the midst of its suffering is not a question of endurance but of condemnation, and as such it is an experience of condemnation that links its consciousness and its speech with the discursive prerogatives of terror: 'In their shoes I'd be content with my knowing what I know, I'd demand no more of me than to know that what I hear is not the innocent and necessary sound of dumb things constrained to endure, but the terror-stricken babble of the condemned to silence' (TN 348). As always, what drives the unnamable forward after pronouncements such as these is its utter disbelief that what it says about itself and about its situation is true. Reduced to being nothing more than the narrative voice of the 'condemned to silence', restrained by its condemnation to speak only the 'terror-stricken babble' of a language incomprehensible except through the terror that provokes it, the unnamable can nevertheless not discredit the suspicion that it is not alone, and that if it is not alone then there is still hope that its condemnation will come to an end and that the babble that it speaks will be substituted and salvaged by the discourse of the company that surrounds it. The unnamable turns to language and to the grammatical freedom that language bequeaths in order to try and extricate itself once and for all from its condemnation in radical suffering: 'I shall not say I again, ever again, it's too farcical. I shall put in its place whenever I hear it, the third person, if I think of it. Anything to please them' (*TN* 348). Even as the unnamable admits straightaway that this gesture of grammatical substitution 'will make no difference', it adds to this narrative of suffering the third-person perspective of the tormentor that pins the unnamable to its tormented existence (*TN* 348).

As it looks down at itself from this third-person perch, the unnamable wonders aloud about what it looks like in its situation and about the observations that can be made about how it makes its way through the narrative. However, the survey the unnamable provides about its physical attributions devolves into a reflection on what is occurring from the perspective of its imaginary tormentors and keepers, who observe the unnamable in what can only be described as a cage fit for the caged beast that the unnamable later in the narrative (as we have already seen) becomes:

> There he is now with breath and nostrils, it only remains for him to suffocate. The thorax rises and falls, the wear and tear are in full spring, the rot spreads downwards, soon he'll have legs, the possibility of crawling. More lies, he doesn't breathe yet, he'll never breathe. Then what is this faint noise, as of air stealthily stirred, recalling the breath of life, to those whom it corrodes? It's a bad example. But these lights that go out hissing? Is it not more likely a great cackle of laughter, at the sight of his terror and distress? To see him flooded with light, then suddenly plunged back into darkness, must strike them as irresistibly funny. But they have been there so long now, on every side, they may have made a hole in the wall, a little hole, to glue their eyes to, turn about. And these lights are perhaps those they shine upon him, from time to time, in order to observe his progress. [. . .] No, in the place where he is he cannot learn, the head cannot work, he knows no more than on the first day, he merely hears, and suffers, uncomprehending, that must be possible. (*TN* 348–9)

That the unnamable 'suffers, uncomprehending' should not produce the conclusion that suffering and thinking, contrary to what Blanchot surmised, are somehow disjoined and reciprocally antithetical. Here it is imperative that we entertain the idea that Beckett selects his words conscientiously, and that 'thinking' does not necessarily equate with 'comprehending' in *The Unnamable*. The terror of thinking articulates as the expression of (metaphysical and epistemological) violence against comprehension, for what demands thinking most imperatively, what alibis literature's (and writing's) right to exist in the world as a discourse that autonomously, sovereignly speaks and thinks, is the unforgettable yet all too widely forgotten presence in the world of essentially unthinkable, unspeakable existences condemned interminably to incomprehension and silence. The terror of thinking is the imperative of thinking *with* such existences, but to do so in a way that does not shy away from plunging headlong into the crisis, the terror of what happens to thinking (and speaking) in its proximity with what is unthinkable (and therefore unspeakable, therefore unnamable) in the experience of such existences.

Blanchot writes that Artaud's '"I cannot think, I cannot manage to think" is a summons to a more profound thought, a constant pressure, an oblivion that, never allowing itself to be forgotten, always demands a more perfect oblivion. Henceforth thinking is this step always to take backwards' (*BC* 39). The act of thinking, in other words, always steps backwards into the destroyed ontological zone of radical suffering from which it had occasion to emerge in the first place. Literature is the preeminent space where this experiment with commencing and continuing thinking in the face of the incapacity to be extricated from radical suffering can be undertaken, and it is Beckett's writing of *The Unnamable* that drives this experiment forward to its most terror-stricken extreme. That Beckett's writing of *The Unnamable* is so intransigently embroiled in the problematic of what this chapter has termed the terror of thinking is precisely what makes it so laborious, so incomprehensible, so visceral, and yet so necessary to read as a principal instance of the terror of literature.

Notes

1. Daniel Katz is of course right that 'to assume there is such a substance, or "voice," in the book *The Unnamable* and to refer to it as 'The Unnamable' is already to violate the conditions under which the text tells us this phenomenon may be discussed. *Perhaps* such a

violation is necessary, even programmed by the text, but even if this is the case, the implications and the economy of such a violation would need to be addressed. And any investigation of this question should recognise the way the prose of *The Unnamable* refuses not only the stability of reference offered by the proper name, but even that of the entire pronominal system with its built-in deictic distinctions between *who is speaking* and *who is being spoken of*' (1999: 79; italics in original). Katz also recognises that 'no discussion of Beckett's refusal of subjectivity and the "I" can ignore Maurice Blanchot's thoughts on this issue', but like most Beckett critics, Katz worries that Blanchot tends towards rendering the neutered subjectivity that speaks through Beckett's writing as one of absolute detachment from referentiality (1999: 24). 'One of the great paradoxes of *The Unnamable*', Katz writes, 'is that although in many ways it seems the perfect model of Blanchot's "neutre," all the same it retains highly determinate relations to inscriptions of gender and also to the specificities of different languages, nationalities, and geographies' (1999: 26). Part of what I want to do in this chapter is to refer Blanchot's notion of the 'narrative voice', or the neutered subjectivity that speaks in Beckett's writing, to a particular historical experience that Blanchot reads out of Antelme's memoir. Blanchot is not as dismissive of referentiality as far too many Beckett critics make him out to be, even when they praise the value of Blanchot's conception of the neutered voice of narrative speech for its capacity to articulate how the figures that inhabit the space of Beckett's writing tend towards engendering impersonal structures of subjectivity that derive from the ontological emphasis in Beckett's writing on textuality and language.
2. This is the experience of what Martin Hägglund advocates in *Radical Atheism* as the atheistic, diachronic temporality of ontological survival, which is derived from what Derrida describes as the work of 'spacing' constitutive of *différance*: '[T]he aspect that is most crucial for radical atheism [. . .] concerns the ontological status of spacing. Derrida repeatedly argues that *différance* (as a name for the spacing of time) not only applies to language or experience or any other delimited region of being. Rather, it is an *absolutely general condition*, which means that there cannot even in principle be anything that is exempt from temporal finitude' (2008: 2–3; italics in original).
3. Christopher Fynsk reminds us that this section of *The Infinite Conversation* on Antelme, which Blanchot titled 'Humankind', is 'coupled to another bearing the subheading "Being Jewish" ("Etre juif") – the latter constituting what is one of Blanchot's most signifi-

cant statements on Judaism. The essays are joined with the chapter title, "The Indestructible." Since "Being Jewish" may be construed as the description of a *form of existence* that bears witness to the exigency to which I have referred, the meaning of Blanchot's gesture of coupling the essays should give us pause' (2013: 35; italics in original). Fynsk is right to read 'Humankind' and 'Being Jewish' as (possibly) disjunctive statements on a single question – what is *autrui*? – and thus his work serves as an important reminder that Blanchot's reflections on the concept of 'the indestructible' are part of a larger context and discussion involving Levinas that unfortunately this chapter does not have the space or indeed the mandate (as a reading of *The Unnamable*) to pursue in any serious way.

4. In his chapter on *The Unnamable* in *Interpreting Narrative in the Novels of Samuel Beckett*, Jonathan Boulter alerts us to a section in Beckett's *Proust* where Beckett insinuates a relation between suffering and interpretation: 'As Beckett suggests in *Proust*, suffering is more than a mere existential condition. It is a condition that tempers and perhaps articulates interpretation, the hermeneutical experience itself: suffering initially is a heuristic "device." [. . .] Suffering – suffering of the Proustian character, the Beckettian character, the writer – thus articulates its own aesthetic, its own framing of specific experiences' (2001: 95).

5. The question of how discrete discourses like philosophy, art and science engage in the act of thinking has been an abiding preoccupation of Deleuze's beginning with *Difference and Repetition* and lasting all the way through to his collaborative work with Guattari in *What is Philosophy?* Accordingly, I am not claiming here that Deleuze is extending his critique of 'true thinking' to literature, at least not from the perspective of *Difference and Repetition*; rather, I am claiming that Beckett too is engaging with the question of what thinking *is* as such, though for Beckett distinctions of genre matter far less (which is not to say they do not matter at all) than they do for Deleuze. Indeed, Rodolphe Gasché treats this dimension of the Deleuzian oeuvre in *The Honor of Thinking*, where he argues that whereas *Difference and Repetition* was 'intent on demarcating true philosophical thought from any image of thought, old and new', '*What is Philosophy?*, by contrast, seems to reconsider the previous condemnation of the image. [. . .] But if Deleuze can thus reconsider the status of the image, is it not because the image of thought as "what thought claims by right" now characterises all philosophy, old and new? Is Deleuze not led to recognise in this later work that at least a minimal element of

the nonphilosophical is essential to philosophical thought as such and that all philosophy thus comes with an image of thought?' (2007: 251). The implication of Gasché's reading of Deleuze is that the question of thinking must be asked not just for philosophy alone, but for all who would engage in the act of thinking, whether philosophically, aesthetically or scientifically.

6. This is not to say that writing in the 'non-historical margins of literature and narrative' commits Beckett to an anti-historical conception of suffering. Deleuze and Guattari's concept of 'minor literature' is helpful for underscoring this distinction, particularly as they argue that literature's contribution to subverting the dominant ideology of a repressive society and politics is to instruct on the possibility of inhabiting its language and its culture as a 'stranger *within*' (1986: 26): 'this is the problem of immigrants, and especially of their children, the problem of minorities, the problem of a minor literature, but also a problem for all of us: how to tear a minor literature away from its own language, allowing it to challenge the language and making it follow a sober revolutionary path?' (1986: 19).

7. There is also of course the earlier episode where the unnamable posits the presence of Malone and considers imagining for him a companion, as in 'the pseudocouple Mercier-Camier. The next time they enter the field, moving slowly towards each other, I shall know they are going to collide, fall and disappear, and this will perhaps enable me to observe them better' (*TN* 291). Accordingly, it may be mistaken to say that Mahood is the unnamable's first companion. However, it is not mistaken in the sense that in the case of Malone, who with his hypothetical companion is positioned to enter 'into collision before me' (*TN* 291), imagines the unnamable, what the unnamable is projecting is an encounter that he observes – 'in a word, I only see what appears immediately in front of me, I only see what appears close beside me, what I best see I see ill' (*TN* 291) – but in which he does not directly participate. Unlike Malone, in other words, Mahood is posited as a 'vice-exister' alongside the unnamable, and it is for this reason that I am privileging the entrance of Mahood in *The Unnamable*.

8. In *Spirals: The Whirled Image in Twentieth-Century Literature and Art*, Nico Israel predicates the image of the spiral on the image *par excellence* of what it means to be thinking in *The Unnamable*. Israel cites Hugh Kenner in the process of arguing that 'a special form of finding, and not finding, the center is at issue in the many spirals that play a significant role in Beckett's writing. Nowhere is this more powerfully the case than in Beckett's most sustained and yet argu-

ably most "concentrated" novel, *L'innommable*. [...] The final novel of the trilogy of the mid- to late 1940s that, as Hugh Kenner notes, "carries the Cartesian process backwards, beginning with a je suis and ending with a bare cogito," *The Unnamable* "concerns itself to no end with a baffling intimacy between discourse and non-existence." It does so, at least in part, through the repeated presentation of spiralled journeys and spiralized thinking' (2015: 163).

2

The Beginning (Again) and Ending (Again) of Terror in *Texts for Nothing*

For beauty is nothing / but the beginning of terror, which we still are just able to / endure, / and we are so awed because it serenely disdains / to annihilate us. Every angel is terrifying.
(Rainer Maria Rilke)

I

It is no secret that Beckett found himself at an impasse following the writing of *The Unnamable*. In the letter to Rosset dated 21 August 1954, we will recall, Beckett remarks that 'I think my writing days are over. *L'Innommable* finished me or expressed my finishedness' (*Letters II* 497). *Texts for Nothing* was meant to be the immediate attempt to escape from this impasse. This proved not to be the case. From Beckett's perspective, as we will again recall from the 1956 interview with Shenker, '[t]he very last thing I wrote – "Textes pour rien" – was an attempt to get out of the attitude of disintegration, but it failed' (cited in Shenker 1999: 148). What Beckett means by 'disintegration' can be read as the realisation in the figure of the unnamable of the utter unworkability in prose of a fragmented narrative subject (or voice) condemned to 'go on' existing, speaking and thinking in the midst of being repetitively effaced of its narrated subjectivity. Accordingly, while it is quite possible that Beckett's reference to 'failure' here could be ironic (since when is failure a bad thing for Beckett?), it is just as likely that it expresses a genuine feeling that his writing of *Texts for Nothing* was being inescapably held hostage by the recurrent ontological impasse of *The Unnamable* – 'I have ten or so little texts written recently, the afterbirth of *L'Innommable* and not to be approached directly' (*Letters II* 300).

As a consequence of Beckett's continuing reliance in *Texts for Nothing* on the poetics of disintegration derived from *The Unnamable*, one of the many challenges of reading *Texts for Nothing* involves determining precisely this work's significance as a transitional moment (or not) within Beckett's oeuvre. H. Porter Abbott has made a compelling case for reading *Texts for Nothing* and *How It Is* as complementary projects in Beckett's commitment to continually reinventing his work in literature after the impasse of *The Unnamable*. Accordingly, Abbott refers to *Texts for Nothing* and *How It Is* as Beckett's most sustained attempts to realise a post-narrative work of literary fiction, such that *The Unnamable* is assessed through its stubborn adherence to what Abbott sees, for all intents and purposes, as a traditional narrative sequence. Rejecting the last residue of the teleological narrative form that remained operative in *The Unnamable* – Abbott argues that 'the *Texts* is Beckett's deliberate abandonment of the very practice that had worked so well in the trilogy and given it so much of its power – its masterful deployment of the quest' – allows Beckett to pass from an 'attitude of disintegration' to what Abbott calls an 'aesthetic of recommencement' (1996: 109).

In his introductory remarks to *The Complete Short Prose*, S.E. Gontarski similarly maintains that *Texts for Nothing* and the 'Four Novellas', 'to use the current historical markers, [...] represent a leap from Modernism to Post-Modernism, from interior voices to exterior voices, from internality to externality' (1995: xxv). This is an argument that relies on Beckett's presumed ability to continuously 'make it new' after impasses like the one his writing confronted at the exasperated ending of *The Unnamable*: 'perhaps it's done already, perhaps they have said me already, perhaps they have carried me to the threshold of my story, before the door that opens my story, that would surprise me, if it opens, it will be I, it will be the silence, where I am, I don't know, I'll never know, in the silence you don't know, you must go on, I can't go on, I'll go on' (*TN* 407). Placed within the boundaries of Beckett's career in prose, these readings, which to a large extent extricate *Texts for Nothing* from the suffocating clutches of *The Unnamable*, discourage (inadvertently or otherwise) efforts at reading *Texts for Nothing* as itself being a critical intervention *into* the impasse of *The Unnamable*, and this in spite of Beckett's avowed recommendation to the contrary.

Writing in the pages of the *Journal of Beckett Studies*, Paul Sheehan bucks this early though no doubt influential trend of separating *Texts for Nothing* from *The Unnamable*. Sheehan adopts the perspective that *Texts for Nothing* indeed intensifies the narrative paralysis that likewise engulfed the speaker of *The Unnamable* in the aporetic density of its speech, its unfulfillable desire for silence, and its (always sceptical) affirmation ultimately of the ontological sovereignty of the nothingness that its narrative subjectivity is on the verge of becoming. In so doing, Sheehan's interpretation of *Texts for Nothing* is, on the one hand, similar to that of Badiou's, according to which *Texts for Nothing* and *The Unnamable* are inseparable in their fatally nihilistic commitment to the terror of phenomenological reflexivity. Unlike Badiou, however, Sheehan sees the relation of disintegration that pins *Texts for Nothing* to *The Unnamable* in positive terms, i.e. as that which makes *Texts for Nothing* such an extraordinarily advanced work of literature. For Sheehan, *Texts for Nothing* can 'easily be seen as a condensed version of the *Trilogy*' (2001: 93): 'The Texts for Nothing are the doubtful underside hinted at all through the *Trilogy*, the necessary emission generated by the suspicion that the earlier work has not plunged far enough down into its dark' (2001: 102). Beckett, Sheehan explains, turns to a musical conception of nothingness (articulated by Sheehan through John Cage's 'Lecture on Nothing') as a more appropriate aesthetic strategy for penetrating into the nothingness of language that perhaps resides beneath what Beckett famously describes in the 1937 letter to Axel Kaun as the 'terrible materiality of the word surface' (*D* 171).

If there is a problem with Sheehan's analysis, however, it does not consist in the observation that *Texts for Nothing* intervenes into the aporetic interstices of speech and silence, or plenitude (something) and nothingness, with a more acutely refined sense of the aesthetic and ontological urgency of breaking through the recalcitrant materiality of language than is otherwise apparent in *The Unnamable*. Its limitation, rather, is that this argument leads Sheehan to conclude all too abstractly and anticlimactically that 'the kind of theorist Samuel Beckett is, in the works that established his name and philosophical outlook, is an explorer of nothing, where nothing operates as both a disrupter of certainty and a shaper of experience. The experience of nothing, in the early works and in the *Texts*, is the experience of theory' (2001: 101). These kinds of conclusions and the theoretical presuppositions that they invariably defend (implicitly or otherwise) – nothingness as the metaphysical crystallisation of dialectical negativity, i.e. 'the kind of negative solidity', writes Daniel Katz, 'which Beckett wished to deny' (1999: 181) – recapitulate ahistorical, hyper-theoretical readings of Beckett that predictably end in a straightforward substantialisation of nothingness.[1] In this and in other readings like it, there is a conspicuous lack of direct and sustained hermeneutical engagement with the texts that are supposed to legitimate such conceptually sure-footed conclusions. Sheehan's reading, in other words, is symptomatic of far too many theoretical interpretations of Beckett, which tend to be overly reliant on *non*-hermeneutical encounters with works like *The Unnamable* and *Texts for Nothing*, encounters that protect the interpretive subjectivity of theoretical criticism from succumbing to the disintegration of comprehension and consciousness that the Beckettian protagonists and narrative voices are not so privileged as to pretend is not happening in the narrative worlds that they are condemned to endure.

The reading of *Texts for Nothing* developed in this chapter involves a hybridisation of the two approaches that have, in large part,[2] dominated its critical reception: *Texts for Nothing* occupies a space of writing and of thinking that at once resists disavowing the sincere intractability of the impasse of *The Unnamable*, but that also resists the accusation of being either a repetitive confirmation of this impasse, or a fatal resignation to its supposedly ahistorical, nihilistic seductions.[3] This incessant doubling and redoubling of compositional protocols that stand in contradiction to one another at the same time that they are reciprocally self-sustaining is a mainstay of the Beckettian rhetoric of writing. We could say, then, in the spirit of Blanchot, that *Texts for Nothing* performs a *step/not beyond* the impasse of *The Unnamable*, at once a prohibition against continuation, and a transgression of this very prohibition.[4] Rather than regard *Texts for Nothing* as the culmination of a project that inevitably delivered Beckett's writing over to narrative and phenomenological paralysis (as in Badiou), the breaking point inaugurating a reinvigorated phase for Beckett on the possibilities latent in the medium of prose (Abbott and Gontarski), or the theoretical success of an analytic exploration of nothingness (Sheehan), perhaps it is time to be a little more precise in negotiating the narrative complexities and historical exigencies of this enigmatic, fragmentary collection of writings.

II

That the critical reception of *Texts for Nothing* should have inspired so much disagreement surrounding how best to situate it relative to the unworkable aftermath of *The Unnamable* is coincidentally symptomatic of the twentieth century's consistent incapacity to distinguish between *its* beginnings and endings too.[5] 'Ultimately', Badiou argues in *The Century*, 'the problem of the century is to exist in the non-dialectical conjunction of the theme of the end and that of the beginning. "Ending" and "beginning" are two terms that, within the century, remain unreconciled' (2007: 37). Badiou points to the discourse promulgated throughout European consciousness at the end of the First World War, which, because of its singular brutality and destructiveness, determined that this, 'the last war', was 'the heinous war that must never again take place – whence the expression "the last of the last"' (2007: 34). The end of the last war of 1914–18 was supposed to inaugurate the beginning of a new peace, except that the constellation of antagonisms (political, historical and economic) that led to the beginning of the last war were never properly reconciled at the end of the last war. The end of the last, bad war to end all bad wars, in other words, required the beginning of a new, good war to lay the foundation for an everlasting (perpetual) peace: 'because it all began in violence and destruction, this violence and destruction must be brought to an end by a superior destruction, by an essential violence' (Badiou 2007: 30). The failure of the last war to begin a new peace, Badiou argues, precipitated the ontological axiom on which the subsequent antagonisms, disagreements and misrecognitions of the twentieth century were essentially predicated. The twentieth century was the century of mislabelled endings and misidentified beginnings, and so what was needed, in the words of *Texts for Nothing*, was a 'new no, to cancel all the others' (*CSP* 147). Beckett's writing of *Texts for Nothing* was entangled in the analogous problematic of catalysing the recommencement of writing fiction vis-à-vis discontinuing the disintegrative narrative protocols of *The Unnamable*, and so regardless of the success or failure of this endeavour, *Texts for Nothing* comes to us from this historical (philosophical, historiographical) perspective articulated by Badiou as a quintessentially twentieth-century work of literature and fiction.

Because 'ending' and 'beginning' constituted an irreconcilable opposition in the historical context of the twentieth century, and because the twentieth century set for itself the single-minded task of nevertheless striving towards reconciling the irreconcilability of 'ending' and 'beginning', it inevitably confronted the question of how to distinguish between authentic beginnings and the semblance of beginnings (i.e. repetitions of endings). Badiou borrows the concept of 'the real' from Jacques Lacan in order to pinpoint the gap, or distance separating one antagonistic pole of opposition from another in this semblance-authenticity continuum of ontological (mis)perception. The real is what the century passionately desired to substantiate in order to pronounce the beginning of the end of the essential antagonisms responsible for twentieth-century crisis, ruin and despair. The whole point of ideology in this schema is to mask what turned out to be the *absence* of the real, making it appear and compelling it to act like something that it constitutively is not. The real precisely and paradoxically *is* the absence of the real, Badiou concludes through Lacan, and this ontological condition of the twentieth century had profound consequences for how the century unfolded politically, scientifically and aesthetically. Because the real is only perceptible through ideological semblances, or fictions of the real, it provided the twentieth century with a dangerously unstable ontological grounding. From out of the projects of reconciliation between the real and its semblance that the century envisioned, the projects it murderously, disastrously enacted, there arose, Badiou observes, 'both horror and enthusiasm, simultaneously lethal and creative' (2007: 32).

What Badiou diagnoses as the century's 'passion for the real' consisted in the century's drive to actualising a reconciliation of the semblance of the real with the oftentimes fanatical supposition of access to the (fantasy of the) real's unmediated authenticity (2007: 48). As Robert Buch describes it in his reading of Badiou, 'the real is a political, and indeed an ethical, category, but what it indicates, above all, is a lack in and of reality, a kind of ontological shortcoming. The twentieth century felt this lack acutely, and its defining passion was to counter it' (2010: 2–3). The twentieth century intuited, in other words, that its ontological ground was, in some sense, missing or absent, or at the very least plastic and manipulable, but rather than accept this as its reality (the reality of the absence of the real), it passionately set to work compensating for this absence with projects designed for circumscribing a new historical, ontological real on which the horizon of the future could be indelibly impressed (through the promise of a Thousand Year Reich, for instance, or through any one of the manifestos,[6] from Marx, Lenin, Mao and Fukuyama, to Breton, Marinetti, Robbe-Grillet and Debord, announcing new paradigms of representing and acting on the present).

The spectre of false beginnings that haunted the twentieth century precipitated the imperative whereby whatever ideological screen the century substituted in place of the real was a screen that required constant pressure and work to convince the world that it was anything but an illusion or a fiction devised solely for obfuscating the terrifying reality, in this 'death of God' historical context of modernity, of the absence of the real. For Badiou, 'the crucial point (as Hegel grasped long ago with regard to revolutionary Terror) is this: the real, conceived in its contingent absoluteness, is never real enough not to be suspected of semblance. The passion for the real is also, of necessity, suspicion. Nothing can attest that the real is the real, nothing but the system of fictions wherein it plays the role of the real' (2007: 52). The conclusion logically follows that 'art provides the first guiding thread to think' through the consequences of having to live through situations of anxiety, suspicion and terror – 'as Hegel grasped long ago' – emanating out of the imbrication of the impossibility and the imperative of deciphering the authenticity or semblance of the beginning and ending of new historical reals, of new historical fictions (2007: 55). The only way to move forward in the twentieth century, accordingly, was through the empowerment of systems of fiction with the authority to unmask and remask the unendingly dissimulating ideological textures of reality:

> What is at stake is the fictionalization of the very power of fiction, in other words, the fact of regarding the efficacy of semblance as real. This is one of the reasons why the art of the twentieth century is a reflexive art, an art that wants to exhibit its own process, an art that wants to visibly idealize its own materiality. Showing the gap between the factitious and the real becomes the principal concern of facticity. [. . .] This is why the twentieth century proposes artistic gestures that were previously impossible, or presents as art what used to be nothing but waste matter. These gestures and presentations testify to the omnipresence of art, inasmuch as the artistic gesture ultimately comes down to an intrusion into semblance – exposing, in its brute state, the gap of the real. (2007: 49–50)

Badiou's thesis is that the twentieth century is the aesthetic century of semblance and fiction, the century of *mise en scène*, and thus the century of the aesthetic imagination. Because of this imagination and its trapping between the real of semblance and the semblance of the real, the twentieth century singularly exposed itself to the fact that there is no possibility of knowledge of the historical and political present, no unmediated access to being in the presence of the real, except through ceaselessly purging and dissolving the older semblances and older fictions through which the appearance and representation of the real is unavoidably mediated. The aesthetic century was as creative and inventive as it was violent and bloody, and these two sides of the twentieth century's accomplishments originate out of the imperative (explicitly acknowledged or not) of exposing the real to the authenticity of its semblance.

Badiou's critique of the century's essential antagonisms (and the century's *thinking* of its antagonisms) circulating between fictions of beginning and fictions of ending is perhaps more apropos for reading Beckett than are Badiou's readings specifically of Beckett. Here we should not forget Beckett's intimate acquaintance with the destructiveness of the century's passionate obsession with new beginnings. Beckett's engagement with the political and social realities of the Second World War through his work with the French Resistance and then, after the war, as an ambulance driver with the Irish Red Cross in 'the capital of the ruins' of France, Saint-Lô, which Beckett notes was 'bombed out of existence in one night' (*CSP* 277), was preceded in 1936–37 by a six-month cultural expedition to Germany. It was during this expedition that Beckett, Mark Nixon explains, no doubt 'experienced a more direct exposure to Nazi ideology' (2011: 86) than he would have experienced during 'his last visit in 1932' (2011: 85). Beckett witnessed first-hand the madness of an ideology that could only think and act on bringing about the beginning of a new national and cultural identity by purging itself of the one that would have preceded (in the retrospective eyes of National Socialism) its historico-political ascendency,[7] for 'when Beckett arrived in Germany in September 1936, he entered a country in which the spheres of literature and the visual arts had been firmly subjugated by politics. The National Socialists had in the three years they had been in power effectively eradicated the autonomy of art and turned it into a vehicle of propaganda' (2011: 84). It goes without saying that art and culture were not the only sectors of society that the Nazis were intent on controlling and purging according to the viciously moralistic criteria of aesthetic degeneracy. Already by 1933, writes Andrew Gibson in his biography of Beckett, 'Germany was caught up in an immense drive to uniformity, and turned putatively on citizens deemed to be racially, mentally or physically defective' (2010b: 76). As we turn now to Beckett's 1937 German Letter to Axel Kaun wherein Beckett announces his commitment to 'a literature of the unword, which is so desirable to me', we would do well to keep in mind that here Beckett is writing from the vantage point of one of the darkest epicentres of the twentieth-century problematic of disavowing the destructions and semblances of the past as well as the present through new acts of destruction and new fictions of authenticity (D 173). What Beckett means by a 'literature of the unword' therefore resonates beyond just a programme of accelerating literature's development in 1937 in pace with more advanced artistic mediums like music or painting (D 173).

Badiou maintains that 'the murderous extremism' perpetrated by National Socialism 'cannot be entirely separated from the idea – widely held in all domains of thought and action – that problems allow for an "absolute" solution' such as the '"final solution" of the supposed "Jewish problem"' (2007: 36). Art continued to betray an analogous conviction, which has been traced by Jean-Luc Nancy, Philippe Lacoue-Labarthe, Walter Benjamin, as well as Blanchot all the way back to the early nineteenth-century literary aesthetics and criticism of German Romanticism, that there is an absolute of art (manifest only through fragments of the absolute) through which art reveals 'itself integrally as art; an art that – taking its own process as its object – is the exposition of what is artistic in art; the articulation, within art, of the end of art itself. In short: the last work of art, in the form of art un-worked' (2007: 36). The point here is certainly not that *all* the solutions devised for twentieth-century problematics are derivative of the Final Solution of the Nazi Terror; rather, the point is that the twentieth century coheres in such a way that its solutions and its problematics, some as destructive and nihilistic as others were creative and affirmative, are all symptomatic of a particular historical epoch that was overdetermined, in Badiou's view, by its quasi-pathological passion for substantialising the semblance and fiction of the real.

Badiou credits Mallarmé, Malevich, Brecht, Mandelstam and Breton for envisioning that aesthetic creativity originates only in the extreme proximity of absolute beginnings and radically decisive endings circumscribed at the void-point of the real, 'and that nothing of value would exist were we not *exposed* to excess' there where the real is unveiled as so many supreme fictions vying for ascendency and power (2007: 143; italics in original). Beckett is not exempt from thinking about the future of literature through this aesthetic consciousness of the imperative for excess, proposing in 1937 that 'as we cannot eliminate language all at once, we should at least leave nothing undone that might contribute to its falling into disrepute' (D 172). The way that this programme of writing should be carried out – with which 'the latest work of Joyce has nothing whatever to do', though 'perhaps the logographs of Gertrude Stein are nearer to what I have in mind', if only 'the unfortunate lady' was not 'doubtlessly still in love with her vehicle' – is by boring 'one hole after another' into 'the vicious nature of the word', 'until what lurks behind it – be it something or nothing – begins to seep through' (D 172). Here Beckett is registering not only a problematic localised within the realms of art and literature, but a problematic, as Badiou helps us to see, that is very much constitutive of twentieth-century political, philosophical and historical experience. The interrelated problematics of how language is to be made to authentically express, i.e. purged of the semblance-character of language (and therefore purged of itself as language), and how literature is to be made to be authentically literary, i.e. empowered only with the dissimulating power of semblance and fiction, converge on a solution that is reciprocally, incommensurably destructive of language *and* literature. Beckett, as Gibson has shown, exhibits a commitment to literature and language that is overdetermined less by a passion than by a *pathos* for the real,[8] what Gibson calls the 'pathos of intermittency', but it is a pathos originating out of a commitment to the *real* of literature and language all the same. Beckett's proposal that language be sacrificed so that literature can be redeemed – 'an assault against words in the name of beauty', as he puts it (D 173) – runs aground against his no less adamant, more evidently ethical refusal of the desire that literature be once and for all purged of the imperative of expression through words. The logics and laws of language and literature assemble in Beckett's writing precisely around this point of incommensurability between the obligation and impossibility of suspending the logic and law of the one without sacrificing the logic and law of the other. The only way around this predicament without disavowing the imperative for its reconciliation is to submit literature to protocols of disintegration, subtraction and disfiguration that are no less unrelenting and severe than the protocols of disintegration, subtraction and disfiguration – protocols of suspicion and terror – that Beckett desires to enact in parallel against language.

Blanchot revisits the phenomenon of terror in *The Infinite Conversation* in order to excavate the origins of literature's twentieth-century inheritance of a neutral, disindividualising form of language and speech, and what he discovers about the interrelation between terror and language, the speech of terror, is useful for enabling us to navigate the twentieth-century protocols of narrative at work in Beckett's *Texts for Nothing*. Like the Revolutionary Terrorists, again something that Hegel grasped long ago, the 'narrative voice' that speaks the language of literature comes into existence via depriving itself of its being yet continuing to exist nevertheless through the anonymous, depersonalised speech of writing. The terroristic fissuring of being, the violent splitting of phenomenological self-presence that *deprives being of its being*, are processes unmistakeably reflective of the fragmentary imperative of writing that has its non-literary, historical as well as political analogue in the revolutionary imperative of terror. Blanchot is as interested as Badiou in accounting for how a particular historical epoch came into existence through the thoughts and aspirations unique to that epoch. The difference, however, is both that Blanchot frames his critique of literature and fiction using the broader historical outlines of the epoch of modernity, albeit (and importantly) from the vantage point of the crises and antagonisms of the twentieth century, and also that, for Blanchot, the terror through which modernity constructed and reflected on its constitution and continuation is not to be so hastily discounted as a force simply of suspicion, destruction and nihilism.

Badiou insists that through his diagnosis of how the twentieth century thought itself, of 'what was thought in the century that was previously unthought – or even unthinkable' (2007: 3), he is not endeavouring to endorse 'the feeble moralising that typifies the contemporary critique of absolute politics'; on the contrary, what he is 'undertaking' is 'the exegesis of a singularity and of the greatness that belongs to it, even if the other side of this greatness, when grasped in terms of its conception of the real, encompasses acts of extraordinary violence' (2007: 53). Blanchot is less concerned than Badiou with the moral expectation of disentangling the phenomenon of extraordinary violence from the phenomenon of extraordinary creativity, although he does aim to take seriously the limitations that the phenomenon of violence imposes on the limits of aesthetic possibility. To do this, Blanchot turns all the way back to the writings of German Romanticism (and Sade, as we have already seen) in order to assess the implications of its contemporaneity with the Reign of Terror on the trajectory and discourse of twentieth-century literature. What Blanchot says about romanticism, particularly in order to shed light on the contradictions and antagonisms resident of the twentieth century, is indeed relevant as well for this chapter's reading of *Texts for Nothing* as a work thoroughly absorbed in the terror of literature through its exacerbation of the protocols of disintegration that so terrorised the figure of the unnamable.

Blanchot begins 'The Athenaeum' essay in *The Infinite Conversation* by cataloguing the ways that German Romanticism has been appropriated and subsequently perverted in the twentieth century to serve multiple ideological agendas. As such, the essay converges with Jean-Luc Nancy and Philippe Lacoue-Labarthe's *The Literary Absolute* in resisting the temptation of 'engaging in an archival enterprise', i.e. 'a monumental or antiquarian history' of the continuing significance of Romanticism (Lacoue-Labarthe and Nancy 1988: 2). The investigation into Romanticism is, in other words, nothing if not an investigation into what it is of Romanticism – its failures and its incoherencies, but also its enthusiasms and its imperatives – that the twentieth century retrospectively inherited. Blanchot notes that Romanticism had been enlisted by Nazi literary theorists, disparaged by figures like Lukács as 'an obscurantist movement' (*IC* 351), celebrated and repackaged by surrealism, excavated by 'French Germanists' like Albert Béguin (who was Swiss) and Henri Lefebvre for having undeniably exerted so profound an influence on the young Hegel and Marx, and denounced by the radical right in France 'because it is romantic and because it is German: irrationalism threatens order; reason is Mediterranean; barbarism comes from the North' (*IC* 351). Whether for reasons political or aesthetic, by intellectuals and ideologues on the Right or on the Left, French or German, Romanticism is ultimately confirmed in its 'vocation of disorder – menace for some, promise for others, and for still others, futile threat or sterile promise' (*IC* 352). The fragmentary poetics of Romanticism, Blanchot wants to argue, acts as a prism of critique into the crises of twentieth-century modernity with which both Blanchot and Beckett were all too intimately acquainted.

Blanchot concludes that Romanticism owes virtually everything it knows and practises to the '*Revolution in person*' that it reincarnates in the space of literature:

> There is no need to insist upon what is well known: the French Revolution is what gave the German romantics this new form constituted by the declarative demand, the brilliance of the manifesto. Between these two movements, the 'political' and the 'literary', there is a very curious exchange. When the French revolutionaries write, they write, or believe they are writing, as the classical writers do; thoroughly imbued with respect for the models of the past, they in no way wish to interfere with the traditional forms. It is not, however, to the revolutionary orators that the romantics will turn for lessons in style, *but to the Revolution in person*, to this language become History that signifies itself through declarative events. (*IC* 355; my italics)

Whereas the Thermidorians convinced themselves of having dispatched into historical oblivion the revolutionary terror along with the decapitated corpse of Robespierre,[9] Romanticism, like the writings of the Marquis de Sade, facilitates the aesthetic reincarnation of what Robespierre represented, and thereby rehabilitates the aspiration for absolute freedom through a new, authentic (political and aesthetic) beginning that revolutionary terror forcibly and violently unleashed into the nascent world of modernity. Not only is the literature of Romanticism all of a sudden speaking in the fragmentary language that it decreed is singularly appropriate for its post-terror aesthetic agenda, but the radical act of speaking in this way – in a movement without term and without determination, and therefore as an *imperative without concept* – forces it into dialogue with the historiographically silenced discourse of revolutionary terror, i.e. that part of 'this language become History' that harnesses the legislative power (not necessarily without the bounds of law) and requisite measure of violence necessary for making this language signify 'through declarative events':

> the Terror, as we well know, was terrible not because of its executions, but because it proclaimed itself in this capital form, *it making terror the measure of history and the logos of the modern era*. The scaffold, the enemies of the people who were presented to the people, the heads

that fell uniquely so they could be shown, the evidence (the grandiloquence) of a death that is null – these constitute not historical facts but a new language: all of this speaks and has remained speaking. (*IC* 355; my italics)

Because there can be no salvation without sacrifice, literature no more than politics is beholden to the requirement that in order for it to begin speaking again anew, to begin legislating again anew, it must first pass through the ordeal of its self-purgation, which invariably commits it to a future predicated traumatically on its violent separation from the past.

So it is that 'if true language is to begin', Blanchot writes in 'Literature and the Right to Death', then 'the life that will carry this language must have experienced its nothingness, must have "trembled in the depths; and everything in it that was fixed and stable must have been shaken"' (*GO* 43). The voice of *Texts for Nothing* is not the voice of 'true language', at least not yet (perhaps not ever), but it is a voice that trembles compulsively where its subjectivity in language and narrative has been so relentlessly submitted to ontological purgation so as to have lost any and all faith in the promise of its (metaphysical) salvation and closure (through finitude, negativity and death). Without the power to cease, the power to begin, the power to go silent or depart, the voice of *Texts for Nothing* is forced to vigilantly embrace the vulnerability that its subjection to ontological purgation engenders. This is likewise the demand of terror, namely that a person's identity be continuously destroyed, again and again, so that they can go on living, again, go on speaking, again, and go on thinking, again, deprived of a memory of life before, of consciousness of the subject they have presently become as a subject of terror, and of faith in the future awaiting their arrival. Writing and terror, in other words, are accomplices in a fragmentary protocol of speech that demands nothing less than the disempowerment of subjectivity and the disintegration of knowledge and memory as conduits of exile and withdrawal from being anachronistically in the world. Terror enforces this lesson not just in the context of the system of fictions that comprised the ideological textures of twentieth-century political discourse, but also in the context of literature specifically as it sets to work on the commencement of a new language adequate for the expression of its sovereignty over the reflexivity of fiction – *the fictionalisation of the very power of fiction.*

If Blanchot's analysis of the historical legacy of terror is correct, namely that twentieth-century literature, precisely as the literature *of* the twentieth century, as Badiou emphasises, inherits the language and *logos* of a terror that 'speaks and has remained speaking', then given that the impasse of *The Unnamable* and its rehabilitated continuation in *Texts for Nothing* is oriented around the presupposition of terror in the Beckettian 'I think' (according to Badiou), surely *Texts for Nothing* can be read through the interpretive matrix of a phenomenological symptomology of terror that surpasses the work of *The Unnamable* through its vigilant repetition. Even so, that the narrative voice of *Texts for Nothing* doubles as the subject and object of the language it destroys, that it is embroiled in what Jonathan Boulter reads as the 'failure to continue to cease speaking (and it is indeed a paradox of *continuing to cease*)', remains nothing short of terrifying for trying to organise an analytical response to the questions of how and why *Texts for Nothing* is positioned relative to the disintegrative aftermath of *The Unnamable* (Boulter 2004: 333; italics in original). Blanchot's identification of this *language become history* spoken so decisively and uninterruptedly through the literary reincarnation of the voice of terror positions the concept of terror as a privileged interpretive lens through which to converse with such literary works as Beckett's that are so manifestly engaged with exposing the depersonalising, perhaps also dehumanising, effects of language on subjectivity precisely where language is taken hold of by literature's sovereign prerogative of expression. The question before us is whether or not the figure of the narrative voice in *Texts for Nothing* is speaking and being spoken by this language of terror that Blanchot diagnoses as a principal origin of twentieth-century literature.

Of particular interest to this chapter's reading of *Texts for Nothing* is the peculiar image of death that converts itself into the nullification of its (hypothetical) arrival, and also the violent metaphysical reaction (forced redemption) that threatens to intervene into the discursive reality of the work's narrative voice in the wake of death's concomitant inaccessibility. It is perhaps not very difficult to imagine a corner of existence where death translates as death's impossibility, but of greater effort of the critical imagination is to devise a language and a logic that is able to converse with a subject, the narrative voice of *Texts for Nothing* in this case, that has been divested of the personal form of its subjectivity, that has

The Beginning (Again) and Ending (Again) of Terror   111

been forced to persist in a space where death is of no more consequence, as Hegel puts it apropos the Terror, than 'cutting off a head of cabbage or swallowing a mouthful of water', and that where being condemned to existence (neutralised in finitude) becomes more traumatic than being sentenced to annihilation (Hegel 1977: 360). Life at the extreme limit of what is (un-)liveable is imposed in *Texts for Nothing* as the permanent reality of its protagonist. This is an existence of terror. As a repetition of the 'attitude of disintegration' consolidated in the unworkable aftermath of *The Unnamable*, *Texts for Nothing* is likewise engulfed in the terror of literature, which articulates for its narrative voice as the tragic imperative of transcending its fictional existence. Let us now consider how *Texts for Nothing* arises as a work of literature wherein its narrative voice speaks through the language of terror.

III

Text 1 of *Texts for Nothing* announces a process that derives from a failure to secure a measure of phenomenological distance between the narrative voice and the place (including the voice's own supposed *ego cogito*) from which it suddenly finds itself speaking. It is a process that is concerned with the poetic decorum of a speaking presence and the preparation of a narrative ground that the voice must secure if it is to confidently and coherently move forward into the projected world of the work's imagined construction. *Texts for Nothing* opens, in other words, with a curious suppression of the most basic prerequisite of narrative: the spatio-temporal distance of a perspective situated between event and narration. The voice's immediate and unwelcome appearance in the opening sequence of Text 1 is quickly taken over by a description of its narrative surroundings that it claims, curiously, is 'unimportant': 'I'll describe the place, that's unimportant' (*CSP* 100). What follows, with apparent disregard for its avowed lack of importance, is a description of an imagined place that quite clearly has no resemblance to the inhospitable dwelling in which the voice finds itself suddenly immersed. Text 1 denies the narrative voice the luxury of a discursively consistent and punctually located identity, and so casts into doubt the textual viability of either a first, second or third-person narrative that the voice could begin to inhabit and/or propel. Nevertheless, the voice is quick to rehearse its narrative options, erratically adopting first, second and third-person instantiations as it desperately searches for its place in the text.

The narrative stalls before it encounters the possibility to begin, and yet it has begun, precisely, by narrating the denial of any subjective coherence to a voice that is already in the midst, it seems, of performing a narrative function. The voice 'knows' this, and with this knowledge it arrives at the first instalment of its attempt to overcome the experience of ontological dispossession predicated on its existence in narrative, saying

> to the body, Up with you now, and I can feel it struggling, like an old hack foundered in the street, struggling no more, struggling again, till it gives up. I say to the head, Leave it alone, stay quiet, it stops breathing, then pants on worse than ever. I am far from all that wrangle, I shouldn't bother with it, I need nothing, neither to go on nor to stay where I am, it's truly all one to me. I should turn away from it all, away from the body, away from the head, let them work it out between them, let them cease, I can't, it's I would have to cease. (*CSP* 100)

Already, then, the voice expresses its desire to leave this place and all of its ontological confusions by giving up on the twin illusions of embodiment and consciousness. The inhospitalities of its 'dwelling-place', however, are not so easily forgotten or ignored (*CSP* 101). The voice is riveted to its dwelling-place as a fragmented cipher of its subjectivity 'gathered together for life' (*CSP* 101). Text 1 reads as a work of narrative and subjective preparation, presupposing that the voice is compelled to consolidate its subjective presence if it is to enter into the temporal sequence of a narrative and into the syntactical demarcation of an identity in language. Text 1 is experimental in this respect, which poses, somewhat surprisingly, very little difficulty for trying to decipher the relation of reconciliation and synthesis between voice and narrative, text and interpretation that it is in the process of establishing, albeit unsuccessfully.

However, things get more complicated when the voice arrives at a formulation that is, this time around, 'all-important': 'And what I'm doing, all-important, breathing in and out and saying, with words like smoke, I can't go, I can't stay, let's see what happens next' (*CSP* 102). The disembodied voice of *Texts for Nothing* is complemented here by the terrifyingly transparent materiality of language ('like smoke'), opening the door for its transmission into the words that will come to comprise its purpose and its reality here in the text. It is not simply the case that the voice speaks with words, though of course it does this too, but rather that it breathes them, lives in them, and relies on them if it is to have any existence at all. Deferring its existence to 'words like smoke' means that if we, readers of *Texts for Nothing*, are to discover a new, ontologically viable, post-unnamable speaking presence here in the text, it will be by observing how the voice materialises and coalesces around the words that it causes, and that also cause the voice, to appear. However, because *Texts for Nothing* is quite explicit that whatever words are spoken by the voice will be as tangible and fleeting as smoke, effaced in the instant of their iteration, the critical desire to discover evidence of a relation between narrative subject and narrated subjectivity cannot but recognise that it, too, is faced with not knowing if the words and concepts it uses to communicate its understanding of the text are not likewise subject to the dissimulating, deconstructive power of smoke. Reading *Texts for Nothing* and translating its ambiguities into concepts amenable to comprehension cannot but seriously entertain the possibility that the impasse of the voice (to exist in words like smoke) is the impasse of hermeneutical subjectivity as well.

So as not to get ahead of ourselves, it is worth pointing out that the voice has not yet revealed that its spectral diffusion into a multiplicity of selves and words is concentrated around a textual space where the enactment of temporality is just as uncertain and ambiguous as is the existence of the narrative voice itself. Its instruction to 'see what happens next' is contextually relevant only up to a point, and indeed this point is illuminated as quickly as it is overshadowed by the declaration that here, in the hermetic inescapability of its 'dwelling-place', 'all mingles, times and tenses' (*CSP* 102). Suddenly, the voice is flooded with scenarios of its death that could only be arrived at from within a functional sequence of narrative temporality: 'I've given myself up for dead all over the place, of hunger, of old age, murdered, drowned, and then for no reason, of tedium, nothing like breathing your last to put new life in you' (*CSP* 103). The narrative voice is trapped in a world that can only permit death, ostensibly as an event *outside* language, if death passes *into* language as a discursive event of absolute negation. Language, though, is precisely what ensures that negation cannot be absolute. But this is not all. Because death presupposes the finite existence of the life that it negates, and because in *Texts for Nothing* no such presupposition obtains, whatever it is of the voice's existence that is susceptible to negation will undoubtedly survive as the discursive trace that it was all along, which it will then be the task of the narrative voice to negate yet again and always if it is to realise the dream of living a life in finitude (and not in the interminable horror of the *il y a*).

Because language has been divested of its subjective and temporal supports – 'time has turned into space and there will be no more time, till I get out of here' (*CSP* 132) – it too has lost all ontological authority over legislating what belongs inside and outside of discourse. The loss of the power to separate language from subjectivity, words from voice, smoke from life, death from existence – 'nothing like breathing your last to put new life in you' – consigns the narrator-protagonist to a textual space of everlasting immanence where it is obliged to repeat what it nevertheless registers as the logical contradictions and metaphysical illusions that only an existence in temporality would reconcile and sublate. Where 'all mingles, times and tenses', the voice can neither presume that it is speaking and breathing *inside* language, nor that it is speaking and breathing from a space that is clearly *outside* of language. Only death and the temporality of finitude, the diachronic time of living in time, could provide it with the certainty of how it is ontologically situated relative to language, but given that the 'time' of narrative, death and finitude is not accessible to the voice, is not welcome inside the dwelling-place of *Texts for Nothing*, it will have no choice except to persist and actively participate in the repetition of an existence given 'up for dead all over the place'. Beckett's staging of repetition; the phenomenon of an 'unworked death' associated by Comay with the phenomenological narrative of terror (2011: 76); subjective anonymity; and interminable narrative paralysis – all of them ingredients of the speech and *logos* of terror that Blanchot diagnoses as the beginning of fragmentary writing – reproduce *Texts for Nothing*, as early as Text 1, as a work that provokes the act of its interpretation to penetrate deeper than is customary into the crevices and cracks of its composition.

Text 2 returns the voice to the nocturnal scene of its dwelling-place expunged of the delusional belief that entry into a recognisably functional narrative sequence is possible. The voice is reminded that 'above is the light, the elements, a kind of light, sufficient to see by, the living find their ways, without too much trouble, avoid one another, unite, avoid the obstacles [. . .]. Here you are under a different glass, not long habitable either, it's time to leave it. You are there, there it is, where you are will never long be habitable. Go then, no, better stay, for where would you go, now that you know? Back above? There are limits' (*CSP* 105). The voice of Text 1 reappears in Text 2 deprived of whatever metaphysical sustenance it may have received from resting under the light of 'that ancient lamp' (*CSP* 104), forced now to find its way 'under a different glass' (*CSP* 105). Where the voice is now, 'down below', is not to be confused as the nocturnal imprint of 'up above', as though *Texts for Nothing* were proposing a simple dichotomy between a reality that is clear and distinct and one that is opaque and obscure. Knowledge of 'life above' does not give the voice any practicable hope of liberation from where it presently resides. This is odd. We would assume that the textual reference to an 'outside' of *Texts for Nothing* would permit the voice to coordinate the dimensions of its dwelling-place as the negative image of 'up above', in which case the 'limits' would apply to an ontologically distinct point of separation between above and below. If the voice's reference to a 'limit' does indeed apply to the ontological distinction between life in the light above, where 'the living find their ways' (*CSP* 105), and life in the darkness below, where phenomenological experience is obscured if not destroyed (but disastrously, without destruction) 'by the excessive light of night' (*CSP* 105), then it would have discovered a potential opening (a distinctly identifiable surface to the tympanum) capable of delivering it into the ontologically quotidian world of temporality and finitude, the ultimate 'destination' of which is the 'tomb, to be trod without a word' (*CSP* 137).

Text 2 demonstrates that the voice has access to memories and ideas of 'life above', though it is far from certain whether these have any operational value with respect to constructing a narrative of its subjective identity by which it would commence/return to a liveable life.[10] Whatever knowledge or recollection the voice might possess concerning memories of 'Mother Calvet' (*CSP* 105), 'the cliffs and the sea' (*CSP* 105), 'Mr. Joly . . . in the belfry' (*CSP* 107), 'Piers pricking his oxen o'er the plain' (*CSP* 107), or 'the farm of the Graves brothers' (*CSP* 107) can no longer be said to form an integral part of the life and world it presently inhabits: 'but one more memory, one last memory, it may help, to abort again' (*CSP* 107). These memory-scraps offer no traction for the beginning of a narrative or of a life (in narrative) that the voice could begin to call its own. The voice has not lost the memories of a life once lived; rather, it has lost the very capacity to exist as a subject around whom such memories could be gathered together in order to define. 'Here at least none of that', we are told, 'no talk of a creator and nothing very definite in the way of creation' (*CSP* 107).

Even if an opening into 'life above' were visible from where the voice is inscribed, passing through such an opening would still be provisional on the voice overcoming what in Text 3 is presented as an insurmountable obstacle of its spectral, anxiety-ridden ontology: 'is it possible to sprout a head at last, all my very own, in which to brew poisons worthy of me, and legs to kick my heels with, I'd be there at last, I could go at last, it's all I ask, no I can't ask anything. Just the head and the two legs, or one, in the middle, I'd go hopping [. . .], what's wrong with that? I don't know, I'm here, that's all I know, and that it's still not me, it's of that the best has to be made. There is no flesh anywhere, nor any way to die' (*CSP* 113). The absence of all that would confirm the voice's identity as a subject (a head, legs, a way to die, etc.) does not mean, then, that there is an absence of what constitutes the subjectivity of its (impossible) role as subject. The voice is in some way present to the images of a corporeal self that continually allow it to 'brew poisons worthy of me', but what keeps it cut off from inhabiting such images, from taking ownership of them, is precisely the ontological constraints that the textual 'here' of its dwelling in terror exercises over the passage into such an identity.

Texts for Nothing is a labyrinth of the openings and closures of a narrative sequence that never quite begins. The voice is tormented by the compulsion to perform the discursive ceremonies that serve little more than to confirm the unapproachable limits of its entrapment in the immanence of narrative. Unfortunately for the voice, the ceremonial repetition of its torment becomes its exclusive haven of consistency in a world that is shot through with contingency and denial: 'Utter, there's nothing else, utter, void yourself of them, here as always, nothing else. But they are failing, true, that's the change, they are failing, that's bad, bad. Or it's the dread of coming to the last, of having said all, your all, before the end, no, for that will be the end, the end of all, not certain' (*CSP* 106). The failure of any recognisably coherent narrative to commence is the structural consequence of the voice having to so thoroughly and completely depend on anachronistic protocols of narrative representation if it is to acquire the type of subjective persona on which narrative, too, ineluctably depends. Such co-dependence is disastrous for the voice's desire of transcending its intimacy with a world that strikingly corresponds with the unliveable space of radical suffering and terror circumscribed by *The Unnamable*. Relying on narrative to consolidate the spectral heterogeneity of the voice, to quell the play of contingency and uncertainty that overwhelms its dwelling-place, and to impute onto its words and language the saving grace of value and meaning, is destined to failure in *Texts for Nothing* in so far as narrative as such is just as dependent on these things having already been coherently envisioned and axiomatically presupposed if it is to properly commence towards their realisation.

The absence of a storyteller, to put it crudely, means that there is no story to be told; conversely, the absence of a story in the detemporalised zone of *Texts for Nothing* means that there is no storyteller to do the telling. What emerges out of this narrative stalemate is an unstoppable outpouring of words, memories and reflections over which the voice of *Texts for Nothing* is powerless to either obstruct or take ownership: 'and beauty, strength, intelligence, the latest, daily, action, poetry, all one price for one and all. If only it could be wiped from knowledge' (*CSP* 106). The stalemate between the narrative voice and the acquisition of a distinct narrative subjectivity, in other words, is surprisingly dynamic and productive of the very narrative discourse this stalemate would seek to deny, and it is one of Beckett's gifts, and perhaps even the tragedy of his writing, that despite the immobility and decay of the narrative sequences, voices and figures that his writings produce, they do not, as a result, conclude in an absolute state of ontological and narrative paralysis.

Texts for Nothing asks of its interpretation that if the terror-stricken site of dwelling exclusively in narrative is to be taken as a serious problem, as of course it must, then so too must dwelling in the fragmented space of language. Having confronted the voice with the impasse of a life in narrative, the impossibility of an existence outside the narrative immanence of terror, the next step taken by *Texts for Nothing* is to bombard language again and again with the voice's insatiable desire to escape into a world where the temporality of finitude that connects birth with death, sign with concept, would be once again ontologically and phenomenologically viable. Text 2 exposes the ideological veil that covers over how language, too, is as dependent as is narrative on the acquisition of a non-terrorised subjectivity (the ontological *a priori* of metaphysical humanism) if it is to practise the dialectical law of negativity that all representation requires. In *Texts for Nothing*, however, both narrative and language are held in abeyance in so far as 'the subject' that is responsible for sustaining the narrative implementation of its subjectivity 'dies before it comes to the verb' (*CSP* 106). Provided solely with words, the voice of *Texts for Nothing* is condemned to seek its existence in the very language that perpetuates its exclusion from life amongst the living. Because language misfires by both exceeding and disappointing its intended use and meaning, it fails to avoid the suspicion that with each word spoken another is required to supplement its impotence; with every word spoken another is required to restrain its referential promiscuity. One of Beckett's more recognisable stylistic strategies is to link each and every proposition and image with its immediate retraction. If no word or image can definitively rule out its negation, however, then the voice can begin to look, hypothetically, outside of language and text for the traces and materials of a post-traumatic (if not post-*traumatising*), post-terror existence.

The notoriously Beckettian impulse towards silence and nothingness is what would afford the narrative voice of *Texts for Nothing* its avenue of escape (transcendence) *out of* the narrative context of terror and *into* the 'life above' of a post-terror world. Its tragic condition, however, is that because it is a being made of words, because its existence resides in words as a purely fictional phenomenon, the voice cannot so easily ignore or escape its prison of words, and thus it is obstructed from enjoying the ontological payoffs of a life predicated on its finitude. Nothing like Levinas's ethical event of transcendence, for instance, or even Badiou's confidence in an event of ontological subtraction, will suffice to cut the narrative voice off from its unworkable existence encased in language and words. More fundamental than the voice's inseparability from the narrative sequence that it can cause to neither end nor begin is thus its intimacy with the hermeticism of its linguistic output. Lacking access to an ontological framework uncontaminated by language and fiction, the voice remains suspended between the subject it cannot become and the consciousness it can never possess. The entire drama of *Texts for Nothing* will turn on how deep the narrative voice is capable of descending into the aporetic vicissitudes of its failure to begin existing other than as

The Beginning (Again) and Ending (Again) of Terror 119

a subject of (self) interrogation, suspicion and terror: 'Did I try everything, ferret in every hold, secretly, silently, patiently, listening? I'm in earnest, as so often, I'd like to be sure I left no stone unturned before reporting me missing and giving up. In every hold, I mean in all those places where there was a chance of my being, where once I used to lurk, waiting for the hour to come when I might venture forth, tried and trusty places, that's all I meant when I said in every hold' (*CSP* 127). It is part of our job as readers of *Texts for Nothing* to assess just how vigilant the voice has been in the passionate, inquisitorial work of its ferreting.

The voice's acquiescence to its subjection to language is emblematic of how literature similarly mounts resistance to the ontological destructiveness of the negativity of language by first capitulating to language's ontological ubiquity:

> leave, I was going to say leave all that. What matter who's speaking, someone said what matter who's speaking. There's going to be a departure, I'll be there, I won't miss it, it won't be me, I'll be here, I'll say I'm far from here, it won't be me, I won't say anything, there's going to be a story, someone's going to try and tell a story. Yes, no more denials, all is false, there is no one, it's understood, there is nothing, no more phrases, let us be dupes, dupes of every time and tense, until it's done, all past and done, and the voices cease, it's only voices, only lies. Here, depart from here and go elsewhere, or stay here, but coming and going. (*CSP* 109)

The question that guides our reading of *Texts for Nothing* does not immediately relate to how the subjectivity of the voice is to be predicated (or not) in relation to the narrative it has constructed (or not), but in response to the quotation above it concerns instead the significance of the work's speaking presence having committed itself so unreservedly to syntactic fragmentation, figural immobility and ontological effacement vis-à-vis the laws of dissimulation constitutive of language. In Text 3 the voice projects its use of language towards retrieving the subjective accoutrement of its existence in a way that short-circuits the path of trying to endlessly recuperate what is otherwise irrecoverable of its life in narrative: 'start by stirring, there must be a body, as of old, I don't deny it, no more denials, I'll say I'm a body, stirring back and forth, up and down, as required. [. . .] I'll call that living, I'll say it's me, I'll get standing, I'll stop thinking, I'll be too busy, getting standing, staying standing, stirring about, holding out' (CSP 109). By so vigilantly embracing its impotence as a point of departure for realising its hope to 'get standing', the voice is able to undermine the metaphysical conviction of language that it is only by way of the negation of alterity that identity in the world can be said to appear. 'Holding out' is not easily reducible in *Texts for Nothing* to an inert refusal of representation. To 'stay here, but coming and going' is precisely what the representational logic of negativity, 'no's knife', cannot tolerate, and so it is precisely this kind of posturing, this refusal of negativity, that is required if ordinary language, language based on negativity as the unavoidable gateway of ontological resurrection in discourse and words, is to be shaken at the core of its application (*CSP* 154).

The narrative voice of *Texts for Nothing*, accordingly, is forced to embrace an inhuman form of existence if it is to somehow function with this idea of 'true language' on its horizon: 'what matter how you describe yourself, here or elsewhere, fixed or mobile, without form or oblong like man, in the dark or the light of the heavens, I don't know, it seems to matter, it's not going to be easy' (*CSP* 110–11). However, because the representation of an inhuman existence is dependent on being excluded from familiar forms of representation, and also because the voice cannot be perpetrator, witness and judge of its inhuman representation simultaneously, determining how an inhuman discourse is practicable can only be conducted by first determining *how* and *where* it can appear in the text. *It's not going to be easy* precisely because in *Texts for Nothing* language is implicated as a site for the fragmentary imperative of writing and terror just as harshly as is the site of narrative. Depending on where the voice finds itself at any one moment during its navigation of the text, indeed where we, readers of *Texts for Nothing*, decide to locate it within or without its dwelling in terror, will determine whether and to what degree (if any) Beckett has escaped the impasse whereby the narrative voice is condemned to repeat the unworkable refrain of the unnamable, 'you must go on, I can't go on, I'll go on' (*TN* 407).

IV

So far the concern in our reading of Text 1 to Text 3 has been to show that the compulsion to narrative in lieu of the impossibility of narrative requires a similar compulsion to language, also in lieu of its impossibility – 'name, no, nothing is namable, tell, no, nothing can be told, what then, I don't know, I shouldn't have begun' (*CSP* 144). The interruption of narrative causes the voice to confront a similar interruption at the site of language, which only serves to exacerbate the necessity of reviving the illusory anticipation of narrative for the voice's acquisition, via language, of anything resembling an identity or an existence that could place it, alas, in suicidal possession of its subjectivity. Confronting the impossibility of narrative, in other words, places a greater emphasis on the necessity of acquiring language as a medium for the recognition of one's existence, and the impossibility of language emphasises, in its infinite turn, the necessity of narrative to perform the same. Herein lies the vicious circle of a life immersed in the inhuman immanence of terror. That there is nevertheless 'something' that is speaking and communicating from out of the pages of *Texts for Nothing*, even if this 'something' is only the inhuman alterity of 'a voice murmuring a trace', obliges that we situate its presence in the text as precisely as is possible in order that we do not let ourselves acquiesce to something as disastrous as this infernal repetition of the voice's destroyed subjectivity (*CSP* 152). The decision to conceptualise the voice's position in *Texts for Nothing* according to a fragmentary poetics of terror intends to avoid this by conjoining the textual and interpretive experiences of narrative impasse – on the one hand, of a voice condemned to the solitude of inexistence, and on the other, the interpretive desire to penetrate and articulate the inner workings of this confinement – around a common point of intelligibility. This 'bed of terror', as it is called in 'The Calmative', points us towards a precise disposition that captures how the voice of *Texts for Nothing* relates to the repetitive destruction and resurrection of its subjectivity: 'I'll tell my story in the past none the less, as though it were a myth, or an old fable, for this evening I need another age, that age to become another age in which I became what I was' (*CSP* 62).

How does a fragmentary poetics of terror articulate in *Texts for Nothing*? Text 4 continues to map out the topographical coordinates of terror at the syntactical level of the voice's internment. Text 4 begins by interrogating the influence of spatiality on the voice's capacity for a transcendental inquiry into the reality of its situation: 'where would I go, if I could go, who would I be, if I could be, what would I say, if I had a voice, who says this, saying it's me?' (*CSP* 114). It is not enough that the voice finds itself immersed, suddenly, 'in the pit of my inexistence, of his, of ours' (*CSP* 114) if it is to outwit the negativity of language that would have it 'dead like the living' (*CSP* 114), but it must *perform* its immersion in this inhuman space of terror as well. A poetics of terror is only possible where its performance is given some semblance of representation, yet it is in the performance of a fragmentary poetics of terror that all forms of representation become unsustainable. At issue is the possibility of representing a subjective presence while simultaneously taking seriously the disseminating effects of language on a subject riven to such ontological extremes by textuality. In light of the argument being advanced here, the transcendental opening of Text 4 is a reflection of the necessity to ensure the voice's ongoing interpellation in narrative, but as the voice of *Texts for Nothing* is not a typical narrative subject already interpellated within a narrative sequence, nor for that matter does it act as a unified voice whose memory and speech are its own, it is denied from coinciding with the category of the subject that all transcendental critiques (Kantian, Husserlian, Heideggerian) are committed in one way or another to exposing. By unveiling what it is that conditions the possibility of meaning, thinking and representation, transcendental critique is inevitably implicated in restoring unity between contingencies of existence and narratives of redemption that religion, art and philosophy have historically conspired in similarly devising. Beckett's writing intends to subtract itself from this conspiracy. Beckett's deployment of a fragmentary poetics of terror, then, which unfolds through the myriad of ways that solipsistic reflexivity is rendered phenomenologically intolerable, is able to generate a narrative sequence where the categories of narrator and protagonist are evacuated of all ontological credibility from within the very sequence that such categories exist in order to ground.

'Sometimes standing in the void, sometimes shivering in the open' (Deleuze 1997: 159), as Deleuze says of Beckett's figures, the voice's exclusion from a narrative of third-person designation – 'if at least he would dignify me with the third person, like his other figments, not he, he'll be satisfied with nothing less than me, for his me' (*CSP* 115) – means that implementing a transcendental critique of its subjectivity is exposed to the contradictory requirement of its absence from the critique at hand – *who says this, saying it's me?* There is no textually neutral perspective that the voice of *Texts for Nothing* could begin to inhabit without abdicating from the textually decreed position of its ontological exile. Despite or perhaps because of its exposure in the void of subjectivity and narrative, the voice nevertheless discovers the (unliveable) context of its interpellation in and through the repetitive re-confirmation of its anonymity. It is not wholly present as a speaking and thinking subject, in other words, but nor is it wholly absent as one, either. As a result of its dissimulated position relative to its use of language and thought, there is no reason why the voice of *Texts for Nothing* cannot be speaking and thinking *at one and the same time* as object of reference and subject of utterance, doubling as the inhabitant of both:

> when he had me, when he was me, he couldn't get rid of me quick enough, I didn't exist, he couldn't have that, that was no kind of life, of course I didn't exist, any more than he did, of course it was no kind of life, now he has it, his kind of life, let him lose it, if he wants to be in peace, with a bit of luck. His life, what a mine, what a life, he can't have that, you can't fool him, ergo it's not his, it's not him, what a thought, treat him like that, like a vulgar Molloy, a common Malone, those mere mortals, happy mortals, have a heart, land him in that shit, who never stirred, who is none but me, all things considered, and what things, and how considered, he had only to keep out of it. (*CSP* 115)

As the voice repetitively encounters avatars of its anonymity, i.e. figments of an imagination intensified by terror, its subjectivity becomes the function of what a transcendental critique cannot include – the perspective of its own implementation. This does not mean that the voice loses all ontological credibility; rather, a life somewhere between his and mine, a life that is not his, not mine, begins to aggrandise around a modicum of ontological credibility predicated on the simple fact that a life that is neither his nor mine, and never matter Molloy's or Malone's, does not simply dissolve into *none at all*: 'there's my life, why not, it is one, if you like, if you must, I don't say no, this evening. There has to be one, it seems, once there is speech, no need of a story, a story is not compulsory, just a life, that's the mistake I made, one of the mistakes, to have wanted a story for myself, whereas life alone is enough' (*CSP* 116).

Whereas Text 4 of *Texts for Nothing* performs an exhaustive refusal of a transcendental critique by which the voice would be rescued from the immanence of terror and 'restored to the feasible', Text 5, with its invocation of a pervasive juridical presence, judges the voice guilty of the ontological crime of desiring to elude the phenomenological grip of terror on which its textual dwelling is predicated:

> I'm the clerk, I'm the scribe, at the hearings of what cause I know not. There it goes again, that's the first question this evening. To be judge and party, witness and advocate, and he, attentive, indifferent, who sits and notes. It's an image, in my helpless head, where all sleeps, all is dead, not yet born, I don't know, or before my eyes, they see the scene, the lids flicker and it's in. An instant and then they close again, to look inside the head, to try and see inside, to look for me there, to look for someone there, in the silence of quite a different justice, in the toils of that obscure assize where *to be is to be guilty*. That is why nothing appears, all is silent, one is frightened to be born, no, one wishes one were, so as to begin to die. (*CSP* 117; my italics)

Text 5 reverberates with an aggressively suspicious tonality that is absent from Text 4. More inquisitorial than inquisitive, in other words, Text 5 signals an abrupt indictment of Text 4's transcendental voyeurism. The incapacity of Text 4 to restore feasibility to the ontological link between the subject and its subjectivity – 'then it goes, all goes, and I'm far again, with a far story again, I wait for me afar for my story to begin, to end, and again this voice cannot be mine' (*CSP* 116) – opens the door for the events of negativity and death to reassert their discursive prerogative over whatever enters into the textual field of iteration and consciousness. Just because the voice is trapped in this inhuman narrative zone of its inexistence, in other words, does not mean that it is thereby exempt from the mortifying effects of the ongoing demand for its textual representation.

The failure of the voice in Text 4 to be restored to the world of ontological feasibility and narrative (re-)constitution means, furthermore, that it has no other choice than to relinquish its claim over the responsibility for its textual existence. Text 4 had taken the obligation seriously that something, anything, must of necessity happen to the voice that would restore it to the feasibility of an ontological subject of narrative, though the responsibility for this 'something', this 'anything', could really only have been derived from what the voice itself was capable of producing. It was trying, in other words, to be the giver of the gift of existence. Text 5, on the other hand, proceeds on the basis of the voice having forfeited the responsibility for its representation as either subject or object of a narrative sequence, and so is a more serious reflection on the ontological consequences of *nothing further happening* in the narrative of *Texts for Nothing*,[11] i.e. of the voice forever inhabiting this terrifying, inhuman domain of its inexistence. Text 5 does this by universally condemning the very idea of the voice's ontological credibility – *to be is to be guilty*.

The scene of Text 5 offers a panoramic view of the voice's agonising transition between obligation and contingency, tormentor and victim, judge and party, and witness and advocate, all the while refusing the unity of perspective that the voice can intuit and even to some degree internalise, but never satisfactorily acquire: 'Ah yes, I hear I have a kind of conscience, and on top of that a kind of sensibility, I trust the orator is not forgetting anything, and without ceasing to listen or drive the old quill I'm afflicted by them, I heard, it's noted. This evening the session is calm, there are long silences when all fix their eyes on me, that's to make me fly off my hinges, I feel on the brink of shrieks, it's noted' (*CSP* 118). What state of mind is the voice of *Texts for Nothing* capable of possessing? To call it madness, psychosis even, is not far off the mark, were it not the case that the voice anticipates and deflates such diagnoses with a disarmingly parodic nod of indifference – *it's noted*. The problem, then, is not one of deciding on the plausibility of any number of conclusions about what the voice is doing or what it is trying to become in the world of *Texts for Nothing*, but of why attaching value, significance or closure to any conclusion whatsoever is ill-advised. Taking *to be is to be guilty* as an *a priori* indictment of representation is a way for Beckett to arrest metaphysical redemption and ontological resurrection before they have the chance to pass from desire to praxis.

What we have here, in other words, is a contradiction that is both ontological and metaphysical: the instant that a decision of guilt is made, the pathway to metaphysical redemption and ontological resurrection is automatically paved. The compactness of the formula *to be is to be guilty* precludes by way of syntactical concentration what its semantic import logically includes by way of connotation: redemption and resurrection. Text 4 did not go far enough in foreclosing the desire for narrative, and thus either for metaphysical or ontological feasibility, and so the next logical step is to short-circuit all the ways that the life-story of the voice is exempted from feasibility and to simply assert that were it to suddenly become feasible (i.e. metaphysically redeemable, ontologically resurrectable and phenomenologically comprehensible), it would be subject to the harshest forms of suspicion and violence that a life in the terror of literature is able to sustain. Text 5 is pivotal in exposing the textual identity of the voice as a cipher of the absolute semblance of its subjectivity. The underlying supposition here is that in order for a subject to consolidate the ontological consistency of its subjectivity, it must have already precipitated and thereby participated in what Blanchot understands in 'Literature and the Right to Death' as 'that deferred assassination which is what my language is' (GO 43). Text 5 works to suspend the mortifying temporality of ontological deferral in order to lock the figure of the voice in the subjectivity of being 'nothing but a voice murmuring a trace' (CSP 152).

Rebecca Comay's dialectical reading of terror in *Mourning Sickness*, through stages of a phenomenological narrative that begins in radical loss and ends in an anxiety-ridden re-possession of subjectivity, helps to reinforce the overall conceptual ambivalence that accompanies the act of thinking through the experience of terror as it is instantiated in *Texts for Nothing*:

> Terror [...] announces the heroic rebirth of the subject from the trauma of its own annihilation. There is a fetishistic component. To suffer the loss of oneself is already to enjoy the consoling fiction that there is or was a self to be lost; we can only regret or fear losing what is there for the losing. And there is a temporal twist. In psychoanalytic terms, we could say that traumatic terror is being rewritten as preemptive anxiety. The shock of unprepared injury is absorbed by the retrospective anxiety that transforms the unmastered past into a pending future. The terrified nonsubject of absolute freedom is reborn as an anxious subject. And anxiety itself reassures us that we still have something to lose. Transforming past into future, anxiety teaches us how to mourn in advance. (2011: 90)

As Comay understands it, terror is directed through its impositions of violence and its exhortations of speech to dissolve as many of the phenomenological coordinates that it can that consciousness requires in order to be oriented epistemologically in the world. To be immersed in a state of terror is therefore to be exiled from the world of phenomenological experience and epistemological security. It is to have lost contact with the temporal dissemination of being-in-the-world, and to be violently separated from one's own consciousness and memory of a life before this existence in terror commenced. Terror works best through confusion and disorientation. Accordingly, when a subject struggles to set epistemological confusion and phenomenological disorientation aright, for instance by pronouncing the judgement of its absolute ontological crimination, terror intervenes all the more forcefully as a repetition of the anxiety that led to terror in the first place. Because terror therefore throws into confusion the diachronic experience of temporality, because it complicates, to say the least, the phenomenological and epistemological acuity of the subjects forced to experience terror first-hand, to truly understand the narrative valences of terror requires the capacity for critiquing situations, precisely like *Texts for Nothing*, where the presence and repetition of terror in narrative leads inexorably to the deconstruction of narrative as such. If to be is to be guilty, is to be *again* not to be guilty of a crime worse than being before? This is the suspicion that impels the narrative movement of *Texts for Nothing* forward from inquisition to inquisition, judgement to judgement, negation to negation, and indeed from Text to Text.

The point to underscore about the dynamic of terror, in other words, particularly as it is operative as the constitutive experience of dwelling exclusively in the space of literature and fiction, is the movement whereby terror encapsulates (conceptually) and propels (experientially) a 'fetishistic circle of self-reifying negation' (Comay 2011: 61). Taking this definition of the movement of terror as an interpretive point of reference for tracing the textual dissemination of the voice in *Texts for Nothing* and the relation it has to the narrative horizon of its repetitively destroyed subjectivity, its traumatic rebirth from Text to Text out of the remnants and traces of its preceding negation in and through discourse, language and words, places Beckett's writing within a larger, though still largely under-analysed context of philosophical and historical significance. Beckett's writing, when viewed through the lens of terror, becomes a space of radical conceptual alterity that it is our job as thinkers of literature to risk approaching without the faith that it will accommodate our analytic demands for comprehension.

The thematic constellation of *Texts for Nothing* is perpetually realigned and reconstituted as it unfolds from Text to Text. The thematic of guilt permeating Text 5, for instance, reappears in Text 8 at the site where the ontologically vicious circle of self-reflexivity is newly set askew. *To think*, more precisely, rather than *to be*, becomes the target of ontological indictment in Text 8: 'if I'm guilty let me be forgiven and graciously authorized to expiate, coming and going in passing time, every day a little purer, a little deader. The mistake I make is to try and think, even the way I do, such as I am I shouldn't be able, even the way I do. But whom can I have offended so grievously, to be punished in this inexplicable way, all is inexplicable, space and time, false and inexplicable, suffering and tears, and even the old convulsive cry, It's not me, it can't be me' (*CSP* 132–3). Let us not underestimate the significance of substituting *thinking* for *being* as the locus of ontological condemnation. That the voice emerges, again and again, as an anonymous representative of the existence and narrative it cannot possess ensures that it is left vulnerable to a far more perniciously ambiguous form of instantiation: 'begging in another dark, another silence, for another alm, that of being or of ceasing, better still, before having been' (*CSP* 135). Presenting itself to the eyes and ears of understanding (of his, of ours, the difference matters little) means that it is susceptible to being forcibly removed from the inconceivable context that *Texts for Nothing* has nevertheless assigned (and which readers must therefore respect) as its dwelling-place.

The inconsistent ontology that prevents the voice from either 'being' or 'ceasing' is evocative of what we would expect of a figure that exists only to the degree that its 'keepers' are able to confirm it accordingly. To place the determination of one's existence in the hands of another, of the voice's in the hands of its 'keepers' – 'my keepers, why keepers, I'm in no danger of stirring an inch, ah I see, it's to make me think I'm a prisoner, frantic with corporeality, rearing to get out and away' (*CSP* 122–3) – is to turn over the power and authority of endless interrogation into one's existence to an external gaze of comprehension. There is evidence throughout *Texts for Nothing* of the voice giving itself over to an external gaze of comprehension only to immediately retreat before the moment of its being made available to its conceptual retrieval. Just as much as the voice is compelled to negotiate the ontological limits of its dependency on language, so too must hermeneutical subjectivity negotiate its dependency on the self-same language that holds *Texts for Nothing* prisoner to the incomprehensibility of the narrative it cannot become.

Epitomising the frustrating experience of reading Beckett is that

The Beginning (Again) and Ending (Again) of Terror 129

not even impotence and misunderstanding can be valorised as the 'secret' to thinking through the textual constructions and figures of his fiction: 'the vacancy is tempting, shall I enthrone my infirmities, give them this chance again, my dream infirmities, that they may take flesh and move, deteriorating, round and round this grandiose square' (*CSP* 134). Marooned somewhere *beyond* the void of understanding, begging in Text 8 *in another dark*, divested yet again of the hope of being, the voice can neither die nor be killed by the assassin's touch of reading and representation. What happens to reading and thinking when they are forced to fabricate death and meaning (meaning *as* death) on behalf of a work that actively blocks the authenticity of such fabrication? The disempowerment not only of the power *to be*, but also, in Text 8, of the power *to think*, has dire consequences for the prospect of transcending the multiplicities of detour and deadlock that *Texts for Nothing* has established. If the trajectory of Beckett's writing is towards an excess of terror then surely it is with *Texts for Nothing* that the destination has been glimpsed.

Texts for Nothing thus appears destined for the purgatorial repetition of 'affirmations and negations invalidated as uttered' (*TN* 285), and thus for recapitulating *The Unnamable*'s attitude of disintegration, unless of course its invocation of a textualised state of terror can be appropriated interpretively as an epistemological horizon of hermeneutical possibility. The onus of responsibility for the crucial task of sustaining an existence in the radical interruption of its ontological feasibility falls to hermeneutical consciousness and the extent to which it is willing to accommodate the fragmented ontological economy of this dwelling in terror that permeates *Texts for Nothing*. Trying to beat the voice at the same impossible game of hitting 'on the right ones, the killers', is destined to repeat the implacable desire to 'hear a story, tell a story, in the true sense of the words, the word hear, the word tell, the word story', but does this mean that we are sentenced to simply throw our hands in the air in an act of hermeneutical resignation (*CSP* 126)? Not necessarily.

Text 9 proceeds on the basis of exhausting the limits to what remains possible with the voice speaking from where it is 'dead and getting born, without having ended, helpless to begin, that's my life' (*CSP* 138). Text 9 emits an accelerated tone of desperation on behalf of the voice as it is in the midst of evading its own spectral presence. How can the voice die in and with the words where death now signifies only the impossibility of dying? 'That's right', says the voice of Text 9, 'wordshit, bury me, avalanche, and let there be no more talk of any creature, nor of a world to leave, nor of a world to reach, in order to have done, with worlds, with creatures, with words, with misery, misery. Which no sooner said, Ah, says I, punctually, if only I could say, There's a way out there, there's a way out somewhere, then all would be said, it would be the first step on the long travelable road, destination tomb, to be trod without a word' (*CSP* 137). It is *this* freedom from death, the freedom to be dead without having died, of having been dead without having lived, that the voice of *Texts for Nothing* would like to transcend, except that having (always already) arrived in a space that signifies only the impossibility of dying, it is no longer possible to traverse the poles of a relation leading from a beginning to an end, the beginning that would signal 'the first step' of its journey to a tomb, and thus of the journey out of the terror of its fictional anonymity. We can turn to Levinas for a sober assessment of what such liminal conditions of existence entail, namely 'the horror of immortality', the 'necessity of forever taking on its burden' (2001: 59).

If there is to be a movement of transcendence into the secure ontology of finitude, a narrative that climaxes with 'the graveyard', indeed a space where it would be possible to 'see the beauties of the skies, and see the stars again', as seems to be the sincere intention of the voice in Text 9, it will be through an event of transcendence deprived of a phenomenological subject, and therefore, paradoxically, barred from enjoyment by the narrative voice of *Texts for Nothing* (*CSP* 140). Blocking the voice from coinciding with the expression of its anonymity is precisely the illusion that here, in the absence of any teleological narrative momentum, death can still be appropriated as an event that shelters the fragility of the finite subject (being-towards-death). Anonymity and finitude are constitutively incompatible as predicates of the subject, yet it is because of the ineffaceable remnants of subjectivity resurrected again and again by the ceaseless compulsion to 'hear a story, tell a story' that all hopes of performing an act of reconciliation on the irreconcilable ontological antagonism between anonymity and finitude are not lost, however much such an event of reconciliation is precluded from occurring *here and now* in *Texts for Nothing* (*CSP* 126).

In Text 10 we are told that there are 'no souls, or bodies, or birth, or life, or death, you've got to go on without any of that junk, that's all dead with words, with excess of words' (*CSP* 142). We are therefore compelled to ask what is behind the compulsion to deny the predicates of subjectivity – souls, bodies, birth, life, death, etc. – in order that it still be possible to 'go on'. One possible explanation is that the speaker of *Texts for Nothing* has been tasked with dissolving the existential coordinates that put being and death into a discursively meaningful relationship – existence in finitude – so that the ubiquitous 'murmuring' of language might flow unceasingly, thus stripping finitude of its sovereignty over death (and, by extension, over life). But how does a finite being become infinite? How does the human become inhuman, and thus become the very truth of its humanity? Beckett attacks the categorical subject of finitude, humanity and subjectivity at the very place where it is most powerful and yet most vulnerable: its capacity to know, to speak and to die. The difficulty is that the desire and drive for knowledge, speech and death persists, and thus what *Texts for Nothing* is embroiled in is the tension that erupts between the obstinate persistence of 'a voice murmuring a trace' and the narrative finality that is no longer possible amidst anonymity's exception to finitude.

There is nothing that prevents the voice from ceasing to speak, ceasing to be, in which case it will 'have done nothing, nothing but go on, doing what, doing what he does, that is to say, I don't know, giving up, that's it, I'll have gone on giving up, having had nothing, not being there' (*CSP* 143). The absolute freedom to not be tied down by ontological structures of subjectivity is the terror of having to exist precisely where these structures of subjectivity engender only the fiction of their continuous self-annulment. It is entirely possible that this is all literature can hope to achieve if it is honest about the repercussions of language having been divested of any transcendent referential authority beyond its own immanent, sovereign capacity for signification. Beckett articulates such a capacity as little more than the capacity for 'lies': 'I'll be able to go on, no, I'll be able to stop, or start, another guzzle of lies but piping hot, it will last my time, it will be my time and place, my voice and silence, a voice of silence, the voice of my silence' (*CSP* 143). Beckett's thorough exhaustion of what could be enlisted in the service of a thematic hope for 'a better idea, to put in the negative, a new no, to cancel all the others', inevitably succeeds in reproducing the content of such a hope as the negative image of what it would be if writing were determined otherwise than according to the fragmentary imperative of the terror of literature (*CSP* 147).

With the disappearance of the voice into the outside of all identity and negativity where death coincides with the interminable disaster of existence, there nevertheless flickers, albeit dimly, a light of possibility for this life in literature to be lived otherwise:

> something better must be found, a better reason, for this to stop, another word, a better idea, to put in the negative, a new no, to cancel all the others, all the old noes that buried me down here, deep in this place which is not one, which is merely a moment for the time being eternal, which is called here, and in this being which is called me and is not one, and in this impossible voice, all the old noes dangling in the dark and swaying like a ladder of smoke, yes, a new no, that none says twice, whose drop will fall and let me down, shadow and babble, to an absence less vain than inexistence. (*CSP* 147)

So as long as the voice is multiply divided from one absence to the next, one word to the next, it will continue to displace rather than destroy the temporal coordinates on which all redemptive logics of relation rely. It is not simply because the narrative voice of *Texts for Nothing* is unknowable and unnamable as a subjective persona that it cannot be re-assigned to an absence less vain than inexistence; rather, the problem of how to position the voice ontologically turns on how it is positioned vis-à-vis the subjectivity of what prolongs the unknowability and unnameability of a life trapped in the terror of this narrative dwelling: 'where am I, to mention only space, and in what semblance, and since when, to mention also time, and till when, and who is this clot who doesn't know where to go, who can't stop, who takes himself for me and for whom I take myself, anything at all, the old jangle' (*CSP* 146).

Text 12 is a distinct addition to the sequence of preceding Texts. It aims at consolidating the voice's resignation to the ontological apathy that has thrust its inexistence into the unceasing inertia of terror: 'what a blessing it's all down the drain, nothing ever as much as begun, nothing ever but nothing and never, nothing ever but lifeless words' (*CSP* 151). The voice is in words, it is made of them, but these words are as lifeless as the pronouns are uninhabitable. Its punishment for the unforgivable crime of desiring an existence predicated on negativity and death is to inhabit the emptiness of language and to have the null image of its alterity reflected in all the 'babble of homeless mes and untenanted hims, this other without number or person whose abandoned being we haunt, nothing. There's a pretty three in one, and what a one, what a no one' (*CSP* 150). Installed as the haunting presence of an empty space is, for the voice, the closest it ever comes to climbing into a body and attaining the hope that it, too, might someday be dead like the living. *Texts for Nothing* articulates a number of problems that resonate historically, politically, philosophically and of course aesthetically, but if there is one that stands out it is perhaps the interrelated problem of *how* and *where* an interpretive perspective is to begin communicating with a textual figure that is permanently undergoing its own self-erasure. Just as disastrous as the conceptual coupling of revolution and violence is to politics, the virtually indecipherable relation that *Texts for Nothing* maintains between voice and silence effectively denies all optimism that the work's ambiguities and aporias can be disentangled and conceptualised coherently. To maintain a semblance of narrative progression that at every turn reconfirms a narrative of inertia is no small or inconsequential achievement. Of even greater consequence, though, is that such a narrative of inertia does not therefore lapse into a blind affirmation of nothingness and despair, otherwise there would be no point at all in Beckett's obsessive conviction to keep writing beyond *The Unnamable*.

Text 13 reads as the summation of what remains of a voice that has exhausted all avenues of coinciding with the verb *to be*. Here we 'learn' that 'there is nothing but a voice murmuring a trace' (*CSP* 152). However, what the terror of literature demands is that the voice is no more to be privileged in *Texts for Nothing* than is its dwelling-place. Its dwelling-place is one of terror, and the voice is both symptom and custodian of this terror. If Blanchot's post-Levinasian appeal to 'speak of a *subjectivity without any subject*' is to be accurately applied to thinking through the ontological predicament of the Beckettian voice and the dwelling of terror that it inhabits, then the preservation of the 'space', cipher or archive of this absent subject must also be taken into account (*WD* 30; italics in original). They are perhaps indistinguishable, the voice and its dwelling-place, the subject and its subjectivity, language and literature, but nevertheless it cannot be denied that there is, at the very least, the semblance of a workable distinction between them: 'unfortunately it is not a question of elsewhere, but of here, ah there are the words out at last, out again, that was the only chance, get out of here and go elsewhere, go where time passes and atoms assemble an instant, where the voice belongs perhaps, where it sometimes says it must have belonged, to be able to speak of such figments. Yes, out of here, but how when here is empty, not a speck of dust, not a breath, the voice's breath alone, it breathes in vain, nothing is made' (*CSP* 153).

All propositions made about the figure of the voice in *Texts for Nothing* circle endlessly around a space where everything is subject to the law of ontological fictionalisation, and as such no proposition escapes the suspicion of beginning to falsely, misleadingly legislate over the sentence of its validity. 'Tire myself out that's the point', utters the speaker of 'The Image' (*CSP* 165). Similarly in *Texts for Nothing*, the very last semblance of a difference between voice and silence collapses into a syntactical fold of indecipherability where nothing is said, nothing is told, and nothing is made in the very acts of speaking, telling and making. This occurs precisely because the difference between the commencement and discontinuation of a narrative of ontological reconciliation with terror has been neutralised throughout *Texts for Nothing* through its exhaustive protocols of decomposing, recomposing and endlessly disseminating the subjectivity of whatever existence or voice has entered into its space of narrative circumscription:

> Is it possible, is that the possible thing at last, the extinction of this black nothing and its impossible shades, the end of the farce of making and the silencing of silence, it wonders, that voice which is silence, or it's me, there's no telling, it's all the same dream, the same silence, it and me, it and him, him and me, and all our train, and all theirs, and all theirs, but whose, whose dream, whose silence, but it's ended, we're ended who never were, soon there will be nothing where there was never anything, last images. (*CSP* 154)

What we find in this passage is a space left open by a topography of smoke, of words like smoke, into which the last images, traces and residues of the voice are destined to fade. Nothingness does not descend with any apocalyptic vigour here, since the site of its arrival is the nothingness that has not ceased precipitating the repetition of its descent. And yet the space of pure semblance, of terror without repose, is what stubbornly (tragically) persists as the *only* haven of possibility for literature amidst its ongoing disintegration and ruin, piling fiction upon fiction and compelling the voice to speak one last time as if it were the first, as if it were 'now, as soon now, when all will be ended, all said, it says, it murmurs' (*CSP* 154).

Notes

1. Alysia E. Garrison is therefore correct to argue that 'as the historicist turn in Beckett studies attests, it is not enough to suggest' that what Beckett is after in the post-war phase of his writing 'is simply a dramatization of nothingness and absence' (2009: 89).
2. Jonathan Boulter's '"Wordshit, bury me": The Waste of Narrative in Samuel Beckett's *Texts for Nothing*' would be the most notable exception to the dominant trend in readings of *Texts for Nothing*. Acknowledging the value of those readings that share an affinity with Porter Abbott, Boulter insists that neither strands of interpretation 'take into account that Beckett's own assessment of *Texts for Nothing* is not necessarily dismissive but may in fact be a canny diagnosis of the work: that is, "failure" is not a negative critical term but functions as a theoretical assessment that may provide a valid starting point in our own critical reading of the work' (2002: 2).
3. John Pilling contextualises Beckett's negotiation of this problematic in relation to Beckett's thinking about Sade, and specifically how Bataille and Blanchot were thinking about Sade during this period of transition between *The Unnamable* and *Texts for Nothing*. Pilling writes that 'roughly half way through the composition of *Textes*, at the end of the first of the two notebooks in which they were written, Beckett jotted down a handful of phrases from Georges Bataille's "Préface" to a limited edition de luxe reprint of Sade's *Justine*. In this preface Bataille [. . .] wryly points out that there is an irresolvable paradox in Blanchot, whose emphasis on negation is difficult to square with him writing so fluently and at such length on what could not be negated without destroying itself. Beckett had been aware of this difficulty in the writing of *Dream* (1931–2) some twenty years earlier, but was obviously now even more alert to the problem, with *L'Innommable* having atomised almost everything and with the *Textes* proving difficult to dig out from under their avalanche of destruction' (2014: 123–4).
4. In *The Step/Not Beyond* Blanchot writes that 'the law', by which he means the law as it is articulated by the fragmentary imperative of writing, 'cannot transgress itself, since it exists only in regard to

its transgression-infraction and through the rupture that this transgression-infraction believes it produces, while the infraction only justifies, renders just what it breaks or defies. The circle of the law is this: there must be a crossing in order for there to be a limit, but only the limit, in as much as uncrossable, summons to cross, affirms the desire (the false step) that has always already, through an unforeseeable movement, crossed the line' (*SNB* 24).

5. Richard Begam takes up a similar line of argumentation in *Samuel Beckett and the End of Modernity*, where he introduces his work as 'focusing on the five major novels Samuel Beckett wrote between 1935 and 1950: *Murphy, Watt, Molloy, Malone Dies*, and *The Unnamable*. It will be my claim', Begam writes 'that these novels provide the earliest and most influential literary expression we have of the "end of modernity"' (1996: 3). The implication here is that Beckett, in signalling the 'end of modernity', inaugurates through literature the beginning of poststructuralism and postmodernism, discourses *par excellence* of the impossibility of ever 'ending' the past in and with the present decisively without remainder. Thus where Begam invokes the image of the 'tympanum' in *The Unnamable*, he is able to argue that 'to occupy the interspace described here, the "without" that is also the "within," is to acknowledge that one never arrives as a point of absolute or final transcendence' (1996: 177). Unfortunately, Begam concludes his reading with *The Unnamable* without considering in any meaningful way whether or not Beckett's post-*Unnamable* prose gets beyond the inertia of ontological indecision.

6. Martin Puchner's *Poetry of the Revolution: Marx, Manifestos, and the Avant-Gardes* articulates well the centrality of the manifesto as the genre *par excellence* of twentieth-century avant-garde aesthetics (the rhetoric and poetics of the twentieth century). For Puchner, it is the *Communist Manifesto*, specifically, that 'invented a poetry of the future revolution, a form that would help revolutionary modernity to know itself, to arrive at itself, to make and to manifest itself [. . .]. The history of successive manifestos is thus also a history of the futures these manifestos sought to predict, prefigure, and realize' (2006: 1–2).

7. According (famously) to Walter Benjamin, the fascist assault against modernist and avant-garde art and aesthetics resulted less in the de-aestheticisation of art than it did in the aestheticisation of politics. He writes in the 'Epilogue' of 'The Work of Art in the Age of Its Technological Reproducibility' essay that 'humankind, which once,

in Homer, was an object of contemplation for the Olympian gods, has now become one for itself. Its self-alienation has reached the point where it can experience its own annihilation as a supreme aesthetic pleasure. *Such is the aestheticizing of politics, as practiced by fascism. Communism responds by politicizing art*' (2003: 270; italics in original).

8. This term belongs to Robert Buch, who explains that his engagement with figures like Bataille, Kafka, Simon, Weiss, Müller and Bacon is indebted to Badiou's assessment of the century at the same time that it tries to add nuance to Badiou's purposefully hyperbolic pronouncement's about the century's unwavering passion for the real. Buch writes that 'the confrontations with violence and destruction at the center of the works' he examines in *Pathos of the Real* 'seem in many respects to instantiate the passion that is supposed [by Badiou] to have animated the century, carrying its greatest ambitions and culminating in its greatest horrors. At the same time, their engagement with the real is far more equivocal than Badiou's evocative formula suggests. [. . .] [T]hey summon us before a similar configuration: the spectacle of suffering that they conjure up in the most vivid terms, urging our gaze to dwell on it' (2010: 7–8). Andrew Gibson argues a similar point vis-à-vis Beckett and Badiou, reminding us that from Badiou's perspective 'the square root of two is a capital event. The accumulation of plague-stricken corpses in the streets of Athens is not.' 'But Beckett', Gibson rejoins, 'urges us to think them together' (2006: 290).

9. David Andress writes that 'the blade that cut short Robespierre's screams on 10 Thermidor could not snuff out the Terror like a candle. The Incorruptible had been processed to his death by the same machinery that had accounted for his victims, and on the next day, 29 July, the guillotine was the busiest it had ever been in Paris, dispatching no fewer than seventy-one members of the Robespierrist hierarchy of the capital' (2005: 345).

10. There is a divergence of critical approaches to *Texts for Nothing* circulating on precisely this point of contention regarding whether or not the subject of *Texts for Nothing* can operate as a subject of history or memory. This divergence is explicitly taken up in the readings of *Texts for Nothing* presented in Jonathan Boulter's 'Does Mourning Require a Subject?' (2004) and in Séan Kennedy's 'Does Beckett Studies Require a Subject?' (2009), which Kennedy frames as a critical riposte to Boulter. Whereas Boulter reads the narrator of Beckett's *Texts for Nothing* as 'unable to present itself as a stable,

unified (or potentially unified) subject' (2004: 333), such that it becomes uncertain whether or not 'the concepts of mourning and trauma', specifically, become 'unworkable in the texts of Samuel Beckett' (2004: 346), Kennedy, in trying to make 'the case for a historicised reading of Beckett's work', is insistent that this sacrificing of the Beckettian subject to the ahistorical paradigm of poststructuralist interpretation (Kennedy cites Boulter's reading as emblematic of this position), 'this eagerness to merely dispense with the subject of history' in Beckett's work, 'can only be a debilitating gesture'. Kennedy asks rhetorically, 'in the absence of history/memory, is an ethical Beckett possible? Does Beckett studies require a subject, and does that subject require a politics?' (2009: 25).
11. Jean-François Lyotard connects terror with a suspension of temporal progression through terror's indissoluble link with experiences of privation: 'Terrors are linked to privation: privation of light, terror of darkness; privation of others, terror of solitude; privation of language, terror of silence; privation of objects, terror of emptiness; privation of life, terror of death. What is terrifying is that the *It happens that* does not happen, that it stops happening' (1991: 99).

3

The Writing of *How It Is* in the Paratactic Delay of Terror

> Hell any positivist can tell you 'does not exist.' There is no such place. But I feel there is an area of act that is hell . . . a place of naming.
>
> (Amiri Baraka)

I

As discussed at the beginning of the preceding chapter, many Beckett scholars agree that *How It Is* represented something of a turning point in Beckett's oeuvre away from the 'attitude of disintegration' that was responsible for the impasse of *The Unnamable* and *Texts for Nothing*. The impasse took the form of Beckett's refusal to write in prose for nearly a decade, during which time he focused largely on his dramatic writing (*Endgame*, *Krapp's Last Tape* and *Happy Days*). Beckett's sojourn from prose came to a decisive end, however, with the publication of *Comment c'est* in 1961 (translated under the title *How It Is* by Beckett and published in English by Grove Press in 1964). Although it is 'ultimately a little-known work', explains Badiou, its publication signalled nothing less than 'a major mutation in the way that Beckett fictioned his thought. This text breaks with the confrontation between the torturing cogito and the neutrality of the black-grey of being' that circumscribed the narrative totality of *The Unnamable* and *Texts for Nothing* (2008: 264). Through the introduction in *How It Is* 'of alterity, of the encounter, of the figure of the Other', Beckett's writing finally 'fissures and displaces solipsistic imprisonment' (2008: 264). No longer able to sustain his compositional focus on the narrative subject's unending paralysis brought on by the terroristic imperative of phenomenological self-mutilation, Beckett discovers through the writing of *How It Is* a mine of creative possibilities in the poetics and ethics of encounter. It is precisely the introduction of the alterity of the other into the narrative texture of *How It Is* that promises an end to the 'reign of terror' that Badiou ascribes to the 'super-ego fury' of *The Unnamable* and *Texts for Nothing* (2008: 261).

Badiou's reading of *How It Is* places him squarely in the 'ethical camp' of Beckett studies by virtue of the emphasis he puts on the subversion of solipsistic terror by the evental encounter with (and care for) the alterity of the other. The encounter with the other that Badiou valorises in *How It Is* is an encounter that promises a decisive interruption of the vicious, autoimmunitary repetitions of speech and silence, pain and laughter, torture and tenderness that otherwise subsume everything said, illsaid, missaid and unsaid in what is perhaps Beckett's most hermeneutically unaccommodating work of fiction. The presence of terror in Beckett's writing no doubt signals a serious threat to the ethical paradigm of its critical reception in so far as terror exerts an oppressive pressure over the life-world of Beckett's narrators and protagonists (often one and the same) that compels them to struggle continuously against the very conditions of vulnerability and victimisation that their weapons of struggle – images, memories, fantasies, desires, thoughts and words – paradoxically refortify. As the unnamable puts it, 'the search for the means to put an end to things, an end to speech, is what enables the discourse to continue' (*TN* 293).

One of the purposes of this chapter is to show that rather than refuse to go along with what Badiou disparages in *The Unnamable* as the 'terrorist commandment to have to maintain what cannot be' (2008: 261), *How It Is* capitulates more intensively than ever to precisely this terrorist commandment that eternally returns to demarcate what is simultaneously most ethically hostile and creatively regenerative in Beckett's writing. It is within and against the ethical paradigm of reading Beckett that Blanchot's account of narrative speech, surrounded and overshadowed by radical violence, 'its fringe and its halo' (*IC* 187), is indispensable for its fashioning of a non-ethical exigency for literature, one that is rooted in a sustained reflection on human relation and capable of explaining why *How It Is*, 'our epic' (*IC* 329), precludes overt attempts like Badiou's at divesting Beckett's narrative voices of the eternal return of terror they ceaselessly speak. With the continuous drama of speech and violence that it stages in the relation between its narrator and the figure of Pim, *How It Is* is the text most inviting of an ethical interpretation at the same time as it is the text that thwarts ethical readings most decisively. The argument here, in other words, is not that *How It Is* marks a repetition without difference of the traumatically unrelenting asceticism – the narrative protocol of terror – of *The Unnamable* and *Texts for Nothing*; rather, *How It Is* doubles down on the terror of literature with an intensity that is inversely proportionate to its desire to escape precisely the terrifying 'solipsistic imprisonment' of Beckett's two previous texts.

As it concerns the question of ethics in relation to Beckett's writing, contemporary Beckett studies has been most indebted to the ethical theories of Theodor Adorno, Jacques Derrida and Emmanuel Levinas (and increasingly of Badiou) for arriving at the virtually unanimous decision that whatever else it is, Beckett's writing is above all ethical in that it confirms, writes Jean-Michel Rabaté, 'the ethical revelation of existence and otherness', 'which applies to the whole of Beckett's work' (2015: 169). In her influential reading of *How It Is*, Ewa Ziarek concurs with this comprehensive assessment of the Beckettian oeuvre, explaining that 'there is no better way to describe the style of Beckett's work than to call it, in Levinas's words, an "interrupted discourse catching up with its own breaks"' (1995: 169). The ethics of such a style is particularly apparent in the rhetoric of parataxis that Beckett uses for the peculiar composition of *How It Is*, the successful deployment of which ensures in advance of the encounter with the other that 'although the body' of Pim, the body of the other, Ziarek argues, 'becomes an arena of subjection to language, this subjection, no matter how violent, fails nonetheless to assimilate the other into what Levinas calls "the order of the same," because language constantly slides from the interior of consciousness to the exterior of the body, from the interiority of voice to the exteriority of writing' (1995: 184). David Kleinberg-Levin voices a similar assessment of the ethical imperative that motivates Beckett's writing, not just of *How It Is*, but across the entirety of Beckett's post-Second World War creative oeuvre, explaining that 'at stake for Beckett as a writer, as a storyteller, is – drawing, here, on the grammar of both the subjective and the objective senses of the genitive – language as the language *of* justice. Language holds the promise of happiness – holds it, however, in a structure of withholding' (2015: 8). Beckett's interminable paratactic prose exacerbates this ethical dimension of language by inscribing a ubiquitous network of unbridgeable fissures between what the narrator seeks to extract from and through Pim, and what the alterity of Pim stubbornly obstructs the narrator from acquiring: communication through coercion, and community through incarceration.

For Ziarek, Beckett's paratactic deployment of dialogue between the narrator and Pim (the self and the other) acts ultimately as a tactic of resistance against the all-too-ready-to-hand solution of violence, torture and extortion to the problematic of the impenetrability of the alterity of the other. 'The monstrous scene of communication' between the narrator and Pim, Ziarek explains,

> stages a violent, though no doubt 'therapeutic', attempt to mend the instabilities of discourse by overcoming the asymmetry between the self and the other. [...] Intertwined with the effort to overcome the opacity of the other, the violence of dialogue brings the other into the light of comprehension. In *How It Is*, violence becomes paradoxically measure of both the success and failure of this linguistic invention: success – because the necessary conditions of communication are inevitably produced and reproduced; failure – because 'successful' communication can no longer maintain the pretensions of reciprocity and openness. (1995: 180)

Faced with the stubborn incommunicability of the other, i.e. the refusal of the other to play the narrator's game of communicative exchange, the narrator frantically resorts to violence against the other in order to more expeditiously 'integrate alterity into the homogeneous socio-linguistic order' that the narrator is so intent on establishing (Ziarek 1995: 187). *How It Is* instructs on the violence of dialogue by reproducing thematically the grisly endgame of a subject-driven construction of the space of communicative sociality. Fortunately for the prospect of salvaging the ethical core of language itself, the dialectical violence of linguistic reification that Beckett stages in Part II, 'with Pim', as the narrative centrepiece of *How It Is* is sabotaged in its third (and perhaps final) section, 'after Pim', which reveals how the deployment of a particular protocol of language, the perseverance from beginning to end of Beckett's paratactic prose, can compensate for the violence of the dialectical appropriation of alterity by withdrawing alterity altogether from the impulse of integrating 'otherness within the social and pedagogical apparatus' (Ziarek 1995: 193). Beckett's paratactic commitment to 'discontinuity, indeterminate temporal and spatial distancing, and the "anxiety" of relation' is taken by Ziarek as evidence that with *How It Is* Beckett is endorsing 'a notion of sociality inaugurated by a perpetual retreat of the other from the common being' (1995: 193). *How It Is* would thus represent a literary treatise on a Beckettian ethics of alterity and the advancement of a concept of community where the alterity that Beckett's writing unveils might ethically and peaceably dwell.

One of the unspoken premises of Ziarek's ethical reading of Beckett, however, is that in order for Beckett's paratactic ethics of alterity to succeed, as Ziarek confidently believes that it does, it is imperative that it is reacting to a narrative situation that stages the conditions of nothing more (but also nothing less) severe than *violence* against alterity. In so far as violence consists 'of a force', writes Jean-Luc Nancy, 'that remains foreign to the dynamic or energetic system into which it intervenes', there will always be the possibility in the face of violence of bringing violence to an end and of returning the system that violence assaults to its functional state such as it was regulated before being targeted for violence (2005: 16). That the tormentors of *How It Is* were once victims, and that the victims of *How It Is* will once again become tormentors – 'these same couples that eternally form and form again all along this immense circuit' (*HII* 121) – suggests, however, that what is so unsettling about *How It Is* is that it stages the conditions of a relation that ends (interminably) where it begins (interminably) in a state of enthrallment before the threatening presence of alterity. This is a relation that is far more problematic from an ethical perspective than a relation that commences with violence against alterity and ends with the affirmation of the resistance of alterity against violence. On the one hand, it is comforting to join Ziarek (as do other Levinasian-inspired Beckettians like Peter Fifield[1] or Carla Locatelli) in believing that thanks to Beckett's paratactic vigilance, alterity is given a perpetual outlet of retreat from the violence implicit in the structures of communicative rationality and ontological totality that are made present in the narrative; on the other hand, there would be little comfort indeed if Beckett is in fact refusing us the knowledge that the destination of the retreat of alterity is not right back into the ontological thresher of coerced communication that precipitated the paratactic retreat of alterity in the first place. The eternally recurring catastrophe of *How It Is* is that there is nowhere for alterity to go where it would not be met yet again and always with violence. The eternal return of violence, the complicity of language and dialogue in perpetuating violence, and the figuration of violence in the narrative's promise of ontological justice to all who inhabit the world of *How It Is*, oblige us to consider that what we are in fact dealing with in *How It Is* is nothing so banal as the writing of undecidability, but rather the writing of a violence in radical excess of violence.

Accordingly, calling the place in which the narrative situation of *How It Is* unfolds a place of *terror* is perhaps a more precise and altogether more disorienting diagnosis of just how thoroughly compromised its writing is by its unending descent into (and incitement of) violence, for as Hannah Arendt explains in *On Violence*, 'terror is not the same as violence'; rather, terror 'comes into being when violence, having destroyed all power, does not abdicate but, on the contrary, remains in full control. [. . .] The climax of terror is reached [. . .] when yesterday's executioner becomes today's victim' (2001: 55). Arendt's account of how violence morphs into terror by transcending its dialectical dependence on the resistance and power of the body and the state that violence targets can help us to begin mapping conceptually such relations in *How It Is* that are so subsumed by violence that the identities assigned to the perpetrators and victims of violence become nothing more than mere place holders to be circulated through unceasingly without any indication of when the violence that mediates these relations will stop: 'what I for Pim Pim for me' (*HII* 60).

Arendt credits none other than 'the Stalinist functionaries themselves' for the realisation that a regime that has successfully converted violence into terror must be stopped at all costs because it would lead, 'not to an insurrection, against which terror is indeed the best safeguard, but to paralysis of the whole country' (2001: 55–6). Both politically and ethically speaking, Arendt is right to advise so vehemently against endorsing the descent of violence into terror, but the same does not necessarily hold when speaking about the capacities of literature and art in the face of violence and terror, particularly if we are on board with Nancy in maintaining that 'art is not a simulacrum or an apotropaic form that would protect us from unjustifiable violence' (2005: 26). Insisting that art and literature must, *necessarily*, represent spaces of ethical possibility is to risk hoping too optimistically that art and literature are not valuable precisely to the degree that they assume the burden of acquiescing to complicity (thus sacrificing their ethical pretensions) in such limit-experiences as terror that we would much rather be spared from experiencing (in the world outside as much as inside the space of literature).

Beckett's writing of *How It Is* emanates continuously (returns and returns again) from a place of paratactic delay where violence against alterity becomes the only mechanism of defence against the very real prospect of alterity evaporating altogether in an unbroken nightmare of ontological paralysis. Beckett coerces his readers into unlocking the open secret that Pim's vulnerability to violence and torture is the only available gateway to exposing Pim's vulnerability to dialogue and speech. Beckett's framing of the relation with Pim in the paratactic delay of terror – that is to say, in a space that is uncannily commensurate with 'an area', writes Giorgio Agamben, 'in which [Primo] Levi succeeded in isolating something like a new ethical element', a 'zone in which the "long chain of conjunction between victim and executioner" comes loose, where the oppressed becomes oppressor and the executioner in turn appears as victim' (2002: 21) – is the surest way of refusing the naive ethical impulse of immunising speech from violence, and alterity from naming. Russell Smith proposes that it is precisely the delineation of Agamben's 'zone of indecipherability' that renders *How It Is* a narrative about the ethics of witnessing. The argument in this chapter departs from Smith's (and Ziarek's) through its insistence that the *repetition* of this zone of indecipherability, i.e. the eternal paratactic recurrence of the moment of its inscription, precludes the position of even an imaginary witness from articulating a place of visibility in proximity to the place of violence and suffering inscribed in the narrative. That narration from the place of suffering is explicitly denied in *How It Is* can therefore be submitted for evidence that this is not in fact a narrative first and foremost of suffering, but rather a narrative of what, in language, makes suffering possible, of what, in language, perhaps makes suffering necessary.

It is within this non-ethical[2] paradigm of art and literature sacrificing their *a priori* ethical (but not necessarily ontological) allegiances to concepts like alterity, dialogue and unconditional justice that we can begin articulating how the writing of *How It Is* unfolds atop the threshold of violence morphing into terror. This is a threshold where the spaces and the identities that separate perpetrators from victims are under permanent ontological threat of indistinction, and where the dialectical energy ordinarily released when the force of violence that confronts the resistance of alterity dissipates (dialectically stalls) into an ever-worsening state of epic paralysis: 'linked thus bodily together each one of us is at the same time Bom and Pim tormentor and tormented pedant and dunce wooer and wooed speechless and reafflicted with speech in the dark the mud nothing to emend there' (*HII* 140). The closing of the distance and distinction between Bom (the narrator) and Pim, between being-speechless and being-reafflicted with speech, represents the imminent denouement in *How It Is* of terror. There is no place more demanding of analytic scrutiny than the instant *before* this denouement, for its passage would (and perhaps does) signal nothing less than the commencement of the ethical disaster of dialectical inoperability, which is intuited in *How It Is* in a place of language – *the* place of language *par excellence* – where the eternal return of violence threatens alterity with the spectre of its absolute effacement. Where there is the terror of a violence in excess of violence, there is no longer any access to the outside of violence from where ethical resistance *against* violence is to be surmounted. Where there is terror, in other words, outside collapses into inside, the security of transcendence morphs into the insecurity of immanence (the horror of the *il y a*), and there is no longer any place to go, no identity left to inhabit, and no words or names left to pronounce whereby subjects of terror would be either innocent or free of the repetition of violence that terror continuously perpetrates. *How It Is* obliges the uncomfortable realisation that the possibility of violence against alterity is a necessary corollary of the desire that there be alterity in the first place, and the way that it impresses this realisation upon its readers (and its narrator) is by threatening the denouement of terror in the place of language where alterity is most vulnerable to violence and speech.

II

Readers who have taken even a passing glance inside the pages of *How It Is* will intuit the difficulty that inheres in the structure and syntax of the work's composition. This is a text that refuses to signpost its grammar, that is broken up into strophic paragraphs, and that reads with a musicality punctuated repeatedly by abrupt paratactic amendments to the speaker's continuous recitation of the stream-of-consciousness-esque (and potentially infinitely reoccurring) discourse it is tasked with (re-)producing. Beckett compensates for the difficulties in stylising the prose of *How It Is* with a plot that is indeed not much more complicated than how he describes it in a letter to Barney Rosset dated 5 May 1959: 'It all "takes place" in the pitch dark and the mud, first part "man" alone, second with another, third alone again. All a problem of rhythm and syntax and weakening of form, nothing more difficult' (*Letters III* 230). *How It Is* begins with a 'man' crawling in the mud and in the dark, on his way to victimise one who patiently awaits his arrival. This is the action of Part I. In Part II, the crawling protagonist reaches his victim, Pim, and the violent ritual of victimisation begins. Part III consists of Pim crawling away from his tormentor (the narrator) in order to victimise another in exactly the same way as he himself has just been victimised. The abandoned narrator is now left lying prone in the mud awaiting his turn to be victimised by Bom in accordance with the infernal mathematical justice that ensures no victim will be deprived of its tormentor and no tormentor deprived of its victim in this 'procession without end or beginning' (*HII* 127).

What we are told about 'the beginning of my life present formulation' is limited in the opening pages of *How It Is* to the 'certainties the mud the dark I recapitulate the sack the tins the mud the dark the silence the solitude nothing else for the moment' (*HII* 8). And yet, the 'moment' of the narrator's certainties quickly gives way to a series of images of a life that it is said to have once lived 'above in the light' (*HII* 9). Because there is no accounting for 'how I got here no question not known not said', readers of *How It Is* are left in the clumsy epistemological position of speculating not only on the catalyst, but also on the consequences for life here in the mud of the fact that the narrator cannot return to the life it imagines itself to have lived before its deportation (its disappearance) into the darkness down below: 'how it was my vanished life then after' (*HII* 20). The presence in *How It Is* of words resurrecting the time of this 'life life the other above in the light said to have been mine' inserts an ontological wedge into the consistency of life here in the mud, and it is on the basis of such a wedge of discontinuity that the narrator is able to produce the images of a life that is fundamentally unliveable in its present ontological condition (*HII* 8).

From the very outset of *How It Is* the narrator is struggling to conjure up an image of its life that would last long enough and that would be compelling enough to reconstitute how it sees and experiences its life going forward in the future of the mud:

'that's all it wasn't a dream I didn't dream that nor a memory I haven't been given memories this time it was an image the kind I see sometimes see in the mud part one sometimes saw' (*HII* 11). The content of these images includes the narrator watching 'some creature or other I watched him after my fashion from afar' (*HII* 9); scissoring 'into slender strips the wings of butterflies' (*HII* 9); seeing a woman who 'stoops to her works' as she 'looks up looks at me the images come at the beginning' (*HII* 10); sitting with his mother 'on a veranda smothered in verbena' (*HII* 15); spying on 'a boy sitting on a bed in the dark or a small old man I can't see with his head be it young or be it old his head in his hands I appropriate that heart' (*HII* 18); and several other imaginings of the 'rags of life in the light' (*HII* 21). These images, which insinuate themselves as redemptive fictions of the imagination, are the narrator's only weapons against the monotony of the crawl on the way towards Pim, but because they have been hijacked and infiltrated by the words that are murmured to the narrator in the mud, they are destined for failure as tokens of independent verification that its life in the mud can be lived otherwise than how the 'ancient voice in me not mine' tyrannically prescribes (*HII* 7): 'the images come at the beginning part one they will cease I say it as I hear it murmur it in the mud the images part one how it was before Pim I see them in the mud a light goes on they will cease' (*HII* 10).

The imminent cessation of images is unfortunate, for what it impresses on the narrator is the sober realisation that its 'wish' early on in Part I 'to be less wretched a little less the wish for a little beauty' will not be granted in so far as the images that it is able to produce in service of this wish 'before Pim' provide nothing more than mere moments of distraction and pause from 'the need to move on the need to shit and vomit and other great needs all my great categories of being' (*HII* 14). Subsisting so passively in the mud as 'a monster of the solitudes' entails that whatever possibility of resistance to the monotony of the crawl the narrator can envision will have to come from somewhere outside of its solipsistic horizon, and until its solipsistic horizon is breached by an external interventionary force capable of reimagining how life 'down below' is to be (re)constituted, it will persist in its myopic journey on this unbearable tract in the mud (*HII* 13). The ancient voice that murmurs the words signifying the narrator's life down below is too adept at overwhelming the interrupted spaces of the narrator's panting in the mud for the narrator's images to have any lasting consequences on reimagining life otherwise than how it is lived in its present formulation: 'the wish for a little beauty no when the panting stops I hear nothing of the kind that's not how I'm told this time' in Part I 'before Pim' (*HII* 12).

Throughout Part I 'before Pim' the narrator behaves as one who has suffered violence at some point in its past, though it is not at all certain that the past in which its subjection to violence occurred can be linked together with the temporal matrix that comprises the 'present formulation' of its life now lived in the mud (*HII* 8). Nevertheless, traces of the unnamed event of violence, which we can reasonably speculate is responsible for the narrator's ontological displacement in this nightmarish narrative, live on in the narrator's peculiar comportment as it is conducted in *How It Is* as a being whose reconstituted essence now consists in having once or yet again (but always for the first time) been violently assaulted. This applies to whether we opt for reading Part I 'before Pim' as the very first citation of life in the mud, that is to say, as the instant where 'life above' ceases and the narrator's recording of 'life below' commences, or for reading it *in medias res* as the latest citation of an epic voice that has been speaking this life in the mud from time immemorial. Whether the narrator has journeyed 'down below' for the first time from 'life above', in other words, or whether it has just been released from its share of victimisation along this infernal tract in the mud, it speaks to us from a position *after* the singular experience of victimisation has occurred, in one (temporal) place or another: 'a most remarkable thing when you come to think of it only the victims journeyed' (*HII* 142). 'From elsewhere or beyond', writes Jean-Luc Nancy, 'violence brandishes another form, if not another meaning' (2005: 16), and it is the unfortunate though irreversible condition of this narrator to have to move forward as the embodiment of some new form, some new name, and with some new meaning of how life is to be lived according to 'this new formulation namely this new life to have done with that' (*HII* 142). Appearing in Part I 'before Pim' as a subject pieced fragilely together with the detritus of the life that remains in the wake of its traumatic victimisation, the narrator is forced to inhabit an ontological reality that obeys new laws and new regulations of how this post-violence, post-victimisation after-life is to be lived and relived according to the voice of its anonymous inscription.

'[T]hat of the four three quarters of our total life only three lend themselves to communication' is no small detail of the narrative, for what the absence of any record or even, and perhaps especially, the *possibility* of a record of the narrator's exposure to the violence it will commit against Pim implies is that in the space (in the time) of How It Is there is therefore neither place nor words through which the voice of victimisation might communicate its tale *qua* narrative of its victimisation (*HII* 131). The voice of the victim is too singular, too vulnerable and too catastrophic for the language that survives its victimisation to be welcomed, without violence, back into the place in discourse that was responsible for grounding the possibility of its victimisation in the first place. Having suffered a great loss – 'losses everywhere' (*HII* 7) – and being brandished in Part I 'before Pim' in another form, the narrator comes into *How It Is* with 'the only thing', as Paul Celan explains (ironically yet mournfully), that remains 'reachable, close and secure amid all losses: language. Yes, language. In spite of everything, it remained secure against loss. But it had to go through its own lack of answers, through terrifying silence, through the thousand darknesses of murderous speech. It went through. It gave [. . .] no words for what was happening, but went through it' (1990: 34).

While it would be a salutary thought to envision the narrative of *How It Is* occupying a time after the end of victimisation, that is to say, a time when language 'could resurface' and be used by the narrator, as it was hoped for by Celan, 'in order to speak, to orient myself, to find out where I was, where I was going, to chart my reality' (1990: 34), the sobering reality of *How It Is* is that with the ancient words at its disposal, it is riveted to a place in language – 'it's the place without knowledge' (*HII* 123) – that foreshadows the horizon of only one outcome that will return and return again: 'quaqua the voice of us all who all all those here before me and to come alone in this wallow or glued together all the Pims tormentors promoted victims past if it ever passes and to come that's sure more than ever by the earth undone its light all those' (*HII* 127). The time of *this* narrative is therefore not the time *after* victimisation when language, amidst the ruins of its irremediable destruction and decay, could begin the infinite task of reassembling itself by 'those who', like Celan, and 'with manmade stars flying overhead, unsheltered even by the traditional tent of the sky, exposed in an unsuspected, terrifying way, carry their existence into language, racked by reality and in search of it' (1990: 35); rather, it is a time that is circumscribed before victimisation has started (again) and after the time it has come (momentarily) to an end.

We can read the emphasis placed on images in Part I of *How It Is* as a symptom of the narrator's distrust of the words that will have been complicit in its return to the place of victimisation. The wager on the ontological (re-)inventiveness of the image is a desperate one, for should its images fail in their promise of envisioning life otherwise, the narrator risks being left alone for the continuation of its journey in a place of language where its vulnerability to violence is perennially exposed. In *The Infinite Conversation* Blanchot refers to such a place as the place where thinking and speaking begin, but in doing so he does not intend to make of the discovery of this place a cause for celebration. This place is a place of fear 'where searching for what is reached in fear, putting oneself at stake in the shaking that is fear', brings 'us closer to a decisive point that, if it escapes philosophy, does so because something decisive escapes philosophy' (*IC* 50). What is decisive is that the one who inhabits this place without any tangible hope of escape comes face-to-face with the 'violence that reveals itself in fear and that threatens to transform him from a frightened man into a violent man; as though he feared less the violence he suffers than the violence he might exercise' (*IC* 50).

The failure of images to disrupt the journey wherein the narrator is condemned to 'keep dying in a dying age' (*HII* 17) nevertheless forces the recognition that pulsating throughout its narrative dwelling are glimmers of redemption – 'the space of a moment the passing moment' (*HII* 16) – that paradoxically flash brightest at the height of their impenetrability. The narrator does not have the inventive power to inscribe an image of life lived otherwise in the mud that the 'voice once without quaqua on all sides then in me when the panting stops' would not coopt into the machinery of words that propel the narrator forward on its panting, fatalistic way towards Pim, but it does at least have the desire that the image will glimpse the possibility of a life lived outside of the fear that would compel the exercise of violence against Pim (*HII* 7). This struggle between the voice – 'in me not mine' (*HII* 7) – and the image – 'the kind I see sometimes see in the mud part one' (*HII* 11) – over what will ground the narrator's vision of what its life is and of what can be hoped for in its life in the mud is a struggle that, alas, the image in this case was set up to lose from the eternally recurring beginning of the narrative. The narrator's images are too nostalgically conceived, too hopelessly pedestrian, and altogether too comprehensible to overturn the sheer incomprehensibility of how the narrator's vision of its life in the mud is refracted by the words of the voice: 'here confused reckonings to the effect I can't have deviated more than a second or so from the direction imparted to me' (*HII* 40). What is interesting here is not *that* the narrator's images fail to extract it for 'more than a second' from down below in the darkness of the mud; rather, it is *how* and *why* they fail in this respect that demands articulation, particularly if we are to understand the consequences of the narrator's imminent substitution of images with the body of Pim *qua* instrument of subverting the epic sovereignty of the ancient voice as it murmurs the narrator into the precarity of its existence from one paratactic interval to the next *ad infinitum*: 'I hear me again murmur me in the mud and am again' (*HII* 126).

In his essay 'Image and Violence', Nancy identifies the 'essential link' that binds the production of images to the phenomenon of violence (2005: 20). Only through acknowledging their reciprocally constitutive filiation with one another do violence and image stand a chance of embodying the essential aspiration of their respective forms:

> If violence is exercised without responsibility to anything other than itself, without reference to any higher authority (including, of course, when violence invokes such a moment of authorisation and justification), this becomes apparent through the essential link that violence maintains with the image. Violence always makes an image of itself, and the image is what, of itself, presses out ahead of itself and authorizes itself. [. . .] Even when the image is mimetic, it must fundamentally, by itself and for itself, count for more than an image; otherwise, it will tend toward being nothing but a shadow or a reflection. (2005: 20)

Just as violence represents transformation through the self-aggrandising power of its excess, so too is the image defined by manifesting a break with the ground of representation from which the image is extracted, and through this break exposing the possibility that the ontological horizon of its representation can be reconstituted precisely according to the ungrounded possibility that preceded its representation in the first place. There is a definitive desire to transcend the ontological law that oversees the place and the manifestation of what violence and image target for constituting (presenting) otherwise, but alas, it is a desire that must go unfulfilled in the prospect of its satisfaction lest violence become the annihilation of life, and image become the optical obliteration of its own ungrounded horizon of possibility. Violence and image are in perennial, dialectical competition with what is, and rather than annihilate the being of what is so as to produce something altogether new, the success of violence and image is limited to realigning the coordinates of how *that which is* traverses the manifestation of its presence in the post-violence, post-image space of its *re*presentation. Violence obstructs the law of a person or thing's ontological functioning so as to make that thing or person do, be or say what is contrary to its habit of existence. The image goes one step further than violence, for it is invoked not just to extract a thing, person or idea from the ground of its presence and expose it to the ungrounded possibility of its being repurposed *in its very being*, but is invoked in order to accomplish this process of extraction *on itself* as well. Every image is an image of violence that doubles as the violence *of itself becoming image*: 'therefore being is torn away from being; and it is the image that tears itself away. It bears within itself the mark of this tearing away: its ground monstrously opened to its very bottom, that is, to the depthless underside of its presentation' (Nancy 2005: 24).

Nancy's reflections on the essential relation between image and violence give some indication of why the images conjured up by the narrator in Part I 'before Pim' were destined to fail. Because their very possibility *qua* images of seeing life otherwise (the optical precondition of *being otherwise*) was predicated on overcoming the optical status quo of life in the mud, they would have had to have manifested an unhealable rift in the ontological ground of the narrative. Juxtaposing itinerant images of 'life above' with the prevailing image of 'life below' is too dialectically innocuous a gesture to have any impactful effect on the ontological law governing the here and now of 'life below' in the mud, which is already predicated according to the paratactic repetition of rifts in the texture of the narrative. It is because of the weakness of images in *How It Is* that we read in Part III 'after Pim' a summary of life in the mud wherein images are unproblematically subsumed into the ontological totality that they had been ostensibly produced to subvert in Part I 'before Pim'. The promise of discontinuity represented in the image is broken by the threat of its redundancy given that the paratactic law of discontinuity that the epic voice of the narrative has installed to oversee how life in the mud is structured is always already immune to what the image is constitutively tasked with provoking: 'here in truth all discontinuous journey images torment even solitude part three when a voice speaks then stops a few scraps then nothing more save the dark the mud all discontinuous save the dark the mud / an image too of this voice ten words fifteen words long silence ten words fifteen words long silence long solitude once without quaqua on all sides vast stretch of time then in me when the panting stops scraps' (*HII* 126). In an ontological regime where the paratactic law of continuous discontinuity is installed as the order of the day, a new image, a new violence is required for the possibility of transcending this law. Images *must be violent* if they are to unground the groundedness of the ontological regime against which the violent becoming of their presence is manifested. The image, like violence, comes into existence for the purpose of altering the organising principle of the place from which and against which it originates. Accordingly, images are doubly dangerous due to 'the ambiguity of the image and of violence – of the violence at work in the image and of the image opening itself in violence' (Nancy 2005: 25): 'if no image can exist without tearing apart a closed intimacy or a non-disclosed immanence, and if no image can exist without plunging into a blind depth – without world or subject – then it must also be admitted that not only violence but the extreme violence of *cruelty* hovers at the edge of the image, of all images' (2005: 24; italics in original).

The point here is not that an image *about* cruelty is a cruelly extreme image of violence, even though the image of the narrator having 'scissored into slender strips the wings of butterflies first one wing then the other sometimes for a change the two abreast never so good since' is undoubtedly an image of the narrator's propensity for cruelty (*HII* 9); rather, it is that the very act of insinuating an image as a new optical modality of perception – *life in the light* – is to invoke the same impulses of denaturation and subversion that compel towards violence. The attraction of the image is its promise of overthrowing a regime of seeing, which is the first step to either directly or indirectly overthrowing a regime of being. This is the case even and especially when a particular optical or ontological regime is repressive, oppressive and altogether suffocating of life, and thus deserving of being targeted by forces of insurrectionary violence (imaginative or corporal).[3] That the image exists on a continuum where it can engender *either* infinite suspension *or* infinite cruelty at the extremity of violence is, then, precisely the point. To risk the image is once again to risk the violence that surrounds the image. It cannot be otherwise; so, in the face of an ontological regime that presents as the monopolisation over the imperative of discontinuity that likewise compels the demand for the image, what is needed is not the momentary irruption of the image, but a wholesale annexation of the right to discontinuity that has hitherto been claimed as the exclusive prerogative in *How It Is* of 'the ancient voice in me not mine' (*HII* 7). The words of the voice must somehow be pre-emptively subjected to the *terrifying silence* of victimisation if the image is to triumphantly announce that 'now it's done I've done the image' (*CSP* 168). Without having actually gone through the wordless ordeal of that one quarter of the life that bookends how it was 'before Pim' and how it will be 'after Pim', i.e. the narrative of how it is *as Pim*, there is, however, no guarantee that the silences inscribed throughout the paratactic delays of the text will be terrifying enough to open up a space in language for the image to sever the ancient voice from its murderous speech of 'how it was I quote before Pim with Pim after Pim how it is three parts I say it as I hear it' (*HII* 7).

III

Writing at the beginning of *The Infinite Conversation*, Blanchot downplays the gravity of a phenomenon that he will proceed to render at once increasingly (predictably) pernicious and alluringly (enigmatically) salvific: the phenomenon of continuous speech. Blanchot enjoins us to 'recall that, in modern literature, the preoccupation with a *profoundly* continuous speech is what first gave rise – with Lautréamont, with Proust, then with surrealism, then with Joyce – to works that were manifestly scandalous. An excess of continuity unsettles the reader, and unsettles the reader's habits of regular comprehension' (*IC* 9; italics in original). The frustration of comprehension and habit is unquestionably what makes modern literature so indispensable in coercing its readers to develop new pathways of thinking and new idioms of speaking whereby the infinite approach of the future does not calcify into the sterile repetition of the past. Literature dies with the succession of habit and comprehension, and so the discovery of a protocol of writing that breaks with habit and comprehension is necessary for the sheer strangeness and discomfort constitutive of literature to survive. Where there is nothing but continuity, however, where continuity ascends to a position of all-encompassing totality over the import and trajectory of language and speech, it is not the survival of literature and writing that is guaranteed, but the uncompromising tyranny of mythical decree. Continuity represents a double threat that it is imperative to know how to decipher. The supreme difficulty of reading Beckett's *How It Is*, however, is that there inheres in the fragile latency of the murmuring voice precisely this ambivalent threat of continuity.

In the later fragments of *How It Is*, the ones preceding what many commentators take to be the greatest challenge in the text to the prospect of the salvation of alterity, namely that all the narrator's previous utterances were 'all balls from start to finish yes this voice quaqua yes all balls yes only one voice here yes mine yes when the panting stops yes' (*HII* 144–5), the narrator resorts to a quasi-theological thought experiment aimed at somehow deferring all ontological responsibility for this life in the mud to a transcendental 'intelligence' (*HII* 137). It asks if the procession of victims and tormentors might be discontinued without sacrificing altogether their life in the mud. Needless to say, the thought experiment quickly fails, but not without exposing the narrator's desire that the catastrophic scenario of the voice's absolute sovereignty be avoided (the catastrophe of the narrator *becoming* the voice) and that the paratactic intervals driving the crawl, the torture, the company, the abandon, 'it's our justice in this muck' (*HII* 112), will continue unabated. For there is nothing stopping 'an intelligence somewhere a love who all along the track at the right places according as we need them deposits our sacks' (*HII* 137–8), 'without which no journey' (*HII* 111), from thinking that perhaps it would be preferable for this journey to come to a halt and cease once and for all. Were this to happen, however, if such an 'intelligence' were to succeed, 'God knows who could blame him', 'if to these perpetual revictuallings narrations and auditions he might not put an end without ceasing to maintain us in some kind of being without end and some kind of justice without flaw who could blame him' (*HII* 139), then the memory, the archive, the 'indelible traces' that 'with the nail then of the right index I carve and when it breaks or falls until it grows again with another on Pim's back intact at the outset from left to right and top to bottom as in our civilisation I carve my Roman capitals' (*HII* 70), would likewise have to be abolished – sacrificed to forgetfulness – in order that the narrative not simply be 'frozen in injustice' (*HII* 137). Such an intelligence, if it exists, would be free to stop depositing sacks and thus to absolve itself from any further complicity in the continuation of the epic citation that has been set perpetually into motion, but doing so will result only in the succession of this responsibility to the crawlers who 'without food to sustain us' will nevertheless continue to 'drag ourselves thus by the mere grace of our united net sufferings from west to east towards an inexistent peace' (*HII* 143).

'Eliminating all journeys all abandons', such an intelligence would thereby be committed to eliminating 'at the same stroke all occasions of sacks and voices' (*HII* 141), but would succeed only in 'eliminat[ing] *him* completely and so admit *him* to that peace at least while rendering *me* in the same breath sole responsible for this unqualifiable murmur' (*HII* 144; my italics). Beckett has structured as an unimpeachable mainstay of *How It Is* the very thing that its paratactic style of composition appears designed to preclude: the interminable murmuring of the ancient voice. According to Blanchot, Beckett's writing unfolds at a peak of ethical ambivalence by embedding a mysterious script in works like *The Unnamable*, *Texts for Nothing* and *How It Is* that bespeaks a language that 'is not in the least a spoken language', but 'the oral style of a non-written speech' (*IC* 329). 'Even though we are at the limit of effacement' in *How It Is*, 'a long way from all that makes din, and even though this murmur is close to monotony, saying in an even, equal manner the uneven equality of all speech, there is an essential rhythm, a modulation, a slightly accentuated movement or cadence marked by returns and at times by refrains. It is a tacit song' (*IC* 329). The song that Blanchot detects in *How It Is* sounds remarkably similar to the incessant, albeit reconfigured continuation of the narrative speech that Blanchot first articulated in his reading of *The Unnamable*: 'a wandering speech, one that is not deprived of meaning, but deprived of center, that does not begin, does not end, yet is greedy, demanding, will never stop, one couldn't stand if it stopped, for that is when one would have to make the terrible discovery that, when it does not speak, it is still speaking, when it ceases, it perseveres, not silently, for in it silence speaks eternally' (*BC* 210). The narrative speech that Blanchot extracts from Beckett's writing is so overwhelming in its opacity, so unrelenting in its incessantness, that it successfully pulls off the delicate, improbable balancing act of displacing both Beckett (the biographical subjectivity of the writer) and the Beckettian narrator (the textual subjectivity of the fictional voice) from their respective seats of narrative authority. Here speaks a disquieting language that renders superfluous the subject of the subjectivity that speaks it, and the authority of the author who composed it. And yet, even in its position of superfluity, the narrator, above all, Blanchot argues, can never evade being 'responsible for this irresponsibility', this *unqualifiable murmur* of the voice (IC 330). 'Even at the level of mud', Blanchot continues, 'this remains the exigency from which no being who hears can stand entirely apart. Strange, strange' (IC 330).

What remains when author and narrator go silent in *How It Is* is the unmistakeable presence of a narrative voice that speaks the epic language of 'biblical speech' (IC 330), and far from being silenced by all the pauses and interruptions, all the absences and gaps in the texture of the narrative, it is a voice that inscribes its transcendental apotheosis precisely in the silence of the paratactic delays of the Beckettian mud. The epic narrative voice that speaks out of the fragmentary spaces of *How It Is*, however, is one that no longer 'attempts to found a community or impart knowledge', according to William S. Allen; rather, speaking out of the opaque depths of paratactic delay, it imparts 'an essential lack of certainty over what determines knowledge as such and differentiates it from anything else' (2016: 238). In so far as the paratactic delays of *How It Is* act as narrative outlets for the epic sovereign modalities of 'biblical speech', 'extending from generation to generation', the work's ethical no less than its ontological responsibility 'is not to prolong' this biblical speech, 'but to put an end to it, to bring the movement to rest' (IC 330). Blanchot asks earlier in *The Infinite Conversation* that we 'remember Hitler's terrible monologues', for they oblige us to recall that 'every head of state participates in the same violence of this *dictare*, the repetition of an imperious monologue, when he enjoys the power of being the only one to speak and, rejoicing in possession of his high solitary word, imposes it without restraint as a superior and supreme speech upon others' (IC 75). Biblical, imperious speech is not a speech that is inclined to mediate the ethical event of conversation and dialogue, but because it is the only speech that the narrative of *How It Is* permits its narrator unequivocally to possess, it is a speech that forces the narrator into a situation of desiring alternative methods of speaking – speaking in dialogue with Pim – whereby the dictatorial violence of the voice that circumscribes its existence in the mud would become vulnerable to an ethical protocol of cessation, silence and wordlessness that cannot be integrated into the totality of the voice's narrative.

IV

The hypothesis put forward in Part II 'with Pim' is that 'with someone to keep me company I would have been a different man more universal' (*HII* 67), but to test this hypothesis and to overcome the ontological distance that separates the narrator from this 'dumb limp lump' body of Pim lying 'flat for ever in the mud' (*HII* 52), the narrator must devise a way 'to cleave' to Pim (*HII* 62), to overcome the 'problem of [Pim's] training' (*HII* 57), and to figure out how best to give Pim 'a name train him up bloody him all over with Roman capitals gorge on his fables unite for life in stoic love' (*HII* 62). The problem of Pim, in other words, is the problem of company, of the imperative of traversing the incommensurability of life in common. Pim's presence in *How It Is* represents the problematic of human relation where it is predicated on the capacity of language to facilitate mediation between self and other. Overcoming this problematic, however, is not necessarily an end in itself in the context of *How It Is*. By shifting our perspective momentarily away from locating the confrontation with Pim as the nerve-centre of the text to the continuous catastrophe – the irreversible denouement of terror – of the voice muttering forever in the mud, this voice that simultaneously archives, dictates and predicts the narrator's arrival in the place of Pim (*as* Pim), we begin to see that the violence committed against the body of Pim is an instrumental form of violence and therefore subject to the ethical limits of its finitude.

The real problematic of *How It Is*, in other words, is not the problematic of the violence committed against Pim, which is violence aimed (and therefore violence with a purpose) at precipitating the interruption of the voice, but the problematic of why this propensity for violence necessarily returns to the place that the body of Pim provisionally inhabits. The problem is not violence; it is violence's return *in the place of relation* with Pim. Before it was the violence against Pim, the violence of *How It Is* was the violence of the image, and the question this violence poses is whether or not that which it targets for discontinuity – the terror of the continuity of the voice – is not in fact worse than the phenomenon of violence that is on explicit display in the episode with Pim. The passage from the aesthetic context of violence in the image to the ethical context of violence in the relation with Pim is far from insignificant, and there can be no doubting that the violence committed against the body of Pim is qualitatively distinct from the violence of the image. Nevertheless, what underwrites both instances of the narrator's perpetration of violence (imaginative and corporal) is the spectre of violence's eternal return, the horizon of the denouement of terror, and it is this dimension of violence that the coming into contact with Pim in the establishment of human relation is staged for the purpose of discontinuing. 'This is a long labor', writes Blanchot on the subject of human relation, and even assuming that this labour is accomplished, that 'the reign of liberty' succeeds in substituting 'itself for the reign of necessity' (*IC* 68), there must necessarily come an accounting of 'what measure of blood, sweat, and tears is required for this' (*IC* 68): 'if he wants me to leave him yes in peace yes without me there is peace yes was peace yes every day no if he thinks I'll leave him no I'll stay where I am yes glued to him yes tormenting him yes eternally yes' (*HII* 98).

Levinas and Blanchot have expended much philosophical capital trying to explicate the human relation, and particularly in ways that converge with Beckett's negotiation of the experience of it in *How It Is*. Given Levinas's considerable influence over the question of ethics asked so frequently of Beckett's writing, there is indeed much value in tracking where Blanchot deviates from Levinas on precisely the prospect of its ethical solution. Levinas's point of departure for conceptualising the ethical transcendence of the human relation is his diagnosis of world history as a secular project where violence and war are the *de jure* (if not *de facto*) condition of the ontological totality that structures the contexts where everyday subjectivity lives and dwells in the presence of others. Levinas contrasts this secular vision refracted by war with an eschatological vision of ethical possibility that is predicated on enacting a protocol of speech and language that cuts into 'the anonymous utterance of history' and 'breaks with the totality of wars and empires in which one does not speak' (1969: 23). Speech is thus the eschatological weapon of ethics in the fight of resistance against war, but before it can be deployed (uttered) with an eye on breaking with the ontological law of totality that excretes war, a place of exteriority must be revealed – and this, ultimately, is for Levinas the philosophical task *par excellence* – where eschatological speech can resound: 'we can proceed from the experience of totality back to a situation where totality breaks up, a situation that conditions the totality itself. Such a situation is the gleam of exteriority or of transcendence in the face of the Other' (1969: 24). If, for Levinas, the way that the violence of totality (the ontology of war) is disarmed is by welcoming the alterity of the other that always already precedes totality (such would be the transcendental *a priori* of Levinasian ethics), and if, for Levinas, the way that this is accomplished is by opening up, in the discourse – the language – of totality, a place for the arrival of the other *qua* the face of the other (the *otherwise* than being), then it is necessary to posit a fundamental opposition between the ethical violence of language and speech and the paralytic violence of war and terror. The violence of ethics is a 'violence which, for a mind, consists in welcoming a being' in its opposition to 'the ideal of autonomy' (1969: 25). The ethical event of justice, then, occurs in 'veritable conversation' between the ideal of autonomy that defines the subjectivity of the self-identical subject – the subject produced in the totality and time of (perpetual) war – and the face of the Other that defines the infinite excess of alterity, an excess that uproots the autonomy of the subject from the ground of the totality that legislates its ontological continuity (1969: 70): '*we call justice this face to face approach, in conversation*' (1969: 71; italics in original).

Levinasian ethics consists in the idea that coming face to face with the alterity of the other commands hospitality towards the alterity of the other. Such a commandment of hospitality is embedded in the image of the face in so far as through the idiosyncrasies of its visage – the face of the face – it 'resists possession, resists my powers' (1969: 197). If the encounter with the other is first and foremost an encounter that precipitates the negation of the alterity of the other, then it is the face of the other that guarantees that 'in its epiphany, in expression, the sensible, still graspable, turns into total resistance to the grasp' (1969: 197). The temporal dynamics of this encounter is significant. Levinas is not saying that the face represents a counter-force to the desire to enjoy, know and ultimately kill the alterity of the other. There is nothing ethical, in other words, in the other summoning the power to defy its objectification in the violent economy of encounter. There is no denying that the encounter with the other ordinarily unfolds as an encounter that begins with the violence threatened by comprehension, calculation and communication, and proceeds dialectically through the resistance and struggle that the other mounts in its labour to be withdrawn from this threat of being known, enjoyed and perhaps ultimately killed.

The *ethics* of resistance consists in something altogether different than the *dialectics* of resistance. It consists, rather, 'not in a greater force' that the other is able to produce in service of its resistance, 'an energy assessable and consequently presenting itself as though it were part of a whole', but rather 'the very *unforeseeableness* of his reaction [. . .], the very transcendence of his being by relation to that whole; not some superlative of power, but precisely the infinity of his transcendence. This infinity, stronger than murder, already resists us in his face, is his face, is the primordial *expression*, is the first word: "you shall not commit murder"' (1969: 199; italics in original). Ethics is inaugurated in the transcendence of the face *outside* the dialectics of the face-to-face. The expression of the face, the face that speaks the first word of ethical relation, is an epiphany that imposes an inviolable limit on how ontologically pervasive is the place of secular interiority where the economy of power, knowledge and violence constitutive of the dialectical encounter with the other is put into play. The face *points to* this place of exteriority *from which* the epiphany of ethics arrives. Levinasian ethics is therefore a cartography of transcendence that is committed to defending the sovereignty of the face over the place of its unkillable (though not untorturable) presence.

It is important that we understand the ontological division that Levinas imposes over the dialectical economy of struggle in the face-to-face encounter with the other, on the one hand, and on the other the place of transcendence from which this struggle is threatened with the dissolution of its reciprocal exchange of violence and power: 'the epiphany of the face is ethical. The struggle this face can threaten *presupposes* the transcendence of expression. The face threatens the eventuality of a struggle, but this threat does not exhaust the epiphany of infinity, does not formulate its first word. War presupposes peace, the antecedent and non-allergic presence of the Other; it does not represent the first event of the encounter' (1969: 199; italics in original). As important as what Levinas *is* saying here is what he is *not* saying, for there in the caveats that he places on what the face does and does not represent are the logical fault lines of Levinasian ethics, particularly as they pertain to the ethics of language that Levinas goes on to articulate as essential to the revelation of ethical transcendence. Levinas is clear: ethics is not a discourse of philosophical invention, subjective commitment, or political design. Ethics simply *is* by transcendental fiat, and it *is* as such in so far as Levinas can successfully build an ontological edifice of transcendence on the basis of the *a priori* presupposition that war is preceded by peace, that behind the face of the other is a trace of the absolute otherness of the face as such. Ethics is the ontological guarantee of its own illimitability as a discourse of transcendence. The tautology that grounds ethics in the presupposition of peace is avoided, Levinas insists, by attributing its constitutive possibility to the image of the face *qua* plenipotentiary of ethics in the finite struggle of relation. There *is* only ethics – the event of ethics, the event of justice – where there is dialectical struggle in the encounter with the other. There is no transcendent reality to ethics if it is not preceded, *in the time of its epiphanic exposure*, by the face-to-face encounter with the other. Violence is disarmed by the face of the other not because the body and person of the other cannot be negated and destroyed, but because it gestures to the transcendence of the outside, to the infinite alterity of the other that exceeds the mortal facticity of the other: 'there is here a relation not with a very great resistance, but with something absolutely *other*: the resistance of what has no resistance – the ethical resistance' (1969: 199).

Levinas is careful here not to rely solely on an ungrounded presupposition of the impossibility of annihilating the infinite alterity of the other. Although Levinasian ethics originates in a *place* of radical transcendence (a place of peace), it commences *in time* where there is violence and resistance between self and other: 'infinity presents itself as a face in the ethical resistance that paralyses my powers and from the depths of defenceless eyes rises firm and absolute in its nudity and destitution. The comprehension of this destitution and this hunger establishes the proximity of the other. But thus the epiphany of infinity is expression and discourse' (1969: 199–200). The ultimate determination that 'language is justice' is predicated on language being coterminous with the measurement of proximity that opens up between self and other in the face-to-face encounter of violence and struggle (1969: 213). Language is the displaced Other of self and other, the exteriority of place where the measurement of the proximity that separates self and the other, having come into contact in an economy of struggle, locates the terms and conditions of overcoming separation in a relation of nonviolent conversation. Language is the gaze of humanity that pinpoints the ethical relation as a relation mediated by words and speech rather than violence and death. Justice, for Levinas, is the possibility, mediated through language, of belonging to humanity and of participating in the widening gaze of its vision:

> This is why the relation with the Other, discourse, is not only the putting into question of my freedom, the appeal coming from the other to call me to responsibility, is not only the speech by which I divest myself of the possession that encircles me by setting forth an objective and common world, but is also sermon, exhortation, the prophetic word. By essence the prophetic word responds to the epiphany of the face, doubles all discourse not as a discourse about moral themes, but as an irreducible movement of a discourse which by essence is aroused by the epiphany of the face inasmuch as it attests to the presence of the third party, the whole of humanity, in the eyes that look at me. (1969: 213)

What would literature have to do with opening up the space of this gaze, the presence in language of the *whole of humanity*? For literature to be ethical, its engagement with language must be aimed at precluding discourse from the closure of proximity, the cessation of dialogue, and the refusal of alterity by the violence and force of its attraction to signification. Levinas is suspicious of the ethics of literature, however, not because literature either distracts or precludes language from answering its essential call to justice, but because if literature were to act ethically on language in this way, literature would be in violation of what Levinas concedes is the essence of literature, its essential responsibility and dwelling in the space of its aesthetic sovereignty.

In one of the concluding sections of *Totality and Infinity*, Levinas reiterates the nonethical responsibilities of art and literature that he had first laid out in *Existence and Existents*. Writing under the sub-heading 'Against the Philosophy of the Neuter', Levinas charges Hegel, Heidegger and none other than Maurice Blanchot with foreclosing the transcendence of ethics by mobilising the concept of 'the Neuter' to announce 'the end of philosophy. For they exalt the obedience that no face commands. Desire in the spell of the Neuter, said to have been revealed to the Presocratics, or desire interpreted as need, and thus bound to the essential violence of action, dismisses philosophy and is gratified only in art or in politics' (1969: 298). Levinas accuses a line of thinking that culminates in Blanchot of establishing too cosy a relationship with violence to be able to separate violence from the essential nonviolence of philosophical thinking. Levinas is convinced that the ethical discourse he has constructed in *Totality and Infinity* has broken decisively 'with the philosophy of the Neuter: with the Heideggerian Being of the existent whose impersonal neutrality the critical work of Blanchot has so much contributed to bring out' (1969: 298). For the purposes of demonstrating the usefulness of Levinasian ethics for reading Beckett, we can take Levinas at his word in the distinction he maintains between his own thinking and the thinking of Blanchot (and before him Hegel and Heidegger), and therefore question if the thought of the Neuter does not in fact bring us into closer proximity with what is happening – with *how it is* – in a work like *How It Is* that is so manifestly about such questions as human relation, language and violence that likewise interest Levinas and Blanchot. The question is this: does the work of literature constitute an opportunity for interrupting the anonymous utterance of neutered speech (the narrative voice)? Has the writing of *How It Is* discovered a way out of the eternal return of terror wherein there is no resistance of alterity to the violence of speech? Does the writing of *How It Is* put an end to this speech, or does it prolong it? Is its desire to have done with this speech the very catalyst of this speech's unending return?

Whereas Levinas predicates peace and justice on the 'aptitude for speech', i.e. on 'the eschatological vision' that 'breaks with the totality of wars and empires in which one does not speak', Blanchot is far more circumspect in recognising that through the simple act of refusing to have faith in 'the eschatological vision', speech cannot be abstracted from its inextricable link with violence (Levinas 1969: 23). This is perhaps what makes Blanchot a more perceptive thinker of twentieth-century modernity than Levinas given that as a distinct historical epoch the twentieth century consisted not so much in a repetition of discrete acts of violence, but rather in a fundamental transformation of violence into radical violence, of violence into terror. Levinas's theologically overdetermined faith in the overcoming of violence is logically consistent with how the not-yet-terror of violence operates. Violence is a finite phenomenon, and as such it is the responsible task of a philosophical ethics to work out the conditions whereby violence can be repurposed as the violence that dethrones the subject of violence from the totality and ground of its ontological continuity. In a world overdetermined by violence, this is an important and realistic task (however difficult), but in a world overdetermined by war and terror, one that does not lend itself to the transcendental presupposition of nonviolence and peace, it is a task that must re-evaluate all of its conditions and methods of possibility, and particularly its faith in the ethical power of language, speech and discourse.

Beckett's writing challenges the theory of the transcendence of peace by holding the place of peace ransom in a narrative of 'how there are three of us four a million and there I am always was with Pim Bom and another and 999997 others journeying alone rotting alone martyring and being martyred oh moderately listlessly a little blood a few cries life above in the light a little blue little scenes for the thirst *for the sake of peace*' (*HII* 127; my italics). The difficulty of transcribing a Levinasian ethics of language onto the narrative sequence of *How It Is* inheres in the fact that the events recited in the narrative are being recited according to a voice that has not ever ceased speaking. Beckett pulls the ontological rug out from under the temporal (and therefore subsequently the spatial) dimension of Levinasian ethics where the expression, *the first word*, of the face is pronounced in an instant of temporal interruption. The place between self and other wherein language *qua* justice would intervene as the gaze of the humanity that mediates proximity in the face-to-face relation is a claustrophobic place in Beckett's writing, for *when the panting stops* there is no persistence of proximity's opening for *veritable conversation* to commence:

> so many words so many lost one every three two every five first the sound then the sense same ratio or else not one not one lost I hear all understand all and live again have lived again I don't say above in the light among the shades in search of shade I say YOUR LIFE HERE in a word my voice otherwise nothing therefore nothing otherwise my voice there my voice so many words strung together [. . .] (*HII* 95)

> YOUR LIFE HERE long pause YOUR LIFE HERE good and deep long pause this dead soul what appal I can imagine YOUR LIFE HERE unfinished for murmur light of day light of night little scene HERE to the quick and someone kneeling or huddled in a corner in the gloom

The Writing of *How It Is* 167

start of little scene in the gloom HERE HERE to the bone the nail breaks quick another in the furrows HERE HERE howls thumps the whole face in the mud mouth nose no more breath and howls still never saw that before his life here howls in the black air and the mud like an old infant's never to be stifled good try again HERE HERE to the marrow howls to drink the solar years no figures until at last good he wins life here this life he can't [. . .] (*HII* 96)

Beckett withdraws the possibility of speech from the place of conversation and replaces it with the materialisation of writing on the body of Pim. There is no doubting the desire for conversation here in the encounter with Pim. However, because the ancient voice is so adept at hijacking the place of conversation and subsuming it with the senselessness of its murmuring words, the narrator is denied the ethical luxury of conversing with Pim through the immaterial (the unmuddied) medium of speech. To speak, Blanchot writes, is 'to give up breath (to run out of breath) rather than to breathe. To speak, in this sense, an ironic sense, is indeed to have the last word, to have it in order no longer to have it' (*SNB* 90). For there to be ethics, then, there must be a last word, for only on the basis of the opening in speech that the last spoken word inscribes can the expression of the face interject the first word of ethics. Were it not for the imperious murmuring of the ancient voice, Beckett's paratactic writing would be in service of the last word opening up a place for the epiphanic first word, but because the ancient voice is ubiquitously here, because the invitation of its dictatorial recommencement is signed at every instant of the narrator's loss (its forfeiture) of breath *when the panting stops*, the only option still available in the dialogue with Pim for seizing on the last word is the act of writing. The narrator deploys the tactic of writing in order to usurp the last word of his speech, thereby preserving its ethical possibility. Paradoxically, Levinasian ethics has no place in *How It Is* because writing in *How It Is* spells out the place – *to the bone the nail breaks quick another* – of the impossibility of conversation. 'Such is, then,' according to Blanchot, 'the dispersed violence of writing, a violence by which speech is always already set apart, effaced in advance and no longer restored, violence, it is true, that is not natural and that also prevents us, dying, from dying a natural death' (*SNB* 90).

Blanchot is perplexed that for Levinas the ethical horizon of conversation is so philosophically comprehensible, and it is so because what mediates the otherwise unmediated relation of transcendence between self and other (*autrui*) in the face-to-face is for Levinas the accompanying presence of speech that equalises the ontological playing field of being in this relation. For Levinas, the threat of violence attached to relation is neutralised through speech, such that when the self is in the presence of the other, of the alterity of the other, turning to speech as the chosen method of being-in-relation becomes the signature of the ethical event *par excellence*. Before the self and the other enter into the ethical relation by opting for speech over violence, however, and this is really where Blanchot's critique of Levinasian ethics begins, they are faced with the irrevocable realisation that subsuming the ethical encounter is a closed interiority that denies that the self and other are *a priori* equal in terms of either social or ontological status.[4] Levinas presupposes the exteriority of peace as the asymptotic horizon towards which human relations that are otherwise ordinarily steeped in totality seek to revert. Blanchot denies precisely the *a priori* of exteriority. In the context of the human relation, Blanchot is committed to an ontology of juridical materialism, which trumps his undeniable sympathy with Levinas's ethical transcendentalism:

> it suffices, in whatever regime, to have heard the 'dialogue' between a man presumed innocent and the magistrate who questions him to what this equality of speech means when it is based upon an inequality of culture, condition, power, and fortune. But each of us, and at every moment, either is or finds himself in the presence of a judge. All speech is a word of command, of terror, of seduction, of resentment, flattery, or aggression; *all speech is violence* – and to pretend to ignore this in claiming to dialogue is to add liberal hypocrisy to the dialectical optimism according to which war is no more than another form of dialogue. (*IC* 81; my italics)

It is not at all certain, in other words, that the drive to equality and justice that Levinas attributes to ethical speech is not after all a benevolently unwitting precipitation of speech into violence. What determines the ethics or non-ethics of speech, i.e. speech as pathway to peace or speech as overture to violence, exceeds both the power and the responsibility of partners in dialogue to predict and control. To think otherwise is to risk attributing too much conscious control of subjects over the social, political and historical narratives of violence that precede and colour each and every one of their choices, acts and responsibilities. We fundamentally misunderstand complicity in acts of violence and injustice if we do not see that between self and other there presides powerful cultural narratives of inequality, suspicion and resentment, otherwise the worst acts of violence that humanity has committed would be all too easily attributable to the monstrously aberrant choices of individuals, institutions and states. We would fundamentally misunderstand, in other words, that the possibility of such choices remains lurking in the background of the continuing narratives we have in common. In a situation where the anonymous speech of a continuing narrative precedes the subjectivity of the subject, where the subject who speaks in *How It Is* appears only to speak by 'lending their lips to an anonymous utterance of history' (Levinas 1969: 23), all that can be hoped for is that the violence of writing intervenes so that the ethical possibility of human relation is kept alive and that the distance between the narrative and narrator does not capitulate to the genocidal terror of absolute commensurability. The promise of deploying language and speech as principles of equalisation between self and other cannot in fact guarantee that equalisation – a relation of the equality of differences between self and other – does not devolve into the catastrophe of neutralisation given that self and other never enter into relation freed from the *a priori* of inequality and violence that likewise precedes our being in social, political and historical existence with others.

According to Blanchot, it is because Levinas privileges speech (the act of conversation) over writing (the space of literature) that he is able to limit the danger that language exerts over both the body of the other and the place of radical exteriority wherein the face of the other is transcendentally inscribed. In writing, the essential question is not that of responding to the invocation of speech that the encounter with the other demands as the precondition of a conversational ethics; rather, it is a question of responding first and foremost to language *as such*, and not to either language or speech as the vanishing intermediary between self and other. Language circumscribes speech in the space of a solipsistic interiority where the only outlet of expression is the outlet called writing, the outlet, namely, that does not necessarily presuppose a relation outside of language. Literature and writing are indifferent to Levinasian ethics precisely because their relation is not primordially with the other, but with the *presence* and *place* of language *qua* this relation of non-relation that the encounter with the other only really exposes after the fact. Blanchot distinguishes himself from Levinas by substituting alterity *qua* other for alterity *qua* 'presence itself; the presence of the infinite', and this presence is the presence of a language that does not, or more exactly that *cannot* privilege ethical speech in conversation *with* the other over the perpetration of radical violence *against* the other that all speech risks precipitating (IC 59).

The human relation in its primacy, in other words, is not an immediate relation with the other. It is, more precisely, a relation with the place of the other, the place of a radical opening between the self and the other where there are not only no guarantees that the other is not a threat that must be confronted with violence, but also where it is necessary that the threatening horizon of the other be maintained so that the possibility of speech *with* the other can be presented precisely as a possibility. Where there is no possibility of violence *against* the other, there is no possibility of speech *with* the other:

> – One would have to say, then, that man facing man like this has no choice but to speak or to kill.
> – It is perhaps the summary brutality of this alternative that would best help us approach such an instant: should the self ever come under this command – speech or death – it will be because it is in the *presence* of *autrui*.
> – But we should also have to say, then, that the absolute distance that 'measures' the relation of *autrui* to me is what calls forth in man the exercise of absolute power: the power to give death. Cain killing Abel is the self that, coming up against the transcendence of *autrui* (what in the other exceeds me absolutely and that is well represented in biblical history by the incomprehensible inequality of divine favor), attempts to confront it by resorting to the transcendence of murder. (IC 61; italics in original)

How do we approach the instant when sites of mediation between self and other dissolve and the human relation is exposed in the full splendour and strangeness of its naked vulnerability? It is when the self finds itself confronted with the presence of the other that it is forced to resort to the command that the other submit to either speech or death. Otherwise, the self will have before it a presence that threatens to usurp the very place of presence that the self and the other all of a sudden share. Without any laws of mediation, any codes of conduct guiding the self and the other in the sacred space of confrontation, the self comes before the other armed with nothing but language and violence to decide on how the relation will continue. The event of the presence of the other, the being-made-present of the other *in the place* of its sudden appearance, is thus what is *most terrible* about the human relation. What is so 'terrifying' about confronting this alternative, in other words, is the absence of external guidance – the absence of ethical or theological lodestars of transcendence – for deciding if the presence of the other is an occasion for speech or violence. 'I stand before the other person', explains Kevin Hart, 'unmediated by anything in the realm of the possible, and must acknowledge that the situation is terrifying' (2004: 208).

The instant of the human relation does not end here for Blanchot. Blanchot's emphasis on the *presence* of the other, the substitution in the place of the other with the presence of the other's alterity, fundamentally transforms the relation between self and other into a relation between self and the *alterity* of the other, its *presence* as radically unknowable and infinitely unapproachable. Suddenly, it is no longer the other who commands my attention, who solicits either a violent or a peaceful response, but the *place* of alterity in which the other stands as its bonded plenipotentiary. The instant of the human relation is marked not only by the abrupt encounter with the command to speak or to kill, but also by the substitution in the place of the other with the alterity of place wherein the other resides: 'as soon as the presence of the other in *autrui* is not received by me as the movement through which the infinite comes to me, as soon as this presence closes around *autrui* as a property of *autrui* established in the world, as soon as it ceases to give rise to speech, the earth ceases to be vast enough to contain at the same time *autrui* and myself, and it is necessary that one of the two reject the other – absolutely' (*IC* 61).

The human relation subsists in precisely this terrifying interval where the presence of the other precipitates the absolute power to speak or kill, that is to say, the absolute power to eliminate the presence of the other through either the annihilating ontological touch of language or the mortal violence of murder. The other's refusal to speak opens it up to a vulnerability that necessarily risks the terrifying reply of absolute violence. The power that the human relation bequeaths to the self in relation to the other is a power that is nevertheless powerless to seize onto presence and eliminate it or signify it such as it is *as such*. The victim of power is the other, and not its place, not its presence. Because its presence persists, however, because the place of the other will return and return again in the place of language, there is no way of ceasing to enter into human relation with the prospect of radical violence against alterity as one of its constitutive possibilities.

Presence is immune to violence, but this does not mean that violence cannot still act on presence as a conduit for reintroducing violence back into dialectical relation with the signification of the other. Presence represents the infinite distance that separates self and other. It is this distance that is *terrifying* and that requires either speech or violence if it is to be crossed (if the abyss of presence is to be traversed). The instant of the human relation lasts only as long as it takes to decide if it will be violence or speech that intervenes between self and other. If violence overpowers speech absolutely, then the relation quite simply comes to an end, but if speech just so happens to win out, or if violence fails in silencing speech absolutely, the relation continues, but it continues by being subject to the threat of violence that continues to be meted out through the dialectical measurement of relation: 'Such would be the speech that measures the relation of man placed face to face with man when there is no other choice than to speak or to kill. A speech as grave, perhaps, as the death it diverts. The alternative speech/murder is not the simple exclusion of the one by the other, as though it were a matter of choosing once and for all between a good speech and a bad death. What sort of speech is this?' (*IC* 62).

The answer that Blanchot's interlocutor gives helps us articulate the value of 'terror' as it is distinguished in *The Infinite Conversation* from what is 'most terrible' in the human relation. If the human relation, such as it presented itself at the very beginning of the section titled 'Keeping to Words', was 'most terrible, but without terror', now that the conversation has progressed it becomes possible to extrapolate the implicit significance (marked by negativity) of terror to the human relation (*IC* 59). Terror, as Blanchot is using it here, would be the speech of measurement that is prompted by what is 'most terrible' about the sacred encounter between self and other. The human relation, the very neutrality of relation, is as terrible as it is intolerable, as unknowable as it is uninhabitable. For this reason, the human relation is just an instant (or instance) of unmediated relation, interrupted by the terror that speaks from out of the grisly alternative *to speak or to kill*:

> – [. . .] What sort of speech is this?
> – This isn't the moment for us to give an account of it. But I will say two things: first, if speech is weighty, it is because, being bare presence, it is what lays presence bare, what thus exposes it to radical violence in reducing it to the fragility of what is without power. To speak at the level of weakness and of destitution – at the level of affliction – is perhaps to challenge force, but also to attract force by refusing it. And second: in this situation, either to speak or to kill, speech does not consist in speaking, but first of all in maintaining the movement of this *either . . . or*; it is what founds the alternative. To speak is always to speak from out of this interval *between* speech and radical violence, separating them, but maintaining each of them in a relation of vicissitude.
> – From which we must conclude that if the relation of man placed in the presence of man is terrible, it is because it confines us within this alternative: either speak or kill, and because, in this alternative, speech is no less grave than death, with which it is conjoined as its reverse side. (IC 62)

Blanchot is not content with the diametric distinction between speaking and killing that the human relation nevertheless maintains in reserve. Through this exchange, which consists in one interlocutor pushing the other to articulate more precisely what is being proposed about the relation between speaking and killing, language and violence, a wedge is thrust between speech and speaking. Neutral speech, speech that comes from the abyssal outside (the most terrifying interiority) of non-relation, is transformed into an *image* of speech that crystallises the alternatives of speech and violence into a relation immune from dialectical separation. To speak without the possibility of violence is to presuppose a relation of unequal inferiority with the other. Either the other transcends my power to kill – i.e. the other is the absolute Other of divine transcendence – or the other is pathetically unworthy of my power to kill (a power that the self nevertheless maintains in reserve). The speech that preserves speaking and killing in 'a relation of vicissitude' is abstracted as much from its utterance by the self as it is from its retort by the other. Self and other, in the speech of the interval, in the desert presence of paratactic delay, designate the flesh and blood border posts between which this speech occurs. Blanchot calls this space *Autrui*, the space (the outside, the fragmentary) of dispossession and unworking, and it is 'there where detour reigns. The presence turned toward me is thus still a presence of separation, of what to me is presence even as I am separated from it, distant and turned away. And, for me, to be facing autrui is always to be in the abrupt presence, without intermediary, of the one who turns toward me in the infinite approach of the detour' (*IC* 62).

In relating the ubiquitous place of paratactic delay in *How It Is* to what Blanchot conceptualises later in *The Infinite Conversation* as the '*delay* that is the site of speech' (*IC* 187; italics in original), we are likewise delivered over to a place in speech where speech is 'infinitely hazardous', that is to say, where 'it is encompassed by terror' (*IC* 187):

> Radical violence is its fringe and its halo; it is one with the obscurity of the night, with the emptiness of the abyss, and so doubtful, so dangerous that this question incessantly returns: why the exigency of such a language? What have we to do with it? What does it bring us in the frightening silence that announces extreme violence but is also the instant at which violence goes silent, becomes silence? What is this communication without community that no power – that is to say, no comprehension – no human or divine presence can anticipate? Would it not be, alluring without attraction, *desire* itself?: the desire become song that opens hell up to Orpheus when what becomes embodied is the absolute of separation, all the while remaining the depth and detour of interval? (*IC* 187)

Blanchot identifies this place *encompassed by terror* as the place where 'speech begins' (*IC* 187), and although the beginning and the beginning again of speech is often cited as a necessary precondition of ending the mute brutality associated with violence, the implication of Blanchot's linking of speech and radical violence precisely where *speech begins, in the infinite approach of the detour,* is that the commencement and recommencement of speech by paratactic fiat is condemned to complicity in consolidating the threat of violence wherever discourse reigns. There is perhaps no better expression of the terror of literature than the designation of writing as the act *par excellence* of vicissitudinal undecidability between speech and radical violence, and thus it is worth quoting

Blanchot's words again where he insists that 'to speak is always to speak from out of this interval *between* speech and radical violence, separating them, but maintaining each of them in a relation of vicissitude' (*IC* 62; italics in original). The desire of the anonymous voice that speaks incessantly in *How It Is* is the desire for the collapse of this relation of vicissitude, for so long as this relation remains open, the circle of victims and tormentors, crawlers and abandoned will not yet have been closed. Conversely, however, the demand for this relation of vicissitude is precisely the demand *that there be radical violence*.

Can such a demand be ethical? It most likely cannot, which is why it is perhaps more appropriate to affirm the terror that lives in it, the terror that precipitates its survival, the terror that encompasses it, the terror that doubles as the terror of literature. We can therefore diagnose *How It Is* as a narrative of terror in the sense that it not only exposes its speakers and its victims to their naked vulnerability in the place of language, but also that it renders their escape from this place complicit in the ontological necessity of this place's return. To disavow this place is to give tacit approval to the imperiousness of the voice and of the narrative that it destines for recitation. Beckett's paratactic writing of *How It Is* is the writing of the withdrawal but also of the return of alterity *from* and *to* the self-same place of the violence of written speech. *How It Is* presents us with a narrative situation torn between privileging the relation between self and other – tormentor and victim – and self and place: 'never anyone never knew anyone always ran fled elsewhere some other place my life above places paths nothing else brief places long paths the quickest way or a thousand detours' (*HII* 78). Entering into the place of the *most terrible* human relation is not a choice. We are always already enlisted ('thrown', in Heideggerian parlance) in such relations by virtue of our common belonging to humanity, our belonging to humanity *through* language, but it is because of this necessity of belonging that Blanchot impresses on us the ever-present threat and reality of violence in every relation in which our choices, our desires, our responsibilities and our dialogues in face of the other are subsumed. Because 'the human relation, as it affirms itself in its primacy, is terrible' (*IC* 59), and because what is so terrible about this relation is that it precludes predicating of either speech or language the ethical status of an intermediary between myself and the other, the only affirmation that can be made about this relation translates into 'the hard language of exigency: one must speak' (*IC* 65).

What is *most terrible* about *How It Is*, then, is not yet simply that a nameless figure should be given a name like 'Pim' so that it can be invited into the violence of dialogue. What is *most terrible* is what is poised to happen in *How It Is* if one like 'Pim' should refuse to identify with the name and to speak the words that have been assigned to it (etched into his back). Pim is nothing more than the name given to 'a fellow-creature more or less but man or woman girl or boy cries have neither' (*HII* 54). It is the name given to an anonymous body that before being nominated as 'Pim' 'had no name any more than I so I gave him one the name Pim for more commodity more convenience' (*HII* 59). Like the name 'BOM scored by finger-nail' into the back of the narrator during its time of victimisation (*HII* 60), so too is Pim's name carved into his back 'with the nail then of the right index in great capitals' (*HII* 70). This is done not simply so that Pim will know his name, that learning to call himself by the name 'Pim' will appeal 'to him he was calling him by it himself in the end' (*HII* 59), but so that in having a name he will have a place in the arena of communication where his ontological training is being (has been and will be) conducted. What is *most terrible*, then, is that dialogue and the invitation to dialogue are complicit in circumscribing the anonymous other in the place of language where there is no protection against the violence of speech, and where the other is therefore most vulnerable to the possibility of its absolute negation.

The *narrative* of terror that *How It Is* enacts is the introduction of temporality into this instant of what is *most terrible* in the human relation, and what it reveals is that where temporality persists, there is no way of maintaining Blanchot's relation of vicissitude on the threshold of the decision on speech or radical violence. In giving Pim his name, in taking advantage of Pim's vulnerability to speech, the narrator invites what Blanchot calls the 'mortal play of the word' into the space of dialogue with Pim (*SNB* 38). The supreme catastrophe of *How It Is* remains the evacuation of the human relation and the accession to ontological sovereignty of the voice of us all, the anonymous voice of interminable utterance. The only hope left to the narrator for avoiding this outcome is the hope of company with Pim, but such a hope is irremediably dashed against the exigency that Pim must speak as a conversant in ethical relation. What is *most terrible* in the human relation is truly what is most unbearable. Not being able to tolerate the silence of Pim's presence one instant longer, the narrator impatiently withdraws Pim from the exteriority of his presence and sets Pim's pedagogical torture into motion. What does Pim gain by being nominated into discourse by and with the narrator? Blanchot might have an answer: 'not the right to be there in person; on the contrary the terrifying obligation by which what would like to preserve itself in the name of a private unhappiness is drawn out into the public square, into the cold and the impoverishment of the outside, with nothing that can assure any refuge' (SNB 38). If Pim (or more precisely Pim's presence) does not comply with the wish of the narrator that he should speak as the narrator requires him to speak, then Pim will have become the embodiment of vulnerability to precisely the mortal play of the word as Blanchot so ominously articulates it.

That the narrator should retain control over the place of language in the aftermath of its torturous assault on Pim is therefore an unequivocally intolerable scenario, for it would entail accepting Pim's continuous victimisation there where Pim's vulnerability in the place of language is laid bare again and again in the demand for speech. At the same time, that the narrator should lose control completely over the place of language, that it should acquiesce to its forfeiture of power over this place to the epic murmuring voice that it continuously recites, would necessitate that what has happened to Pim and what will happen to the narrator be excluded from all memory and anticipation of its narrative (re)inscription. If it turns out that the narrator is alone, that the final words of *How It Is* come to a close by confirming that the narrator is without company as it quotes the words of the preceding narrative, and thus that its voice is after all synonymous from beginning to end with the imperious 'voice of us all quaqua', then the prospective ontological coup of this voice will have been irreversibly executed and the narrator condemned to the solipsistic hell of its eternal citation (HII 76). Should it transpire that 'all these calculations yes explanations yes the whole story from beginning to end yes completely false yes', then what we will have witnessed in reading *How It Is* is the absolute disaster of continuity triumphing over discontinuity, the totalitarian terror of the citational voice acceding to a position of absolute ontological sovereignty over life in the mud (HII 144).

The threat of Pim's refusal to speak confronts the narrator as the threat of the voice's continuation, which prompts it to expedite a method for the commencement of dialogue designed to avoid precisely this refusal. One such method is to 'stab' Pim 'simply in the arse that is to say speak and he will say anything what he can whereas proof I need proof so stab him in a certain way signifying answer once and for all which I do therefore what an improvement how I've improved' (*HII* 71). The narrator commences a methodical programme of violence and torture with the sole purpose of extracting 'in the case of Pim a few words what he can now and then I am not a monster [. . .] merely that he sing or speak and not even this rather than that in the early stages merely speak what he will what he can now and then a few words nothing more' (*HII* 64–5). Prior to the advent of Part II 'with Pim', however, the narrator can be sure of only one fact of its life in the mud: that the murmuring of the ancient voice is unceasing. Accordingly, if the ancient murmur is to cease, as indeed it must for the narrator to confirm that a denouement of terror like the one against which Arendt cautions has not yet transpired, it will have to be because in the approaching encounter with Pim, Pim has engaged the narrator precisely in a conversation to put an end to the imperious voice of epic citation. Part II 'with Pim' is about Pim's capacity to interrupt the citational speech of the narrative voice, which the narrator is otherwise condemned to passively recite. In order to do so Pim must overcome the power imbalance through which he is victimised and tortured by this narrator who demands precisely that Pim speak in commencement of an ethical economy of conversation with the narrator. The narrator is reacting to a situation where proof of the possibility of a life that the 'ancient voice in me not mine' aspires to annihilate can only be predicated on extracting speech from the *uncorpsed* body of Pim *in* and *at* every instant of the paratactic delay of its iteration (*HII* 7).

Pim is not a lifeless corpse, and as such he is confronted by the narrator as a subject that is immediately vulnerable not only to violence, but also to the demand for speech that violence in this case is being implemented to pronounce. Pim's vulnerability to violence is the common denominator in his presentation to the narrator as a victim of torture and a perpetrator of speech. Pim is nameless, faceless and mute at the instant he meets with the narrator. Torturing Pim only up to the limit where Pim would lose the power to speak and therefore become 'a true corpse untorturable' is the narrator's tactical way of confirming that in crossing the narrative divide into Part II 'with Pim', the words at its disposal have not been divested of the power to coerce dialogue outside of the anonymous utterances of the ancient voice (*HII* 101). The narrator's exchange with Pim is thus not 'sadism pure and simple' (*HII* 63). The paratactic unfolding of its textual dwelling in the presence of Pim – 'suddenly like all that was not then is I go not because of the shit and vomit something else not known not said whence preparatives sudden series subject object subject object quick succession and away' (*HII* 11) – ensures that every word spoken in conversation with Pim exposes the narrator to the 'impenetrable dark' of the intervals between words, which calls upon yet another word (*we're talking of words*, after all) to jump-start again and again the narrative of Pim's ontological vulnerability (*HII* 26). Dialogue in *How It Is* thus begins with a discovery that is indeed far more terrifying than just that the 'encountered companion can speak and sing', as Ziarek argues (1995: 181). The terrible discovery that unveils the imperative of speech, the *hard language of exigency*, rather, is that the companion can speak and sing *because* the companion is vulnerable to violence and cruelty, and vice versa: 'the voice extorted a few words life because of cry that's the proof good and deep no more is needed a little cry all is not dead' (*HII* 122).

We can read the paratactic delays that punctuate the narrative discourse of *How It Is*, 'its paratactic rhetoric', explains Smith, as enabling the work to 'open a space for alterity to appear without being submitted to aesthetic or representational synthesis' (2008: 357). Such would be the ethical trace that attaches itself to the unbroken series of paratactic delays in *How It Is*, the trace that keeps the place of language open to the unnamable, unrepresentable, and ideally the ontologically inviolable presence of alterity. But there is an alternative reading of the ethical significance of this place in language of paratactic delay, a reading obliging that we be attentive to the persistence of the ancient murmuring voice that the paratactic delays are powerless to muzzle precisely because they double as the unending source of its repetitive resurgence. This voice is pervasive, but its speech is not always perceptible. It is only heard, the narrator tells us, 'when the panting stops' (*HII* 113), and yet there is no doubting that behind the narrator's panting in the mud is the murmuring persistence of what the narrator, even when it pants, can never convince itself of having delivered completely to silence. One of the reasons why the narrator craves the encounter with Pim is that dialogue with Pim is a possible way to suture the paratactic gaps in discourse wherein the narrator risks dwelling eternally and terrifyingly alone with nothing but the murmuring voice to keep it company: 'only me yes alone yes with my voice yes my murmur yes when the panting stops yes all that holds yes panting yes worse and worse no answer WORSE AND WORSE yes' (*HII* 146).

It is ominous enough that in all the little instants where Pim threatens to reply with silence to the narrator's regime of 'basic stimuli one sing nails in armpit two speak blade in arse three stop thump on skull four louder pestle on kidney' (*HII* 69), there is the prospect, as Blanchot puts it, 'that there is nothing but desert', that *'the desert is growing'* between the narrator and Pim (*IC* 171; italics in original). Worse than silence becoming 'more and more longer silences vast tracts of time we at a loss more and more he for answers I for questions sick of life' would be that the silence of Pim, the power not to speak that Pim holds in reserve, will disappear altogether and the ancient murmuring voice that impatiently awaits either Pim's temporary departure or his permanent annihilation will re-usurp the place of speech and subject the narrator once and for all to the totalising violence of its murderously incessant speech (*HII* 73). The terror that the 'Stalinist functionaries themselves' feared, we will recall from Arendt, is reflected in the imperious ubiquity of this voice that never ceases (2001: 55). We can sanction the narrator for the method it adopts in extorting speech from Pim, but we should perhaps be cautious in sanctioning its *desire* that Pim must speak *by whatever means necessary*, for the alternative to Pim's withdrawal from this dangerous place of speech is perhaps something far more disquieting. The paratactic delay exposes speech to the place *in* speech where speech is not yet decipherable from silence. Accordingly, 'what I did to him' can be met not just by 'what he said to me', but also by the return of the ancient voice that threatens me *from the place where Pim is silent* (*HII* 16). The threat of Pim's silence, in other words, exposes the narrator to what Blanchot describes in the desert-space of language as the 'decisive test' of the human relation (*IC* 68), the test, that is to say, of maintaining the paratactic delay wherein we encounter 'our companion in an infinite and infinitely deserted space where, by a marvelous chance, he had suddenly appeared at our side' (*IC* 171). What is the decisive test? Blanchot: 'Whoever has reached the desert where there reigns the absence of relations exposes himself to this test, and exposes to it the one he encounters: here you must kill the companion (or let him kill you, happily the choice exists) in order to recognize and verify his presence' (*IC* 183). This is the test of language *as such* where language, speaking out of the silent interval of paratactic delay, 'outside all power to represent and to signify, [...] does not push hell back, but makes its way into it, speaking at the level of the abyss and thereby giving word to it; giving a hearing to what can have no hearing' (*IC* 183–4).

Through Blanchot, we are able to delve just a little deeper into the space of Beckett's narrative where the refusal of the ethical redemption of the terror of literature is situated most intransigently. Let us understand by the *terror of literature* the imperative, following Blanchot, to preserve the act of writing in a relation of vicissitude *between* speech and radical violence, to plunge ever deeper into the abyss of presence where speech is *not yet* decipherable from violence (*IC* 62). This is an imperative that writing dwell at the threshold of the denouement of a terror that is not to be confused with (but nor is it to be decisively separated from) the terror of literature. It is an imperative demanding that violence be welcomed into language because it foresees the catastrophe that awaits language where there is no longer any possibility of violence, for this would be the time when violence, which does not cease, has won its victory over all possibility of resistance. The terror of literature is nothing to celebrate, because violence is nothing to celebrate, but surely the terror of the imperious continuity of speech that literature fears most is something to dread. Beckett's paratactic writing of *How It Is* is a strategy that precludes the denouement of terror, but the price it pays for its success is to preserve the threat, or delay, of this denouement as the inevitable horizon towards which its writing is directed. Beckett's refusal to be unburdened of the weightiness of the past (the archive of suffering), to refuse to redirect the temporal movement of a voice that speaks from the interminable nightmare of historical temporality, derives from his tragic awareness that neither the voice nor the past can be discontinued without in the same stroke disavowing the memory and narrative of all that survives in the light of their continuation. Looking forward to the narrator's unnarratable suffering at the hands of his tormentor is the only alibi required for desiring to see this narrative and this voice terminated, but accepting that there is no outside of the time of the voice, that there is no outside of the narrative in *How It Is* – there is no outside of the catastrophe of history – commits Beckett's paratactic writing of *How It Is* ultimately to thwart the desire it continuously resurrects, namely that there *be* an otherwise than being in *How It Is*.

Notes

1. Fifield begins his book *Late Modernist Style in Samuel Beckett and Emmanuel Levinas* by diagnosing what he sees as 'the deafness of the ethical turn in literary studies to critical voices' (2013: 2). Fifield is referring in this passage to critical voices like Levinas's that do not *a priori* presume that literature is constitutively indebted to the ethical protection of alterity: 'literature for Levinas is [. . .] *un*ethical' (2013: 2; italics in original). With this counter-intuitive proposition Fifield attempts to re-read Levinas in such a way that the poetics of his philosophical style of writing converges with Beckettian formalisms around the unspeakable presence in language of alterity and otherness. What distinguishes Levinas as a theorist of literature is that Levinas's philosophical writing is designed specifically to supplement for literature's unethical shortcomings. Through a comparison of stylistics in Levinas and Beckett, Fifield goes on to argue that Beckett's proto-deconstructive credentials consist precisely in undermining Levinas's suspicions about literature's suitability for employing language ethically. In starting from what is *un*ethical about literature according to Levinas, Fifield arrives at what is decidedly *ethical* in the work of Beckett.
2. Thanks to the work of Michael Marder, we do have the option of referring to the ontological discourse of the ethical in *How It Is* as the *terror* of the ethical in recognition of how the narrator's intermediation of the ancient voice that murmurs the words recorded in the narrative, and the faceless, anonymous body of Pim, mimics how the ethical as such works, i.e. by merging the 'redoubled work of the negative that struggles on two fronts: against the unnamed singularity of the Other and against the nameless generality of the void' (Marder 2008). However, the way that Marder situates the ethical in relation to the *terror* of the ethical is through the temporalisation of the *il y a*, of 'the nameless generality of the void', and unfortunately it is not a modality of temporalisation that can be supported by the paratactic movement of *How It Is*. The temporality that Marder attributes to the terror of the ethical is closer to the diachronic temporality of the time of survival that Hägglund uses, as we have already noted, for estab-

lishing the ethics of finitude proper to deconstruction. The paratactic time of *How It Is*, rather, is more like the time of synchronic suspension to which Blanchot implicitly refers in circumscribing the primacy of the human relation.
3. In a richly detailed essay on how controversies surrounding human rights, torture, interrogation and the Algerian War informed Beckett's writing of *Comment c'est*, Adam Piette notes that 'when Beckett first started thinking about *Comment c'est*, voices were being raised in protest against the hypocrisy of a state that advocated universal human rights and practised torture in evil repetition of Gestapo brutality' (2016: 158).
4. Levinas remarks in 'The Proximity of the Other' that it was Martin Buber who first 'pushed me to engage in a phenomenology of sociality, which is more than the human. Sociality is, for me, the better-than-human. It is the good, not the makeshift of an impossible fusion. Within the alterity of the face, the for-the-other commands the I. So it is a matter, finally, of founding justice – which hides the face – upon the obligation to the face, to the extraordinary exteriority of the face' (2002: 215).

4

The Terror of Passivity in *Company*, *Ill Seen Ill Said* and *Worstward Ho*

> It is necessary to approach always closer to the moment when language will reveal its absolute power, by giving birth, through each of its feeble words, to terror.
>
> (Michel Foucault)

I

In the 1961 interview with Tom Driver, which appeared the same year *Comment c'est* was published, Beckett was asked whether or not his work dealt with the 'same facets of experience' as those that are dealt with by religion (Driver 1979: 221). Beckett replied, 'yes, for they deal with distress', and he elaborated on why this must be so:

> At a party an English intellectual – so-called – asked me why I write always about distress. As if it were perverse to do so! He wanted to know if my father had beaten me or my mother had run away from home to give me an unhappy childhood. I told him no, that I had had a very happy childhood. Then he thought me more perverse than ever. I left the party as soon as possible and got into a taxi. On the glass partition between me and the driver were three signs: one asked for help for the blind, another, help for orphans, and the third for relief for the war refugees. One does not have to look for distress. It is screaming at you in the taxis of London. (cited in Driver 1979: 221)

Although Beckett withholds expounding on the particulars of how he negotiates the migration of distress into his writing, his remarks in this interview with Driver nevertheless extend a useful interpretive foothold for readers (and audiences, viewers and listeners) by asserting that it is the sociohistorical phenomenon of distress that is responsible for the ubiquitous presence of distress in his work. Beckett's writing responds to the distress of the contemporary world, we can begin to speculate, not by providing it with redemptive or cathartic outlets of figuration through the voice(s) of literature; rather, Beckett's response to the screaming voicelessness of distress is the riskiest of responses, for it demands that his writing be complicit in precisely the distress that its narrators and its protagonists, its subjects and its figures, are constrained to endure in and by Beckett's writing. Beckett retrofits the space of literature with a responsibility to distress that is wary of becoming opportunistically parasitic (i.e. guilty of either reification or commodification) on the distress that has occurred and that continues to occur in the sociohistorical spaces outside of literature. Beckett thus intuits the ethical *a priori* of post-Second World War aesthetic and philosophical comportment as it is phrased by Adorno in the opening section of *Negative Dialectics*, namely that 'the need to lend a voice to suffering is a condition of all truth' (2005b: 17–18). The way that Beckett's writing negotiates distress, in other words, is by allowing the voicelessness of distress to cross over into literature in order to uphold the ethical imperative of lending a voice to suffering, on the one hand, and on the other by translating this voicelessness through the disfiguring language that literature singularly speaks in accordance with the modern aesthetic imperative of creatively destructive negativity.

Adorno is no doubt useful for addressing this double imperative at the level of its philosophical conceptualisation. However, the philosophical paradigm of (dialectical) negativity on which Adorno's thinking consistently relies is ultimately ill-equipped for helping us advance as far as we need to go in grappling with the particular predicament of distress that Beckett's writing faces. Michael Rothberg is perhaps right that Adorno's philosophical project is most productively assessed through its ethical-pedagogical rather than its aesthetic-theoretical contributions, for what Adorno ultimately demands of contemporary discourses of art, literature and criticism is that they collaborate in demarcating a haven of reconciliation and redemption to which the sociohistorical world can continue to turn in order not to fall irretrievably into nihilism and despair.[1] With respect specifically to Beckett, Adorno is too invested in ensuring that Beckett's writing stands firm as the 'last haven of hope' against the ideological pressures of the fascist politics of totalitarianism still lurking in the shadows (and sometimes right out in the open) of late modernity, as well as in late capitalism's dehumanising pursuit of instrumentalising virtually all aspects of public and private existence (Adorno 2005b: 381). Beckett's writing matters above so much else to Adorno (notwithstanding his comparable investment in the atonal modernism of Schoenberg or the sociopoetic negativity of Celan[2]) in so far as it keeps vigil over the historical archive of messianic possibility where the redemptive hope of reconciliation is unattainably yet everlastingly encrypted.[3]

For Adorno, as Jean-Michel Rabaté succinctly explains, 'Beckett always exemplifies the spirit of resistance in art, a spirit of obstinate ethical perseverance facing barbarism' (2010: 104). There is of course inestimable value in this view of Beckett as a literary exemplar of an aesthetics of resistance, a view that is fundamental to defending Beckett against any and all accusations of absurdity, nihilism, or even tacit indifference vis-à-vis the suffering, violence and distress of late modernity. Beckett's writings are at the vanguard of artworks that turn away from the world in disgust at the world, but they do so in the name of the world and for what they think (and perhaps know) is best for the world. The reason why we must leave Adorno behind in preference of Blanchot as we pursue Beckett's writing all the way down into the depths of the terror of literature that it approaches, however, is that Adorno's thinking is too optimistically invested in the redemptive potentialities of Beckett's writing to accommodate its admixture of compassion and complicity in and with the suffering and distress of its textual figures. If we can show that the price Beckett's writing is obliged to pay for facing up so courageously to what Terry Eagleton, echoing Adorno, describes as 'fascism's megalomaniac totalities' (2006b: 70) is the sacrificial offering of his textual figures to conditions not unlike the barbarous realities his writing exists in order to defy, then there is the very real risk that even this last haven of hope, the literary space of Beckett's writing where the unreconciled promise of reconciliation still has a chance at being glimpsed, Adorno desperately believes, may have already been thoroughly infiltrated by the crisis – the terror – of absolute dehumanisation clamouring without.

II

In his essay 'Maurice Blanchot: The Thought of the Outside', Michel Foucault praises Blanchot for exposing the dissimulating power over discourses of meaning and conceptions of truth implicit in language when language is taken hold of by the fragmentary imperative of writing:

> language, in its attentive and forgetful being, with its power of dissimulation that effaces every determinate meaning and even the existence of the speaker, in the gray neutrality that constitutes the essential place of all being and thereby frees the space of the image – is neither truth nor time, neither eternity nor man; it is instead the always undone form of the outside. [. . .] And what language *is* (not what it means, not the form in which it says what it means), what language is in its being, is that softest of voices, that nearly imperceptible retreat, that weakness deep inside and surrounding every thing and every face. (1987: 57)

Blanchot's legacy from the perspective of contemporary critical theory consists largely in the discoveries his writing and thinking made about the neutral authority of language over subverting and disrupting philosophically determinate discourses of meaning, representation and truth. Foucault first published this essay in 1966 in the journal *Critique*, and so it pre-dates Blanchot's 1980 publication of *L'écriture du désastre/The Writing of the Disaster*.[4] It is worth pointing this out in order to begin appreciating the subtle pivoting of emphasis occurring in this later text of Blanchot's. Blanchot never stops privileging the subversive powers of language and writing in his lifelong insurgency against the desires of philosophical and post-Romantic discourse for conceptual systematisation and attainment of the absolute. Nevertheless, by the time he gets around to *The Writing of the Disaster*, language and writing no longer keep exclusive watch over the thought of the outside where, as Foucault puts it, 'the sovereignty of the "I speak"' (1987: 10) is substituted with 'the void language takes as its space when', after its arrival (an immobilised movement internal to language as such) in the outside, 'it articulates itself in the *nakedness* of "I speak"' (1987: 12; my italics).

The passage from sovereignty to nakedness through the movement of language to the outside, which is the event of what is called *literature*, is a passage that, beginning most explicitly with *The Infinite Conversation* and continuing through *The Step/Not Beyond* and into *The Writing of the Disaster*, Blanchot becomes more vocal in recognising is a passage all too frequently (coercively, violently) undertaken by persons exiled by political and sociohistorical circumstances to this (non-)place of the outside. Through literature, or writing according to the fragmentary imperative, language is cut off from itself, made to trespass onto places of silent expressivity that the quotidian laws of language otherwise forbid it to go for fear that the communicative and conceptual edifices language props up (whether it is credited with this function or not) will collapse. Blanchot prefaces *The Infinite Conversation* by acknowledging that writing under the law of the fragmentary imperative is therefore 'a terrible responsibility. Invisibly, writing is called upon to undo the discourse in which, however unhappy we believe ourselves to be, we who have it at our disposal remain comfortably installed. From this point of view writing is the greatest violence, for it transgresses the law, every law, and also its own' (*IC* xii). Juxtaposing the movement of language into the outside where meaning and identity are continually effaced (*via* the violence of writing) with the movement of social and ontological dispossession experienced daily by persons classified as migrants, exiles, refugees, prisoners, *häftlings*, etc., exposes writing not only to a responsibility of establishing a relation of compassion with the dispossessed, but also to the disquieting coincidence of enacting in the space of literature the very expressions of violence responsible for dispossession in the sociohistorical arena of suffering and distress.

Blanchot is no less uncompromising in trying to accompany writing to the extreme limits of its transgressions of the laws of language and literature than he is in trying to render dispossessed persons visible at the extreme limits of their invisibility and silence (to knowledge, language, memory and compassion). Leslie Hill explains that, 'for Blanchot', to write is 'always to address the unknown other: the other in so far as it is unknown, the unknown in so far as it is radically other' (1997: 195–6). Or, as Blanchot translates the concept of the 'unknown other' in the vocabulary assembled for *The Writing of the Disaster*, to write is always to make contact with persons subject to the 'absolute passiveness of total abjection', the experience of 'dispossession' where 'the self is wrested from itself', subjected to 'the detachment whereby one is detached from detachment, or again the fall (neither chosen nor accepted) outside the self'. It is 'these situations', again according to Blanchot, situated as they are 'at the limit of the knowable', that thereby designate the 'hidden face of humanity' (*WD* 15). Blanchot decides to call these (silent) voices and these (dissimulated) faces of figures exiled to the limits of the knowable, figures of *passivity*, noting however that if such faces appear, and if such voices speak, they do so 'hardly at all of what we seek to understand by letting this characterless word be pronounced, *passivity*' (WD 15; italics in original). Addressing the 'unknown other' through writing would *ordinarily* be undertaken with a view on reversing the damage of the other's invisibility and silence perpetrated by the violences that led to the other's dispossession of visibility and speech, but because Blanchot remains ever attentive to the demand of writing's perpetration of violence against itself and language, writing's approach to passivity is necessarily always a threatening one. Writing cannot be disarmed of its propensity for disfiguration and violence. We can almost say that there is no such thing as an act of writing that did not perpetrate some measure of violence against language, image, concept or word, and consequently against its figurations of subjectivity and otherness. Nevertheless, writing cannot likewise skirt its responsibility to the 'unknown other' because it is a responsibility that writing is powerless to dispel, for it arises out of the coincidental inscription of writing and passivity in the fragmentary, inhuman *outside* of language, history and indeed our common belonging to humanity.

In the context of *The Writing of the Disaster*, the figure of passivity is therefore poised to become the epicentre of this ethical and aesthetic conundrum of the capacity for *violence against* passivity and *compassion for* passivity inherent in the act of writing. Accordingly, writing's promise to the voicelessness of passivity, or to the screaming silence of distressed subjectivities somehow still speaking to Beckett in the taxis of London, cannot preclude the possibility that writing, in delivering on its promise to passivity, will not devolve into a set of relations with passivity predicated analogously on the extortion of memory, identity and speech typical of such sociohistorical phenomena as interrogation and torture. One of the reasons we take offence to 'the use of force that we call torture', Blanchot posits in *The Infinite Conversation*, is that we sometimes realise that writing and torture are in secret alliance[5] over the necessity they both exhibit of a

> recourse to violence – always in the form of a technique – with a view to making speak. This violence, perfected or camouflaged by technique, wants one to speak, wants speech. Which speech? Not the speech of violence – unspeaking, false through and through, logically the only

one it can hope to obtain – but a true speech, free and pure of all violence. This contradiction offends us, but also unsettles us. Because in the equality it establishes, and in the contact it re-establishes between violence and speech, it revives and provokes the terrible violence that is the silent intimacy of all speaking words; and thus it calls again into question the truth of our language understood as dialogue, and of dialogue understood as a space of force exercised without violence and struggling against force. (*IC* 42–3)

The only difference (albeit a crucial one) between the recourse of writing and torture to the violence of speech is that writing, unlike the act of torture, is beholden not only to transgressing the laws that are otherwise enacted to keep us safe from violences like torture, but also to the violence of transgressing the laws of writing itself. This second order of violence responds to the literary imperative of aesthetic, linguistic and syntactic disfiguration that demands of writing that it internalise the very same violence that torture perpetrates against the tortured, against silence in the extraction of speech, as a violence that must be turned inward as well. This is the quintessential violence of questioning without end, of art defined as 'pure interrogation, rhetorical question less the rhetoric', says Beckett (*D* 91), and while sometimes this modality of questioning is applied inquisitively, at other times, and particularly in the space of the outside that writing cohabits (incommensurably) with passivity, it is deployed much more ominously, much more *inquisitorially*.

As Blanchot describes it in *The Writing of the Disaster*, this is the inquisitorial violence that circulates, as its 'fringe and its halo' (*IC* 187), we will recall from *The Infinite Conversation*, throughout the ethical relation between self and other as Levinas economises its metaphysical distributions of dialogue and power. When viewed from the perspective of the violence through which writing communes with passivity, the *place* of the unknown other, there where the other is exposed and exposes *me* through its proximity to the 'absolute nakedness' of passivity, becomes a place that 'calls me into question to the point of stripping me of myself' and where there issues forth 'the entreaty which disqualifies the me in me until it becomes *sheer torture*' (*WD* 23; my italics). Blanchot's disquisition on passivity in *The Writing of the Disaster* cannot therefore be coded in such a way that it unproblematically recalls writing to its ethical responsibility before the 'unknown other' subjected to radical dispossession, suffering and distress. Blanchot cannot help but see in the word 'responsibility' the obligation to violence to which writing is perennially subjected in its movement towards the outside of language. If writing is predicated by a responsibility to transgress every law, even and perhaps especially its own, and if this is what makes of writing the greatest violence, then in the event that an analogous form of responsibility appears elsewhere than in the space of writing, i.e. in the space of the ethics of human relation, must we not entertain that here too is an invitation to a violence no less totalising and severe in its demands? Just as the responsibility of writing to the fragmentary imperative imposes on writing an obligation to always be overturning its laws and withdrawing itself from its generic securities and protocols (the laws of genre), so too does

> *My* responsibility for the Other presuppose an overturning such that it can only be marked by a change in the status of 'me', a change in time and perhaps in language. Responsibility, which withdraws me from my order – perhaps from all orders and from order itself – responsibility, which separates me from myself (from the 'me' that is mastery and power, from the free, speaking subject) and reveals the other *in place* of me, requires that I answer for absence, for passivity. It requires, that is to say, that I answer for the impossibility of being responsible – to which it has always already consigned me by holding me accountable and also discounting me altogether. (WD 25; italics in original)

This instant of overturning and withdrawal that responsibility in the face of the other precipitates is the instant where writing and passivity converge as expressions of the fragmentary imperative that neither writing nor passivity can outmanoeuvre. Here Blanchot alights on the inappropriateness of reconciling the accursed ontological share (*pace* Bataille) of passivity with the ethico-epistemological economy (*pace* Levinas) of responsiveness to the call of the other, though he does so without rejecting that we continue to desire precisely such an event of reconciliation. Writing's exacerbation of this inappropriateness or incapacity is what subjects it to the interminable question of just why it is that writing is so shot through by this incapacity or inappropriateness.

When writing is put to the question by the violence of questioning in this way it is backed into the infinitely receding corner of responding with a modality of speech 'which cannot be seized by an affirmation, nor refused by a negation, nor raised up to possibility by interrogation, nor restored to being through a response. *It is speech as detour.* Questioning is this detour that speaks as a detour of speech' (*IC* 21; italics in original). Writing becomes fragmentary the instant it is impelled by the unendurable force of its interrogative demands to begin speaking in a voice dispelled from the community of language and speech, which must have its answers, which must have its reasons. What begins speaking, in other words, is the voice of (sociohistorical) figures of passivity that has no words expressive enough to signify or explain what it is undergoing and why subsequent to its exposure to a violence oftentimes no less extreme than the violence turned inward so ferociously on writing. Where violence is doubly imbricated in this way through writing's not-so-secretive alliance with the violence of torture and the violence of aesthetic (self-)transgression, we are forced to disclose that nothing and no one is sacred and safe in the fragmentary space of literature, least of all passive figures of dispossession and silence. So it is that if Blanchot speaks about the 'relation between writing and passivity' in *The Writing of the Disaster* (*WD* 14), and if he feels 'bound to say something about passivity' as he has likewise been bound in so many works prior to *The Writing of the Disaster* to say something about writing, then it 'is because passivity', like writing, 'matters to man without moving him over into the realm of things that matter – and also because, escaping our power to speak of it as well as our power to test it (to try or experience it), passivity is posed or deposed as that which would interrupt our reason, our speech, our experience' (*WD* 16).

In *The Writing of the Disaster* Blanchot revisits the concept of suffering that he had developed so provocatively in *The Infinite Conversation* through his reading of Antelme (and which we discussed at length in Chapter 1 of this book), noting that 'the word suffering is too ambiguous' for capturing the (non-)experience of dispossessed subjectivity at the outermost limits of its dispossession, alienation and exile. The word passivity is preferable to the word suffering in this crisis of subjectivity and experience because, unlike the word suffering, it does not incline towards reconnecting with the time (or subjectivity) before or after suffering. Passivity is more recalcitrantly indescribable and unconvertible into the narrative of its apotheosis precisely as the irreconcilable, irredeemable *disaster* of there being no longer any subject to experience or recollect the dispossession of its subjectivity. However, no sooner does Blanchot propose the word passivity for conveying the experience of what he has been referring up to this point in *The Writing of the Disaster* as the experience of a 'suffering such that I could not suffer it' (WD 14), than is he compelled to acknowledge that the connotative asceticism of the word 'passivity' comes perhaps at too high a cost, for it presents as a word that is callously disconnected from such historically immanent ordeals (voiceless cries) of suffering that survivors like Antelme implored we never forget. For passivity not to lapse into a word that has been purged of its metonymic relation with sociohistorical experiences of suffering (like Antelme's) and distress (of the voices screaming at Beckett), it is necessary that it be seized on in such a way that it never ceases pinpointing that which the word 'suffering' is too ambiguous (because too overused and therefore clichéd) to circumscribe, conceptualise and communicate.

In the process of substituting suffering with passivity, Blanchot concedes that it remains 'very difficult for us – and thus all the more important – to speak of passivity, *for it does not belong to the world*, and we know nothing which would be utterly passive (if we did, we would inevitably transform it)' (WD 15; my italics). Blanchot is not advocating that we speak of passivity in the place of suffering because passivity, as opposed to suffering, does not so obviously belong to the world or that passivity is in a sense more at home in the homelessness of the outside of language, memory and experience than is suffering; rather, he is proposing that we speak of passivity *precisely because* in not belonging so obviously to the world it demands reflection on its relation to the world all the more imperatively:

> we can evoke as situations of passivity: affliction; the final, crushing force of the totalitarian State, with its camps; the servitude of the slave bereft of master, fallen beneath need; or dying, forgetfulness of death. In all these cases we recognise, even though it be with a falsifying, approximating knowledge, common traits: anonymity, loss of self; loss of all sovereignty but also of all subordination; utter uprootedness, exile, the impossibility of presence, dispersion (separation). (WD 17–18)

What is filtered through these situations of passivity is not the subject either purified or deposed of its subjectivity; far more disastrously, it is the subjectivity that ceaselessly, indestructibly perseveres throughout the event of the subject's ontological dispossession.

We can begin to understand the supreme value of Blanchot's reflections on fragmentary writing and passivity to reading Beckett by zeroing in on instances in Beckett's work where the relation of the fragmentary protocols of his writing and the appearance in the spaces of this writing of figures of passivity articulates on the basis of the violent extortion of speech perpetrated by the one (fragmentary writing) collapsing into and therefore intermingling with the refusal of speech predicated on the other (passivity). According to Gerald L. Bruns, it is Beckett's 'late fictions – *Company* (1980), *Ill Seen Ill Said* (1981), and *Worstward Ho* (1982)' – specifically, that take the fragmentary imperative of writing as Blanchot articulates it as *the impossible experience of words* (the title of Bruns's essay) 'to the extreme limits of lassitude. These are, like *The Unnamable* and *How It Is*, extracted utterances – words or voices that overtake, define, and deplete the subjects that suffer them' (Bruns 2015: 91). Unfortunately, Bruns attends only to the philological but not figural symmetries between Blanchot's theorisation of the fragmentary imperative and Beckett's performance of a fragmentary aesthetic (in *Worstward Ho*). In order to build on Bruns's comparative analysis of Beckett and Blanchot, this chapter investigates how the figure of passivity that Blanchot so intricately articulates as a figure of radical suffering *and* as a figure of the fragmentary imperative of writing in *The Writing of the Disaster* opens up new ways of thinking about the terror that overshadows *Company*, *Ill Seen Ill Said* and *Worstward Ho*. Apprehending figures of passivity is indispensable to establishing a responsiveness to the antithetical demands of fragmentary writing (no aggregation without dispersion, no dissolution without unification). As it figures specifically in Beckett's late novels, passivity acts as a conceptual stepping stone for analysing how the voice that speaks in the place of the nameless other immobile and mute on his back in the dark of *Company*, the figure of the old woman not speaking because not being given to be seen in *Ill Seen Ill Said*, and language itself becoming the disfigured figure of passivity *par excellence* in *Worstward Ho* are quintessential ingredients in the terror of literature.

III

Company begins with the pronouncement (and injunction) that 'a voice comes to one in the dark. Imagine' (*NO* 3). That both the reader and the hearer are ordered by the voice to 'imagine' this opening scene is what establishes a relation between the two that threatens to implicate each as recipients of the voice's implicit and explicit directives throughout. One of its implicit directives early on in *Company* is that reader and hearer acquiesce to the presupposition that the voice originates from somewhere other than where the hearer – voiceless, immobile and anonymous on his back in the dark – is patiently awaiting the voice's arrival at the onset of the narrative. The voice comes *here* and *now* to one on his back in the dark, in other words, necessarily from a place and a time that is *not* here and now. A spatio-temporal border has been crossed by the intrusion of the voice that precipitates the hearer and reader having to decide both on the voice's unremarked provenance as well as on the uncertainty regarding which figure – reader or hearer – is being targeted as the privileged recipient of its directives: *Imagine*. Why must the provenance of the voice as well as the recipient of the voice's directives be investigated? So that the hearer can know if the voice is speaking to it or to another, and also so that the reader can know if the voice is speaking as the voice of *this* hearer or as the voice of another textual figure in this dark or in another.

These are the minimum of determinations required for assessing whether or not the figure of the hearer in *Company* is confronted by the reader and by the voice as a figure of passivity. If this figure is indeed a figure of passivity, its presence as such *prior to* the onset of the narrative will have retroactively circumscribed the protocols of representation necessary for its subsequent figuration in the writing of *Company*. The consequences of determining just how voiceless, anonymous and powerless is the hearer relative to the commanding presence of the voice visited upon it as it lies immobile and mute in the dark are therefore quite grave, for not only do they pertain to where the emphasis of reading should be placed in its passage through *Company* – on the figure of the hearer, on the figure of the voice (or on the figure of the deviser), or both (or all three)? – but they pertain also to deciding whether and to what degree Beckett's writing of *Company* is necessarily complicit in keeping this textual figure in its position of voicelessness, facelessness and powerlessness relative to the domineering presence of the voice.[6] Only with this knowledge can the figure of the hearer be apprehended in light of the textual regulations responsible for its figuration in subservience to the voice that speaks *to*, *of* and *at* the hearer throughout *Company*:

> if the voice is not speaking to him it must be speaking to another. So with what reason remains he reasons. To another of that other. Or of him. Or of another still. To another of that other or of him or of another still. To one on his back in the dark in any case. Of one on his back in the dark whether the same or another. So with what reason remains he reasons ill. For were the voice speaking not to him but to another then it must be of that other it is speaking and not of him or of another still. Since it speaks in the second person. Were it not of him to whom it is speaking speaking but of another it would not speak in the second person but in the third. For example, He first saw the light on such and such a day and now he is on his back in the dark. It is clear therefore that if it is not to him the voice is speaking but to another it is not of him either but of that other and none other to that other. So with what reason remains he reasons ill. (*NO* 6–7)

While the hearer understandably bases its decision that the voice is speaking exclusively to it on the evidence of the voice's use of the second person pronoun, the reader is left wondering whether or not the voice speaking exclusively to, of and at the hearer does not mean that the voice is the voice of none other than the hearer on its back in the dark. That the provenance of the voice can very well double as the voice's recipient – the voice of the hearer – would be proof positive that the voice speaking and the hearer being spoken to, of and at by the voice are the same figure. But what kind of figure is this? What distinguishes it as the figure dwelling specifically in *Company*? In what sense can we coherently say that the voice and the hearer (and soon the deviser) are and are not one and the same figure: 'And you as you always were. / Alone' (*NO* 46)? This is the question that the word *passivity* enables us to approach (though not necessarily answer).

Referring to the hearer and the voice as a self-same figure of passivity is a promising first step to addressing the question of how and why the hearer/voice pseudo-couple is figured as such in *Company* as a passive, vulnerable figure that doubles as the figure of an active, accusative voice. Doing so can only be a viable critical gesture, however, if we are convinced that both Beckett and Blanchot are concerned with the complexities of manufacturing voices for the voicelessness of the distressed subjectivity that modernity seems ceaselessly to be (re)producing. The argument here is that the figure dwelling in *Company* is not only an invention of Beckett's, although it is without question an invention of Beckett's as well. It is a fictional figure, in other words, that, like words in general, we learn from *Worstward Ho*, somehow rings true as a figure corresponding with figures belonging to the world outside of literature and fiction. To be a figure of passivity who has not been annihilated absolutely from either history or literature is to speak, according to Blanchot, with the voice of the suffering other that one has somehow, somewhere, and at some time become. We can say that *Company* presents its readers with a figure of passivity precisely because the hearer and the voice, though dialectically inseparable, cannot ever be reconciled except through a nostalgic and therefore ontologically misleading return to a past (and therefore projection into the future) where hearer and voice were presumably one and the same.[7] The terror of passivity is that figures of passivity cannot ever be reconciled with the knowledge, speech and identities required for accepting them back into the humanising fold of subjectivity, and as such their enduring presence outside the ontological community of humanity, their instantiation as the faceless, voiceless, inhuman truth of humanity itself, will always threaten to overturn such criteria for belonging to humanity as the supposedly civilising discourses of rationality, language, memory and community (the social equivalent of *company*) prescribe.

There nevertheless persists in the continuously interrupted existence that passivity reflects an irrepressible craving for the interruption of residing (absently) incessantly in passivity. Because passage out of passivity and back into the community of humanity cannot be enacted except by forfeiting one's responsibility for speaking in the place of the unknown other (one's self, the hearer, *you*) to whom one has been introduced and subsequently become precisely through passivity, the crisis of coming into contact with the other in passivity can only be reconciled by usurping the place of the other "*in place* of me" (WD 25; italics in original). By reading *Company* from the mute, voiceless perspective of the hearer, we are invited to conclude that the voice approaches it in the dark from a place outside of the dark where the voice, in contradistinction to the hearer, has not (yet) been divested of its power of speech (otherwise it would not now be speaking in *Company*). The relation that this absolute disparity in the power to speak establishes between hearer and voice is not a relation where the place of the other in this relation, the hearer, is provided with a voice so that it can begin narrating its arrival and dwelling in the dark from the voice's more ontologically secure perspective. The voice does not speak *for* the hearer; rather, it speaks *to, of* and *at* the hearer with a measure of pronominal violence that will be more than sufficient for transfiguring the hearer's voiceless presence into the blank ontological slate required for it to begin dwelling narratively as the voice's tortured (self-)creation.

Company reworks several of the narrative premises foregrounded, interrogated and thoroughly deconstructed in Beckett's writing of *The Unnamable*, but what distinguishes it decidedly from *The Unnamable*, and thus what makes it symptomatic of containing a figure of passivity more so than a figure of radical suffering, is its emphatic refusal of ever activating the first person pronoun *I*, and in its place opting only for the use of the second person accusative pronoun *you* and the impersonal third person pronoun *he* as the text's exclusive narrative operators: 'Use of the second person marks the voice. That of the third that cankerous other. Could he speak to and of whom the voice speaks there would be a first. But he cannot. He shall not. You cannot. You shall not' (*NO* 4). The principle effect of having banished the first person pronoun from the ontological horizon of possibility in this narrative is that the abrupt appearance of the anonymous hearer, the 'one on his back in the dark' (*NO* 3), excuses the narrative from having to expend any compositional capital at all in accounting for the hearer's arrival in this place of radical ontological dispossession, which would otherwise threaten the ensuing narrative with the prospect that ceaselessly plagued the discourse of *The Unnamable*, namely that the 'I [will] resurrect and begin again' (*TN* 387). That things were not always so for this figure of passivity is irrelevant to the ontological severity of its situation in *Company*, for although 'slowly he entered dark and silence' presumably from a place not limned all around by the darkness and silence of its dwelling in *Company*, nevertheless 'he lay there for so long that with what judgment remained he judged them to be final. Till one day the voice. One day! Till in the end the voice saying, You are on your back in the dark. Those its first words' (*NO* 11). On the one hand, then, the voice is enlisted in the ethically meritorious work of returning the hearer to the ontological context of figures in possession of a voice, a memory and perhaps even an identity, but on the other hand, the hearer's (passive) reluctance to submit to this programme of ontological resurrection is symptomatic of something having happened (*is* happening) to the hearer that has permanently dislocated it from the temporal sequence of a present moving diachronically out of a past and leading inexorably towards a future where its voice would be heard, its presence would be visible, and its life would be salvaged from the disaster of passivity.

The ceaseless interruption of memory, identity and speech that the voice visits upon the hearer reveals the latter's utter powerlessness to secure a place within the discourse of its narrative existence. Nothing is allowed by the voice to be stably linked together so as to begin materialising the fantasy of ontological coherence. Confronting the abyss of temporal alienation as repetitively and insistently as does the hearer places the hearer in a relation with the voice that ensures the transfer of all power of ontological coordination to the voice that speaks in the place of the hearer-become-the-unknown-other of a figure of passivity. This is the event of transfer to be expected when figures like the hearer of *Company* have been inherited by (and thus re-exiled to) the fragmentary space of writing circumscribed in *Company*. Blanchot describes the 'distinguishing characteristic of fragmentary writing' accordingly:

> The interruption of the incessant: this is the distinguishing characteristic of fragmentary writing: interruption's having somehow the same meaning as that which does not cease. Both are effects of passivity. Where power does not reign – nor initiative, nor the cutting edge of a decision – there, dying is living. There dying is the passivity of life – of life escaped from itself and confounded with the disaster of a time without present which we endure by waiting, by awaiting a misfortune which is still not to come, but which has already come upon us and which cannot be present. In this sense, the future and the past come to the same, since both are without present. So it is that men who are destroyed (destroyed without destruction) are as though incapable of appearing, and invisible even when one sees them. And if they speak, it is with the voice of others, a voice always other than theirs which somehow accuses them, interrogates and obliges them to answer for a silent affliction which they bear without witness. (WD 21–2)

Passivity represents a de-temporalised, incessantly unseeable, unsayable, immemorial and ultimately unthinkable modality of existence that writing is in the singular position of interrupting and reinvesting with the power to be seen, to speak, to be remembered, and to be known. The catch, however, is that the only way writing can do this is by usurping the prerogative to speak on behalf of figures deprived of voice. Beckett stages the conditions of just this situation of a figure (the hearer) that without being accosted by the voice would be incapable of appearing because incapable of speaking. Its utter passivity in the encounter with the voice is a condition that the voice is too impatient to tolerate for its incapacity for speech, and so when it does begin speaking from the place of the hearer, it does so, unsurprisingly from the perspective of Blanchot, as the voice of another. Already by the second fragment of *Company*, the voice has begun speaking as the voice *par excellence* of interrogation and torture, demanding of the hearer that it have a memory and a voice, that it confess to having memories and a voice.

The voice's command that 'the hearer have a past and acknowledge it' (*NO* 24), that the hearer say, 'yes I remember', marks a moment of interruption wherein the hearer is suspended in the space between having-forgotten and being-coerced into remembering its past: 'You were born on an Easter Friday after long labour. *Yes I remember*. The sun had not long sunk behind the larches. *Yes I remember*' (*NO* 24–5; my italics). Were the voice to succeed not just in forcing the hearer's capitulation to recalling the voice's manufactured memories, but also in coercing the hearer into *believing* and therefore *confessing* that its remembrance of these memories is volitional, the voice would threaten to undergo an ominous transfiguration from an external to an internal voice. This is the transfiguration that Blanchot associates in the fragment excerpted above from *The Writing of the Disaster* with the commencement of passivity and the event of fragmentary writing. Such a transfiguration would be convincingly unveiled were the hearer successfully to internalise this voice that had arrived in *Company* ostensibly from a place outside of *Company*. Were the hearer to accomplish this and reveal that either the voice has been the voice of the hearer all along or that it has now *become* the voice of the hearer after dwelling so long in the interval of darkness and silence in *Company*, it will have countermanded the voice's abiding injunction that so long as this narrative continues there will be no access to the first person singular pronoun that, throughout *Company*, it taunts the anonymous hearer with adopting: 'huddled thus you find yourself imagining you are not alone knowing full well that nothing has occurred to make this possible. The process continues none the less lapped as it were in its meaninglessness. You do not murmur in so many words, I know this doomed to fail and yet persist. No. For the first personal singular and a fortiori plural pronoun had never any place in your vocabulary' (*NO* 17). Because we are dealing with a figure of passivity in *Company*, in other words, the only way such a figure can begin speaking is with a voice that speaks in order to recall it to the affliction of separation from the voice, the memory, and ultimately the identity it can never possess.

What stands in the way of the hearer adopting the first personal singular pronoun is that it cannot after all internalise the voice and begin speaking as though it were the subject of the voice. It cannot do this for the simple reason that the voice speaks incessantly in denial of the hearer taking a turn in dialogue. The first person singular pronoun is the pronoun of a subject who can say *I speak*, but in *Company* it is not only that such a pronouncement is the prerogative only of the voice, but also, and far more disastrously, that there has never been a time in the existence (its existence in *Company*) of the hearer when the pronouncement *I speak* was part of its vocabulary. This is the temporal paradox of *Company*, namely the past of the hearer and its future have been collapsed into the time and space of textual presence where its past survives and its future arrives here where it can be transfigured (re-humanised) by neither. The hearer speaks in *Company* because the voice speaks in *Company*, but the hearer is not the voice, the hearer is, speaking through the voice, a figure of passivity that is 'nowhere to be found. Nowhere to be sought':

> For why or? Why in another dark or in the same? And whose voice asking this? Who asks, Whose voice asking this? And answers, His soever who devises it all. In the same dark as his creature or in another. For company. Who asks in the end, Who asks? And in the end answers as above? And adds long after to himself, Unless another still. Nowhere to be found. Nowhere to be sought. The unthinkable last of all. Unnamable. Last person. I. Quick leave him. (*NO* 16–17)

The closer the hearer gets to internalising the voice as its own, the more the discourse through which it would carry out this operation of finding and resuscitating the 'Last person. I' begins to fragment under the weight of knowing that this will do nothing to restore the hearer to a time and a place where it would not be bombarded by accusations of its exclusion from company. The only world the hearer knows and can remember is the world of *Company*, and it is this knowledge that obliges the interminable interrogation of who, where, how, when and why this voice is speaking with words reinforcing its voiceless alterity for no other reason than that as words belonging only to the voice they cannot do otherwise.

Through the pronominal austerity of *Company*, Beckett complicates the constitutive problematic of narrative that Blanchot articulates in *The Infinite Conversation* as the unpredictable, unretraceable passage from the sociohistorical determinacy of the autobiographical, first person 'I' to the neutered indeterminacy of the fictional, third person 'he' [*il*], which does not, in its radical ontological spectrality, 'simply designate another me' as the ontological substitute of the 'me' preceding it (*IC* 380). Nevertheless, the process of ontological dispossession that Blanchot articulates from the *I* to the *he* as the condition of possibility for the commencement of narrative leaves open the possibility that there was an autobiographical *I* somewhere in the past from which the narrative *he* has emerged as the presence of the narrative voice. The pronominal restriction in *Company* to the use of the accusative *you* and the narrative *he* works to evacuate any viability from the prospect that the one on his back in the dark and the voice that plagues it with manufactured memories of the voice's creation might be assigned an autobiographical origin independently of the voice's inquisitorial initiative:[8] 'How current situation arrived at unclear. No that then to compare to this now' (*NO* 33). The use of the third person alone would have been enough to preserve the genealogical origins of narrative speech prefigured in autobiographical subjectivity, because use of the third person exclusively would neither foreclose the presupposition of an 'I' that no longer is, nor eliminate traces of the 'I' that will have survived its passage through the ontological detour of narrative speech (as a secret archive of the autobiographical provenance of the narrative voice). The voice's repetitive use of the second person pronoun acts as an indomitable force of repetitive ontological dispossession, precluding the hearer from rebuilding its ruined subjectivity with the tenuous autobiographical mortar of the memory-scraps produced always vicariously as the voice's inventions.

Through the excessive use of the second person accusative pronoun *you*, *Company* is purged of any remnants of a chthonic autobiographical identity, specifically, that the hearer would be able to *voluntarily* adopt as belonging to its past and of therefore being used for reconstituting its identity in the future. The tyranny of the accusative *you* is such that all the memory-scraps the voice recycles to 'temper his nothingness', some of which are drawn directly from Beckett's own autobiographical repertoire, are there only to sustain the illusion that the monotonous continuation of the voice is susceptible to interruption, silence and departure *via* an ontological *coup d'état* initiated by the hearer (*NO* 33). The hearer's absolute capitulation to autobiographical amnesia,[9] coupled with its ontological exile into the fragmentary space of dwelling in passivity, means that when a memory, a synecdoche of the past, does (re-)appear on the horizon of the narrative, it does so violently by being imposed upon the hearer's imagination by the dynastic tyranny of the voice.[10]

The situation in *Company* is far more severe than in *What Where* because here we are not dealing with figures of victimisation and violence, but with a figure of passivity. In *What Where*, the one who is given 'the works until he confesses' does eventually pass out from the exhaustion of its suffering, and when this happens its inquisitor proves quite unable to 'revive him' (*CP* 313). The torturer's failure to revive its victim in *What Where* is what permits the session of torture to come to an end, albeit to an end that recatalyses the infinite circulation of 'the last five' through their interchangeable roles as torturers (the inquisitors) and victims (the interrogated) *ad infinitum* (*CP* 313). Because 'the need for company' proves to be 'not continuous' in *Company*, the voice is obliged to suspend its accusative speech and not only to 'let the hearer' have a name, 'named H', but to 'let him know his name' too (*NO* 22). The voice's generosity is duplicitous (and sadistic in the extreme), however, for no sooner does it permit the hearer to have a name than does it question whether or not having a name in this space where the figure of the deviser too is condemned by the ceaseless interruptions of the voice to be always on his back in the dark will improve on its measure of companionability. The voice refuses that such an improvement is likely, and so decides to 'let him not be named H. Let him be again as he was. The hearer. Unnamable. You' (*NO* 22–3). We can say that this situation is more severe than the situations of *What Where* or even of *How It Is* in so far as the hearer's victimisation by the pronominal violence of the voice only ever ebbs and flows within an uninterrupted continuum of intensification.

One of the consequences of the voice's reluctance to forgo its exclusive prerogative over the second person accusative pronoun is that the hearer is rendered permanently condemned to its ontological exile in *Company*. The problem with the voice's fanatical devotion to its pronominal asceticism, however, is that in the event of the hearer's absolute acquiescence to ontological dispossession, the voice too would be robbed of the recipient of its pronominal fury, and thus therefore of its power to perpetrate its act of pronominal violence indefinitely. Only where there is a recipient of violence who can still 'display a certain mental activity', though 'it need not be of a high order', will the voice be able to continue pursuing its agenda of having the hearer 'confess, Yes I remember. Perhaps even to have a voice. To murmur, Yes I remember. What an addition to company that would be! A voice in the first person singular. Murmuring now and then, Yes I remember' (*NO* 10). The voice shows little interest in forgoing its recourse to the pronominal violence of the *you*,[11] but this does not mean that the recipient of its pronominal violence will persevere as its victim *ad infinitum*. Without a recipient of that violence, the voice would wither into the voice of no one and nothing. This risks happening after several sessions of memory acquisition in *Company*: 'bloom of adulthood. Imagine a whiff of that. On your back in the dark you remember. Ah you you remember. Cloudless May day. She joins you in the little summerhouse' (*NO* 29). In this fragment where we read the repetition of the *you* – 'Ah you you remember' (*NO* 29) – there commences one of several pronominal transitions in *Company* from the second to third person pronoun, and it is in the space opened up by these transitions, these pronominal detours, that the metafictional figure of the deviser suddenly appears in place of the voice empowered with the third person pronoun *he*.

The subsequent fragment of narrative begins with the hearer, 'wearied by such stretch of imagining', suspending its need for company and thus making good on the threat implicit throughout *Company* – 'need for company not continuous' (*NO* 22) – of depriving the accusative voice of the victimised recipient fuelling its tyrannical pronominal reign. The deviser in place of the voice is inclined where the voice was not to have the hearer be part of a narrative predicated on traces of an autobiographical identity: 'till feeling the need for company again he tells himself to call the hearer M at least. For readier reference. Himself some other character. W. Devising it all himself included for company' (*NO* 31). The fragments where the hearer passes out from its subjection to the voice due to sheer weariness of the burden its subjection entails are instructive for noting that while the hearer, the voice and (now) the deviser are distributed in *Company* as discrete textual figures, their textual cohabitation means that from the claustrophobic perspective of their textual dwelling they are in fact indistinguishable as disseminated expressions of a single perseverant figure: 'deviser of the voice and of its hearer and of himself. Deviser of himself for company. Leave it at that' (*NO* 18).

That the devised deviser is in a position to disarm the pronominal violence of the *you* is a consolatory illusion that *Company* is nevertheless powerless to definitively dispel, for only when the hearer collapses out of utter exhaustion at having been pushed beyond the limit of its tolerance for pronominal violence and the torture of memory does the voice relent and permit the fiction of identity to take momentary hold of the hearer: 'let the hearer be named H. Aspirate. Haitch. You Haitch are on your back in the dark' (*NO* 22). The voice allows this moment of respite in order only to revive in the hearer the dreaded need for company that alibis the presence of the voice. From the perspective of the pronominal tyranny of the voice, the hearer's ontological aggrandisement as the deviser of its dispersed subjectivity is productive of nothing more promising than replenishing its vulnerability to continuous ontological pulverisation. The fact that the hearer must 'display a certain mental activity', though 'it need not be of a high order', in order to be subjected to the pressures of the voice means that the hope is not extinguished that ceasing its mental activity once and for all will signal the discontinuation once and for all of the voice's tyrannical persistence (*NO* 7). To 'submit, more corpse-obliging than ever' (*TN* 343), as the unnamable puts it, to the ontological destructiveness of the voice's pronominal violence, is precisely what is required as the first (suicidal) step to extricating itself from its nightmarish dwelling in *Company* where to be is to be always lying, crawling, falling and misremembering from (the endlessness of) the beginning of its life in narrative.

It is when the hearer is named M and the deviser named W that the hypothesis presents itself to the third person deviser of choosing to 'move out of the dark he chose when last heard of and away from his creature into another' (*NO* 31–2). What is won by this manoeuver is the possibility that the tyranny of the voice has been neutralised in *Company*, and although such news would be welcome indeed by the figure of the hearer-*cum*-deviser, it would signal nothing nobler than the displacement of the voice's pronominal violence onto another hearer. The solace of uncertainty over whether or not the continuation of the voice is 'addressed to him or to another sharing his situation' provokes in him a 'vague distress at the vague thought of his perhaps overhearing a confidence when he hears for example, You are on your back in the dark. Doubts gradually dashed as voice from questing far and wide closes in upon him' (*NO* 32). It is a narcissistic red herring for the hearer (i.e. the hearer that the deviser has just become, again) to believe that 'not till hearing cease will this voice cease' (*NO* 11), for the prerogative of deciding on the cessation of the voice is not with the hearer as it is accosted by the voice, any more than it would be for victims of torture to have a say over when their torturers will relent in the programme of their torture, or the persecuted in the ordeal of their persecution; rather, it is because the voice, the hearer and the deviser have been committed to a narrative order predicated on the implantation and extraction of memory and speech that the voice is in the inherited position of demanding that there be always, continuously, a hearer, whether in the same dark as *this* hearer or in an adjacent dark with another. The fault, in other words, is not (entirely) with the voice, but with the place – the place *ipso facto* of fragmentary writing – wherein the voice's pronouncements interminably and ubiquitously reverberate.

Not yet ready to reinvest pronominal authority exclusively in the voice, however, the deviser gives up on the redemptive autobiographical fiction of naming the hearer M and himself W: 'so W reminds himself of his creature as so far created. W? But W too is creature. Figment' (*NO* 33). The deviser, 'in panic to himself', leaves these avatars of ontological coherence behind and acquiesces once and for all to dwelling 'in the same figment dark as his figments' (*NO* 33). There is in this gesture of turning back to the darkness and the silence where the hearer dwells a responsiveness to the ethical call of responsibility for the prospective multitudes of hearers that the deviser's cowardly fleeing from the scene of the voice (the scene of *Company*) would compel into living the tortured existence of life as it is accusatively, precariously lived in

Company. The gesture of persevering in place of the hearer would be a courageous one, an unambiguous sign of the devised deviser figuring itself as a figure of ethical responsibility for the prospective affliction of the suffering other visited upon by the voice in this dark or in another. However, the voice, the hearer and the deviser are all (perhaps) one and the same, and so whatever measure of compassion the deviser exhibits for the imaginary hearers who will be automatically interpellated by the pronominal violence of the voice should the deviser renege on its decision not to move out of this darkness, will be reciprocally proportional to its measure of complicity in *this* hearer's pronominal (re-)affliction should it make good on its promise to stay.

Turning back to the darkness where it lies, becoming again the hearer in whom the desire for the company of the voice is revived, is what implicates the deviser in its exasperated return to the voiceless terror of passivity. The return of the voice (of the use of the second person pronoun) is symptomatic of this return to passivity, and it is the deviser's complicity in its self-reconfiguration as the voiceless figure (the destroyed subjectivity) of passivity – the hearer – that ensures it will never get out of this 'fable of one with you in the dark. The fable of one fabling of one with you in the dark. And how better in the end labour lost and silence. And you as you always were. / Alone' (*NO* 46). The situation of *Company* is this: to have compassion for (itself as) the distressed subjectivity of the hearer, the deviser must banish the voice to another dark, but doing this is to become complicit in the displacement of violence and distress onto another. The situation of *Company* is expressive of the terror of literature the instant that the deviser, desiring to save *other* hearers from the tyranny of the voice, condemns *this* hearer to the continuation of the voice that has plagued it from the very beginning. What keeps this vicious circle circulating *ad infinitum* is that Beckett forecloses the possibility of absolute certainty that the voice that speaks, the hearer that hears, and the deviser devising it all for company are in fact perfectly coherent expressions of a single ontological subject who is 'alone' in the silence and the dark of *Company*.

We can read the figure of passivity that dwells in *Company* as a more analytically fleshed out distillation of the 'three in one, and what a one, what a no one' referenced in *Texts for Nothing* (*CSP* 150). The difference in *Company*, however, is that this 'three in one' is no longer a hypothesis of what remains of the unnamable subjectivity that Beckett had just barely managed to salvage in the compositional (catastrophic) aftermath of *The Unnamable*. Here, in *Company*, the three-in-one is afflicted with embodiment and made to endure a static, timeless sequence of pronominal violence that has only figural displacements of itself as its provenance and recipient. This is a narrative of the terror of passivity in so far as it submits the figure of passivity – the hearer, the voice and the deviser all collapsed into one – to a narrative sequence that will continue 'without end' and that articulates temporally as a narrative 'separated from every other present by an inexhaustible and empty infinite, the very infinite of suffering, and thus dispossessed of any future: a present without end and yet impossible as a present' (*IC* 44).

We can be sure that we have encountered the terror of literature where the pronominal violence of a voice speaking *to* and (in the place) *of* figures suffering in passivity doubles as the only voice passivity can possess for the expression of its suffering. When subjects have been pushed to the threshold of passivity, they can only complete the passage all the way into passivity once they assume (through a choice that is never theirs) the responsibility for compelling their transgression of the ontological boundary that otherwise separates them from entering once and for all the outside of passivity. So it is that the deviser of *Company*, crawling again and falling again, arriving at the limit of its perseverance in the anguished space of *Company*, begins to welcome its replacement by the voice that speaks only in the pronominal register of interrogating the hearer over the ontological crime of its voiceless anonymity. And so will begin (again) the deviser's having to answer for the voicelessness of one who has entered into passivity and who will be made to answer for memories it cannot voluntarily remember:

> Crawls and falls. Lies. Lies in the dark with closed eyes resting from his crawl. Recovering. Physically and from his disappointment at having crawled in vain. Perhaps saying to himself, Why crawl at all? Why not just lie in the dark with closed eyes and give up? Give up all. Have done with all. With bootless crawl and figments comfortless. But if on occasion so disheartened it is seldom for long. For little by little as he lies the craving for company revives. In which to escape from his own. The need to hear the voice again. If only saying again, You are on your back in the dark. (*NO* 40)

The exhaustion of crawling and falling without respite compels the deviser to wonder if all this should end. Unfortunately, it is when the deviser reaches the limit of its exhaustion in this way that the 'craving for company' is recatalysed and the voice begins all over again. It is in such moments of ontological inversion whereby the figure interpellated as the object of the third person pronoun (spoken by that cankerous other) reverts back to the figure interpellated as the object of the second person pronoun (spoken by the voice) that the deviser, the hearer and the voice have (re)entered the outside of passivity. Beckett's compositional strategy for writing *Company* is fragmentary in the extreme in so far as it is quite unable not to oblige the textual figure it represents to dwell forever at this pronominal turning point, or detour, where it must be the object and subject of the voice that commands throughout it can only ever be neither.

Our trouble reading *Company* does not end with the decision that the figure of *Company* around which voice, hearer and deviser cohere is a figure of passivity, for what this decision succeeds in accomplishing is nothing more decisive than bringing into view the source of analytic disorientation that the figuration of passivity will never cease exacerbating. *Company* is Beckett's most thorough investigation into what happens to figures of passivity where writing decides on behalf of these figures that their 'renunciation of the first-person subject', according to Blanchot, 'is not a voluntary renunciation, nor, thus, is it an involuntary abdication' (*WD* 29). 'When the subject becomes absence', as it no doubt threatens to do in its narrative passage through the fragmentary detours of memory and speech in *Company*, 'then the absence of a subject, or dying as subject, subverts the whole sequence of existence, causes time to take leave of its order, opens life to its passivity, exposing it to the unknown, to the stranger – to the friendship that never is declared' (*WD* 29). This is the fate of the hearer of *Company*, the devised deviser of *Company*, as it empowers the voice with the measure of pronominal authority required to coerce its participation in its repetitive, interminable return to the ontological desert of passivity. We cannot therefore unburden ourselves of the suspicion that the voice has in fact succeeded in dividing itself into three distinct textual figures. If it has done so, however, it will only be as figures who have neither renounced their desire for ontological reconstitution as subjects who can say, 'Yes I remember. That was I. That was I then' (*NO* 13), nor abdicated their responsibility for terminating the textual programme of ontological dispossession to which deviser, hearer and voice are all being (vicariously) subjected. The analytical value of a notion like passivity is precisely that it permits of the ethical and epistemological dissonance demanded in the encounter with such voices as we encounter in *Company* that speak the language and instantiate the figuration of the terror of passivity.

IV

One of the reasons why critics like Marco Bernini and Jeff Fort have been able to present the 'fable of one fabling alone in the dark' in *Company* as a 'cruel narrative torture' (Bernini 2015: 46), or more specifically the scenes in the dark between fragments of memory as adding up collectively to 'a scene of torture, whether as the *extraction* of a confession from an unspeaking body, or as the sheer *imposition* on it of a history that has never been its' (Fort 2014: 337; italics in original), is that *Company* belongs to a period in Beckett's writing where its figures are as if claustrophobically confined to spaces of imaginative and corporal distress.[12] The existence of Beckett's late fictional figures is an existence encased by the disfiguring frames of anonymity and voicelessness that predicate the terms of their confinement, and no matter how 'reason-ridden' Beckett's figures stubbornly and undeniably are, there is little chance indeed that they will find themselves so suddenly ontologically empowered as to extricate themselves from their terrifying situation. Paradoxically, however, it is precisely because Beckett's figures are so ontologically disempowered that when they do speak, they do so with voices that assume responsibility and ensure the continuation of their confinement to passivity. The space of figural containment where Beckett's writing unfolds is a space commanding the figuration of passivity (dispossession, exile, anonymity) and that consequently precludes being straightforwardly in tune with a literature of either ontological restoration, metaphysical redemption or ethical immunisation against the disfiguring protocols of violence, torture and terror.

The work of creating the place where these figures 'crawl and fall' is work distinctly characteristic of the fragmentary imperative in response to which Beckett's figures of passivity are the quintessential symptomatic heirs. There is a reason why Beckett's figures are so tragically resilient to ontological reconstitution, for they crawl and fall into and out of the fragmentary gaps that repetitively, insistently erupt out of Beckett's writing (through such rhetorical tropes as aporia, parataxis and epanorthosis) whenever and wherever language and speech are as though weaponised by this writing to perforate and puncture the word surface of Beckett's unsilenceable prose. By the time of the *Nohow On* novels, Beckett had exceeded merely questioning whether or not 'that terrible materiality of the word surface should not be capable of being dissolved' *en route* to a 'literature of the unword', indeed if writing should not be able to commit unreservedly 'to bore one hole after another in it, until what lurks behind it – be it something or nothing – begins to seep through' (*D* 172–3). Once this search for a literature of the unword is underway, there is no turning back to a time or place prior to departure, for what such a literature unearths beneath the surface of language is nothing as ontologically opaque as 'nothing' or as ethically noncommittal as 'something' (*D* 172). What is unearthed is the terror of the fragmentary imperative of writing that saturates the space of literature and discloses, as Blanchot puts it, a region of experience where 'speech is surrounded by empty horror, the error of empty night', and where 'violence itself seems to become neutralized, *seems* for a moment to become calm, like the extreme immobile movement at the center of the maelstrom' (*IC* 184; italics in original). This is the tragic curse of literature whereby in seeking to give voice to voicelessness and visibility to invisibility, in working so diligently at carving out spaces in language where distressed subjectivities might speak and dwell without fear of coercion or manipulation (of retraumatisation), it must first repress its own constitutive predilections for violence and therefore naively disavow the inevitability that these violences will return and be revisited on the figures it had initially hoped to rescue from passivity.

Carla Locatelli wisely seeks to distinguish Beckett from 'postmodernist writers' on the grounds that Beckett 'is not primarily interested in the production of metafiction: after all, most metanarratives challenge only the language of literary narration. Beckett's critical mimesis regards the representation of the unrepresented, not only the representation of representation' (1990: 211). We can take Locatelli's insistence on Beckett's exception to postmodernist writing a step further by adding that there is in Beckett's writing an imperative to represent not just what has hitherto gone unrepresented, but also an imperative to represent what is fundamentally, immanently destructive of writing's normative protocols, or frames of representation.[13] Working within the twenty-first-century context of persons and lives subjected to marginalisation, dehumanisation and technological precipitations of vulnerability to violence (i.e. the context of our perpetual, self-defeating war against terror), Judith Butler proposes that we begin speaking about such persons and such lives with respect to their 'figural form' (2009: 7):

> The figure lays claim to no certain ontological status, and though it can be apprehended as 'living', it is not always recognized as a life. In fact, a living figure outside the norms of life not only becomes the problem to be managed by normativity, but seems to be that which normativity is bound to reproduce: it is living, but not a life. It falls outside the frame furnished by the norm, but only as a relentless double whose ontology cannot be secured, but whose living status is open to apprehension. (2009: 7–8)

Butler is more explicit than Blanchot in cataloguing figural forms of life that have been reduced (reframed) through violence, crisis and war to living invisibly on the ontological outskirts of officially recognised existence. While Butler is attempting to move the question of figures of passivity over into 'the realm of things that matter' (*WD* 16), to borrow from the vocabulary of *The Writing of the Disaster*, Blanchot is compelled by the opposite though no less urgent desire to see this question play out in a context that does not so explicitly matter as do the real-world contexts of torture, violence and war to which Butler points her reader's attention. Blanchot's context is the context of writing, and it is Blanchot's understanding of this context as one that is shot through with the imperative of fragmentation that permits Blanchot to posit that there will always be a destination for the anonymous, traumatised subjectivity that outlasts the destruction, and therefore exposes us to (the return of) the disaster, of the 'always already deported' subject, or figural form, of passivity (*WD* 79). Beckett's unpresentable figures, present textually even when they do not textually appear, are likewise not just 'problems to be managed', but are also representative of the problematic whereby the strategies devised by Beckett's writing for dealing with such figures ceaselessly reproduce such figures across the Beckettian oeuvre.

This is another way of saying that Beckett's writing, by dealing

The Terror of Passivity   213

always, in some way, with distress, has no other choice except to be inextricably connected with all the recalcitrant archives (unknowable, unrepresentable, immemorial) of voices, images and experiences sacrificed (without salvation) to the disquieting silence of passivity. However, because 'silence is a paradoxical word' in so far as 'surely we feel that it is linked to the cry, to the voiceless cry', according to Blanchot (*WD* 51), of figures living 'outside the norms of life', according this time to Butler (2009: 8), there is in the inevitable violation of silence – the staging of silence's mimetic critique – that all acts of writing invariably commit, an analogous affront against the mute cry of the suffering other. But if writing were to refuse responsibility to answer in the place of the voiceless other, it would not thereby win an ethical victory over the silence of the cry it did not dare to violate. Conversely, writing does not succeed aesthetically by severing its ethical relation with the silence of the suffering cry reverberating in the darknesses of the world (of the normative frames of the world) outside of literature. For writing to succeed ethically as much as it strives to succeed aesthetically, it must risk encountering voicelessness there where voicelessness as such speaks, that is to say, where writing is called upon to let itself be traversed by the fragmentary imperative that passivity, in its silent, imperceptible destruction of reason, experience and speech, likewise compels writing to internalise as the unending interruption – the interminable inquisition – of its protocols of representation. The question that Beckett's writing poses is whether or not the expression of passivity out of the essentially mute cry of a scream can survive the passage of translation or transfiguration through to the side of literary visibility intact, i.e. without loss of the uncanny expressiveness of passivity that perhaps only 'the silence at the eye of the scream' can authentically, voicelessly, articulate (*NO* 64).

This is one of the questions taken up in the second of the *Nohow On* trilogy of novels, *Ill Seen Ill Said*. The problematic that this text negotiates vis-à-vis the terror of passivity articulates as the problematic of delineating a frame of figuration wherein the voiceless figure of a manifestly distressed subjectivity can be admitted into a space of ontological appearance and epistemological apprehension without recourse, in the words of Adorno, to 'velleity or violence' (2005a: 263). The protagonist, or figural form, at the onset of *Ill Seen Ill Said* is an old woman who, with 'impassive face', 'stares as if shocked still by some ancient horror. Or by its continuance.

Or by another. That leaves the face stonecold' (*NO* 64). The horror imprinted on this woman's face is rendered exempt from any temporal sequence that would let it be convincingly invested with the narrative of its autobiographical provenance (it is both ancient and continuing). This is a horror rendered visible, in other words, only as the image of a horror stripped bare of its autobiographical (and perhaps by extension sociohistorical) particularity in the memory and life of this woman. It is the horror of an image impressed so indelibly on the face of this textual figure that the only way she can be accurately grasped, 'as had she the misfortune to be still of this world', is as a figure veiled by the disfigurations of her invisibility and silence: 'there then she sits as though turned to stone face to the night' (*NO* 50).

The scene of *Ill Seen Ill Said* is divided into 'two zones' that 'form a roughly circular whole' (*NO* 51), and when the woman leaves the first zone, the cabin, and 'crosses' over into 'the zone of stones and is there', surrounded by twelve staring figures, 'wherewith to furnish the horizon's narrow round' (*NO* 52), she triggers the narrative eye's aggressive injunction to 'seize her where she is best to be seized. In the pastures far from shelter' (*NO* 55). The order 'but quick seize her where she is best to be seized' (*NO* 55) is given not by any one of the figures of the twelve, who are part of this scene, but by the voice speaking on behalf of the 'filthy eye of flesh' that is here in order to see this woman (*NO* 65), to behold her face and to see her presence translated in its transfigured visibility 'from eye to mind' (*NO* 72). What motivates the gaze of this eye is thus the forcible withdrawal of the figure of the woman from the place where she is *not* best to be seized to a place where she *is* best to be seized from the eye's point of view. Hers is a textual figure that oscillates back and forth from visibility to invisibility under the ill-seeing gazes of the twelve tasked with transgressing the essential opacity of her figuration.

This scene approximates the event of two gazes meeting in the zone of stones, the woman's and the twelve's, but while the gaze of the twelve is omnipresent in its ill-seeing manifestation, it cannot therefore overcome the woman's figural inviolability: 'something forbids. Just time to begin to glimpse a fringe of black veil. The face must wait. Just time before the eye cast down. Where nothing to be seen in the grazing rays but snow. And how all about little by little her footprints are effaced' (*NO* 55). The gaze of the woman and of the twelve cannot meet because where they would meet, the only place that *Ill Seen Ill Said* will let them meet, i.e. under the ontological prerogative of the narrative eye, is shrouded so heavily and thickly by the blinding, melancholic whiteness of snow, that it admits only fragments of visibility from either side of the scopic barrier separating the woman from the twelve to escape. Her presence is registered by this scene as an indomitable spectre of effaced corporeality, and as such she figures here as an embodiment of ontological fragmentation that can be neither seen nor said to be seen except precisely as fragment, as what, *pace* Blanchot, fragments the powers of vision and speech to behold her in her spectral presence accordingly.

The figure of the woman, precisely as a figure of passivity, occupies a melancholic space where there is no temporal continuity between the person she perhaps once was and the figural form of a person – the figure of passivity – that she has now disastrously become. There is no possibility of mourning because there is no trace of a loss, no traumatic aftermath of a destruction: 'with herself she has no more converse. Never had much. Now none. As had she the misfortune to be still of this world' (*NO* 53). This is not a figure easy to grasp ontologically or apprehend epistemologically. It is *as if* she is not there at all, so marginalised has she become from the frames of visibility available to the eye in its vigil to seize her presence by whatever means necessary through the gaze of the twelve. Her absence from visibility is symptomatic of her exile from life (the misfortune of this world), but rendering her visible only where she is best to be seized by the illuminating power of the eye would be to exploit her ontological vulnerability in support of the eye's creative prowess. If this figure can only be seen by being transfigured and therefore disfigured by the eye, then she cannot really be seen at all such as she is. This figure's existence irrevocably is, returning to the language of Butler, an 'ungrievable', unliveable existence that lives on nevertheless, one of those lives best defined as the *figure* of a life, the disastrous figure of passivity, 'that cannot be lost, and cannot be destroyed, because they already inhabit a lost and destroyed zone; they are, ontologically, and from the start, already lost and destroyed' (Butler 2009: xix). The eye too occupies the zone of destroyed perception circumscribed in *Ill Seen Ill Said*, and so is unsurprisingly continuously obsessed with relocating her presence to a zone of visibility as yet untouched by destruction. Unfortunately, her figuration here in *Ill Seen Ill Said* is such that she cannot accommodate the eye's desire not to have its vision contaminated – to become 'itself but haze' (*NO* 78) – by what cannot ever be seen because cannot ever be said (and vice versa):

> She is vanishing. With the rest. The already ill seen bedimmed and ill seen again annulled. The mind betrays the treacherous eyes and the treacherous word their treacheries. Haze sole certitude. The same that reigns beyond the pastures. It gains them already. It will gain the zone of stones. Then the dwelling through all its chinks. The eye will close in vain. To see but haze. Not even. Be itself but haze. How can it ever be said? Quick how ever ill said before it submerges all. Light. In one treacherous word. Dazzling haze. Light in its might at last. Where no more to be seen. To be said. Gently gently. (*NO* 78)

It is when we consider the visually obscured (ill seen) figure of this woman in relation to the limits on figuration that her figural presence as such represents that we can begin to see how figures of passivity are inextricably linked (as catalyst and symptom both) with the fragmentary imperative of writing. What, if not Beckett's deployment of fragmentary writing, of speech as repetitive, unpredictable, eternally recurring detour of ill-saying as ill-seen and ill-seeing as ill-said – 'how [only] ever ill said' (*NO* 78) – is responsible for the figure of this woman being so irredeemably inscribed in this incessantly destroyed, eternally melancholic narrative 'zone' of *Ill Seen Ill Said*?

Blanchot comments on the ontological peculiarity of images in *The Infinite Conversation* by positing that

> the image is the duplicity of revelation. The image is what veils by revealing; it is the veil that reveals by reveiling in all the ambiguous indecision of the word reveal. The image is image by means of this duplicity, being not the object's double, but the initial division that then permits the thing to be figured; still further back than this doubling is a folding, a turn of the turning, the 'version' that is always in the process of inverting itself and that in itself bears the back and forth of a divergence. (*IC* 30)

Transposing Blanchot's analysis of 'image' onto the figure of the woman in *Ill Seen Ill Said* needs to be done with caution in so far as doing so too heavy-handedly risks eliding her singular figuration in Beckett's text. The 'filthy eye of flesh' desires to 'seize her' where she is most vulnerable to being seized. Is this not tantamount to desiring that her figural presence, otherwise ill-seen by the eye, be transfigured (and therefore destroyed) as an image that the eye will be able to apprehend and see anew? Is this not a desire to reveal the unseen figural form of the woman precisely by reveiling her presence as the presence of an image of the eye's devising? The eye surely does not desire to see this woman in all the blinding splendour of her invisibility. What it desires is an image of this figure of the woman that corresponds with images that ordinarily confirm the eye's power of vision. So far we can only say that the act of forcing an image into view and violating the veil of imperceptibility is perpetrated solely by the 'filthy eye of flesh' that desires to seize this figure of passivity where it is not (permanently and ubiquitously) inclined to being seized. Through Blanchot, however, we must acknowledge that this figure's vulnerability to optic seizure is, *still further back*, an intrinsic condition of its figuration as something even marginally more substantial than just pure figment: 'if only she could be pure figment. Unalloyed. This old so dying woman. So dead. In the madhouse of the skull and nowhere else' (*NO* 58).

Her stubborn persistence to be seemingly always there, even when the eye is not looking, preserves her as if frozen in the time and the space circumscribed by the fragmentary protocols of *Ill Seen Ill Said*: 'she is there. Again. [. . .] She still without stopping. On her way without starting. Gone without going. Back without returning' (*NO* 58). She is the sole source, it would appear, of the shameful incapacity of writing, seeing and thinking to transfigure her mute incomprehensibility into a presence more malleable, transformable and translatable – indeed torturable – through the powers of imagination and fiction.[14] In this state of being always dying without quite being always living, the figure of the woman figures in *Ill Seen Ill Said* as a fragment that the eye can see only by taking the detour of the image around this fragment's unrepresentability, for as Blanchot understands them, 'fragments, destined partly to the blank that separates them, [. . .] are always ready to let themselves be worked upon by indefatigable reason, instead of remaining as fallen utterances, left aside, the secret void of mystery which no elaboration could ever fill' (*WD* 58). It is not enough that this woman be written as fragment or that the narrative sequence of her figuration be comprised as a series of broken, juxtaposed fragments of language and vision in order for us to say (as we are unquestionably compelled to do) that Beckett's writing is writing according to the fragmentary imperative. The fragmentary imperative is not just an imperative for syntactical or ontological incompleteness for the simple reason that the incompletion of the fragment automatically triggers the 'indefatigable' work of visibility and speech.

The figure of the woman in *Ill Seen Ill Said* presents as both a figure of passivity and a figure of fragmentation. Indeed, it is because she is a figure of passivity that her presence in the text can only be ill-seen and ill-said, and in this ill-seeing and ill-saying that cannot contain her presence in the image of a figure well-seen and well-said, she will be approached again and again in vision and in speech according to the imperative of fragmentary writing. From the perspective of the interrogating gaze that wants little else than to seize the figure of this woman, rendered by the fragmentary imperative of writing as a gaze that ill-sees and ill-says whatever it subsequently beholds, there can and should be no hope that objects or persons placed before the eye of the gaze will cooperate with its nostalgic epistemological aspirations of seeing well on the way to saying well in order subsequently to know well: 'Was it ever over and done with questions? Dead the whole brood no sooner hatched. Long before. In the egg. Long before. Over and done with answering. With not being able. With not being able not to want to know. With not being able. No. Never. A dream. Question answered' (*NO* 70).

The scopic interrogation of passivity is so exhausting in its inexhaustibility, its 'deposition' of passivity never quite 'done' (*NO* 84), that it is tempting to forgive the narrative eye for its panicked refusal to accept the presence of this figure in its ontologically disastrous state of passivity. In its refusal not to want to know (not to want to see and to say), the eye recognises its complicity in the reproduction of this figure that so long as it cannot be transfigured as image or figment, will continue poisoning the eye's power of perception with its faceless inexpressibility. This the eye cannot abide, and so it decides that its only recourse is to expedite an image of this woman that will inoculate the eye from the infection of passivity: 'Not possible any longer except as figment. Not endurable. Nothing for it but to close the eye for good and see her. Her and the rest. Close it for good and all and see her to death. Unremittent. In the shack. Over the stones. In the pastures. The haze. At the tomb. And back. And the rest. For good and all. To death. Be shut of it all. On to the next. Next figment. Close it for good this filthy eye of flesh. What forbids? Careful' (*NO* 65).

Because the entrapment of the narrative eye in a space of visual ruination, its exposure 'to such vicissitude[s] of hardly there and wholly gone' is not sustainable, that is to say, because the eye is simply not up to the task of a fidelity to blindness (failure) otherwise required by proximity to passivity, there is once again every reason to forgive the eye's desire that everything be transfigured (neutralised) into figment and fiction (*NO* 71). Desiring to be rid of the responsibility of welcoming into the field of perception the figural embodiment of what promises to metastasise as the catalyst of perception's suicidal passage into inoperability and blindness is not something that a perspective not directly exposed to passivity is in a position to indict. This is the sensible paranoiac nightmare of the narrative eye, which is either unwilling or incapable or both of acknowledging that it cannot behold passivity as the figure *par excellence* of that which is incommensurable with the imperative of its figuration (its conceptualisation, its being-said). Seeing the woman exclusively as figment, which is the first self-delusional step in seeing 'her vanish', 'for good' with 'all the rest' (*NO* 66), is the narrative eye's panicked solution for devising a 'counter-poison' to what is so real about the unreality of her figural presence: 'such the confusion now between real and – how say its contrary? No matter. That old tandem. Such now the confusion between them once so twain. And such the farrago from eye to mind. For it to make what sad sense of it may. No matter how. Such equal liars both. Real and – how ill say its contrary? The counter-poison' (*NO* 72). There is no getting away from both the necessity and the impossibility – the impasse – of seizing the figure of this woman as a figure that has trespassed out of the misfortunate reality of the world and into the inhospitable space of literature and fiction. The ontological concatenation of her visible-invisible presence would be far easier to disentangle if her ontological provenance could be decided definitively on the side of figment and fiction (if that is the right wrong word for the contrary of the real). Unfortunately, this is not a viable option for overcoming the problematic of representation (of perception) in *Ill Seen Ill Said* in so far as the pervasive illness of vision and speech that prevails throughout is sourced genealogically to the figural spectrality of the woman and of the function her ontologically disastrous, visible-invisible presence plays in poisoning

– fragmenting – the textual grounds of representation (of perception) as such.

What begins as a scopic interrogation tasked with the seizure of the unspeakable namelessness of the figure of the woman is pursued so thoroughly and unsuccessfully in *Ill Seen Ill Said* that the narrative sequence can continue only by interrogating perception itself, 'dazed in its turn', as the work's newly transfigured protagonist (*NO* 72). The eye eventually opens onto the woman there where she is

> dead still on her back evening and night. [. . .] Hidden from chin to foot under a black covering she offers her face alone. Alone! Face defenceless evening and night. Quick the eyes. The moment they open. Suddenly they are there. Nothing having stirred. One is enough. One staring eye. Gaping pupil thinly nimbed with washen blue. No trace of humour. None any more. Unseeing. As if dazed by what seen behind the lids. The other plumbs its dark. Then opens in its turn. Dazed in its turn. (*NO* 71–2)

The projection of scopic impoverishment onto the woman's unseeing staring eye implicates the narrative eye as symptom of her unseeing because unseeable passivity. The future awaiting the narrative eye as an eye enriched in its power of perception is a future that can be glimpsed only at the expense of the unseeing eye of the woman 'vanishing' irretrievably from the field of its visibility. She must vanish if the narrative eye is to have its perceptive powers restored, she 'with [all] the rest' that the eye suspects are responsible for its descent into blindness (*NO* 78). What the eye cannot abide is that this figure's unseeable presence, there in the anamorphic epicentre of this zone of imperceptibility, entails the eye's repetitive return to the site of the unending error of 'the optical imperative' that 'has', according to Blanchot, 'for thousands of years, [. . .] subjugated our approach to things, and induced us to think under the guaranty [sic] of light or under the threat of its absence' (*IC* 27). Such is the imperative according to which 'to speak truly, one must think according to the measure of the eye' (*IC* 27). There is an internecine struggle being waged in *Ill Seen Ill Said* between how best the figure of the woman is to be seized, whether through vision or through speech, and given vision's long-standing epistemological hubris to be always seeing well before speech has the chance of saying well, it is not a struggle that can be won on the side of speech (nor should it be) without first confirming this woman's disappearance from any light whatsoever of her visibility: 'No shock were she already dead. As of course she is. But in the meantime more convenient not. Still living then she lies hidden. Having for some reason covered her head. Or for no reason. Night. When not evening night. Winter night. No snow' (*NO* 73).

What threatens the eye with the prospect of returning, again and again, 'to the scene of its betrayals' (*NO* 63), is this figure's stubborn materiality, 'her tenacious trace' (*NO* 86), that the eye is powerless wholly to efface. Blinded by its errors, its treacheries of vision, the eye is vulnerable to defeat in this struggle with speech to *seize her where she is best to be seized*, except that her seizure by language cannot be any more successful than her seizure by vision if it is not to reproduce a treachery of words no less treacherous than the treachery of images. The only way to overcome the treacheries of this 'filthy eye of flesh' is through a modality of speech that would not simply, naively and hubristically substitute for vision; rather, it is through a speech speaking only and always from this place of 'error', which is revealed here in *Ill Seen Ill Said* by exposure of the eye's disastrous proximity to passivity. Beckett is decidedly not one of those 'novelist[s]' who 'lifts up the rooftops and gives his characters over to a penetrating gaze', and who therefore take 'language as not just another vision, but as an absolute one' (*IC* 29). In proximity with figures of passivity, all speech, all vision and all knowledge will be in error, and their representations of passivity diverted through the eternally recurring detours of fragmentation. Accordingly, it is not 'just any language' or any error (any failure) that Blanchot and Beckett are after for supplementing the treacherous blind spots of the optical imperative, 'but the one in which "error" speaks: the speech of detour' (*IC* 29).

Here we must resist the temptation of looking away from the collateral damage left in the aftermath of writing's (deeply ambivalent) victory over vision on answering the question of how best to err in expressing ill the 'tenacious trace' of a figure like the woman of *Ill Seen Ill Said* (*NO* 86). The fragmentary space of the detour of speech is not, in the world of Beckett (nor is it for Blanchot), a depopulated place, as the penultimate fragment of *Ill Seen Ill Said* dashes any hope that the problematic of the woman's figural presence has been resolved by the eye's defeat and that something as definitively unpronounceable as the ethical event of language has been declared:

> Absence supreme good and yet. Illumination then go again and on return no more trace. On earth's face. Of what was never. And if by mishap some left then go again. For good again. So on. Till no more trace. On earth's face. Instead of always the same place. Slaving away forever in the same place. At this and that trace. And what if the eye could not? No more tear itself away from the remains of trace. Of what was never. Quick say it suddenly can and farewell say say farewell. If only to the face. Of her tenacious trace. (NO 85–6)

Stumbling upon the fragmentary imperative of writing by way of the eye's defeat signals the discovery that in order for there to be fragmentary writing at all, there must first be the presence of a figure so elusive and opaque in its passivity that it stands in for the detours of speech wherein fragmentary writing intervenes. The fragmentary imperative must have figures of passivity, otherwise it would wither aesthetically as nothing more ambitious than a rhetorical exercise in metafictional (postmodernist) deconstruction. Fragmentary writing, on the contrary, is nothing if not the striving after an aptly manufactured frame of expression for figures of passivity, and where it succeeds, the only way it can succeed, is where it reproduces in the space of literature analogous zones or frames of violence, destruction and distress that led these figural forms (*pace* Butler) into passivity in the first place. Fragmentary writing is precarious, uncertain and utterly disruptive of the knowledge and indeed of the *fact* that it is occurring, here and now, in the space of literature; but no less precarious, uncertain and disqualifying of affirmations of ethical and metaphysical reconciliation are the ill-seen, ill-said (after-)lives of figures of passivity, of figures, that is to say in this context of *Ill Seen Ill Said*, 'of her tenacious trace'.

V

Approaching (late) Beckett in this way via Blanchot's suturing of fragmentary writing to figures of passivity in *The Writing of the Disaster* (and *The Infinite Conversation*) compels us to engage finally with Badiou's philosophically systematic (and demanding) reading of *Worstward Ho* as a 'recapitulatory text [...] of the whole of Samuel Beckett's intellectual enterprise' (2005a: 90). For Badiou, the Beckettian aesthetic articulates according to an unwavering commitment to the 'figural preparation' of evental subtraction from the ontological status quo: 'having been figurally prepared' through the literary condition attached to the name 'Beckett', 'an event is what happens so that the latest state of being will not be the last' (2005a: 121). Beckett's incomparable value for Badiou is thus that Beckett's writing (culminating with *Worstward Ho*) is able to 'sustain' the figural preparation of the event 'without naming it. To sustain the "on" and to sustain it to the extreme, incandescent point at which its sole apparent content is: "nohow on"' (2005a: 121). One of the polemical edges of this chapter's reading of *Company*, *Ill Seen Ill Said* and *Worstward Ho* touches on the credibility of the figural ontology that Badiou constructs for coming to philosophical terms with the subtractive (minimalist) orientation of these late fictional writings of Beckett's.

Badiou evacuates all traces of the figuration of lives exiled to passivity in *Worstward Ho* and replaces them with conceptual metaphors extracted from the thematic surface of the text and which are designed to communicate what Badiou reads as Beckett's critique of onto-epistemological nihilism, i.e. the defeatist ethic of perseverance in what is known, secure and consistent in the history of one's everyday existence. Badiou is of course right in principle that Beckett is nowhere endorsing a nihilist outlook on the impossibility of an event, the sudden, unpredictable arrival of a future that disqualifies the oppressive laws of the present, such that while there is 'a horizon of absolute disappearance, thinkable in the statement "dim can go"', which is present throughout *Worstward Ho*, it is decidedly contrary 'to the entire protocol of the text' (2005a: 111). Beckett is aware of the absolute illimitability of the nihilist threat of perseverance in existence, but he does not let this awareness preclude working diligently against the continuous actualisation of this threat. The way that Beckett accomplishes this supreme ethical task is by condensing the subject of the possibility of an event into the subject instantiated by the writing of *Worstward Ho*. Through a phenomenological strategy that reverses the Husserlian method of subtracting the world from the subject, Beckett proceeds in *Worstward Ho* by 'subtracting or suspending the subject so as to see what then happens to being' (Badiou 2005a: 117). Badiou operates from the presupposition that the subjective presence circumscribed by *Worstward Ho* is a presence manufactured exclusively for the purpose of becoming the figure responsible for simultaneously directing and performing the narrative of Beckett's onto-phenomenological critique not only of being, but of the being of an event (and indirectly the impossibility of nihilism).

By opening *Worstward Ho* from the perspective precisely of 'existence', i.e. 'the generic attribute of what is capable of worsening' – 'what can worsen exists', Badiou says succinctly (2005a: 99) – Beckett sets *Worstward Ho* into motion towards the point of a radical interruption in the subject's nihilist perseverance in existence. This is the point where the protocols of worsening become inoperable and mute, and what remains is only the question – the ethical question *par excellence* – of whether or not to persevere radically anew on the basis of this interruption, or to revert back to persevering nihilistically in what has become one's ontologically antiquated existence subsequent to the event. Readers finally 'witness the production of an event in the strict sense – a discontinuity, an event prepared by what Beckett calls a *last state*' in *Worstward Ho*, according to Badiou (2005a: 118; italics in original) – in the scene (to which we will return shortly) of 'the altogether unpredictable metamorphosis of the one-woman into the gravestone', and it is 'on the stoop of this gravestone' where 'the subject is now given only in the erasure of its name, in the crossing out of its name and date of existence' (2005a: 120). This is the point beyond which, however, *Worstward Ho* can go no further along the path of Badiou's narrative schema of the event, for it remains committed to the imperative of subtracting the subject from its existence through protocols of seeing and saying increasingly ill (the unsilenceable protocols of worsening words). Beckett's writing is ultimately too overburdened by its ontological insomnia, its eternal vigilance over spaces, zones or frames of interruption, to awake ontologically reinvigorated on the shores '*beyond* the last state of being' (Badiou 2005a: 121; my italics) where the event will have truly commenced: 'Then, and only then, can I and must I continue. Unless, in order to recreate the conditions for obeying this imperative, one must fall asleep a little – the time needed to conjoin, in a simulacrum of the void, the dim half-light of being and the intoxication of the event' (2005a: 121).

That Badiou resists the urge to project his theory of the event onto the poetics of *Worstward Ho tout court* is undoubtedly to his intellectual credit, but even before Badiou leaves Beckett in favour of Mallarmé – 'perhaps the entire difference between Beckett and Mallarmé lies here. The first forbids sleep, as he forbids death. One must remain awake. For the second, after the work of poetry, one can also return to the shade – through the suspension of the question, through the saving interruption' (2005a: 121) – he has already superimposed a reading onto *Worstward Ho* that risks effacing, or at the very least risks pacifying or evading, what it is that embroils *Worstward Ho* so intransigently in the terror of literature that Badiou's thinking opts strategically not to encounter in any meaningful way. What embroils Beckett's writing of *Worstward Ho* in the terror of literature is precisely that the figural presence that stands behind its protocols of expression, the figure that commands the imperative of saying when the saying as such is drained of all concept or content of the said – 'the void. How try say? How try fail? No try no fail. Say only –' (*NO* 96) – is a figure that Beckett's writing both *is* and *is not* responsible for having it inscribed in the 'what for when words gone' of *Worstward Ho* (*NO* 104).

The figural forms of passivity encased in Beckett's writing are there, in other words, not only because Beckett has purposefully left traces and consciously staged a critique in literature of their unseeable, unspeakable and unthinkable presence as it manifests as a presence subtracted from regimes of representation and existence; rather, it is because these are figural forms responsible for the imperative in the first place that the ideological textures that hold language, memory and knowledge together be torn asunder by protocols of fragmentary writing. It cannot only be that the impoverishment and worsening of words in *Worstward Ho* reflects an affirmation of joy, according to Badiou, over there being so little left to say now that Beckett's writing has penetrated into the void of language, has perched itself at the furthermost limits of the void in the 'dim shades', which are, ontologically speaking, 'all' that 'cannot go' for good: 'Joy, in the end, is on the side of words. To rejoice is to rejoice that there are so few words to say what there is to say. Joy is always the joy of the poverty of words' (2005a: 116). Badiou interprets Beckett's arrival in the impoverishment of words as evidence that Beckett's intertextual narrative of subtraction is moving in the right direction towards the void, but in order to say this, Badiou first separates the phenomenon of the impoverishment of words in *Worstward Ho* from the pain inflicted on the body of its textual figures: 'pain is of the body (while joy comes from words)' (2005a: 115). This idea that words cannot be pained is not one that is easily sustainable in light of what is happening to language in *Worstward Ho*.

What we gain by reading Beckett through Blanchot rather than through Badiou is a heightened sensitivity to the way that figural forms of existences (subjectivities) sentenced to passivity are made accessible through fragmentary protocols of writing, particularly such protocols as Beckett so meticulously exploits in *Worstward Ho*. As Blanchot deploys the term in *The Writing of the Disaster*, passivity does not refer to an *exclusively* literary figural form, nor is the fragmentary imperative of writing an imperative to which *only* writing is responsive. Passivity is a condition of being lost in and to the fragmentary separations of time and space, and if we understand language as being intrinsically fragmentary by virtue of the ruptures it is poised to introduce into ideologically normative frames of existence, then we can say too that even and especially when figures of passivity are rendered absent from knowledge and perception, their presence continues to live on according to 'the simple fact', as Christopher Fynsk exclaims, '*that there is language*' (1996b: 1; italics in original). What language registers of the presence of passivity, in other words, are the discursive aftershocks, or rather tremors of passivity's screaming unrepresentability. The singular role of literature in all of this is to exacerbate where, in language, these unsilenceable little tremors of unrepresentable passivity are most likely to be detectable. Where literature is at its most ambitious in respect of this task is where it extracts these tremors from historical and ontological discontinuities of existence in such a way that the whole of language, according to the minoritarian logic of literature emphasised by Deleuze (and Guattari), is made to 'scream, stutter, stammer, or murmur' (1997: 110).

Worstward Ho is haunted by its refusal to admit onto its plane of discourse the presence of either a speaking or spoken subjectivity. What distinguishes it from *Company* and *Ill Seen Ill Said* is that it foregoes the economics of relation between the figure of the voice (or eye) and the figure of a subjectivity tormented, surveilled and disfigured by the voice's pronouncements and pronunciations. *Worstward Ho* does not gaze through the perforated screen of language from the perspective of the voice, nor does it register the event or experience of figural entrapment outside language and visibility that the voices speaking in *Company* and

Ill Seen Ill Said (tyrannically, shamefully) facilitate; rather, its perspective is the perspective of what Blanchot calls 'the (mute) language of beginning all over again' (*WD* 30). This is a language that punctuates the measurement of passivity where passivity is synonymous with 'that which is not compatible with humanity', with the figural apotheosis of 'our being indestructible because always and infinitely destroyed. The infinite of our destruction, this is the measure of passivity' (*WD* 30). From the perspective of passivity, *Worstward Ho* is still sincerely asking 'whose words?' even though it knows from the start that we can only 'ask' such a question 'in vain. Or not in vain if say no knowing. No saying. No words for him whose words. Him? One. No words for one whose words. One? It. No words for it whose words. Better worse so' (*NO* 98). The ontological 'worsening' of a figure predicated first by 'him', then as 'one', and (perhaps) finally as 'it' reflects back on the idea that where there is language, or rather where language is being produced, reproduced and repetitively regenerated anew, there is outside of language the presence of figures threatening words, concepts and images with the wounds and with the scars not only of unrepresentability, but also of language's disavowal that 'it' is the reason *that there is* the beginning (again) of language in the first place.

Levying the question 'whose words?' with the sanction against 'knowing what it is the words it secretes say' (*NO* 105) is the surest way to bypassing (without transcending) the aporetic relation between the 'two languages, or two requirements', according to Blanchot, that legislate over the inquiry into passivity (and the disaster): 'one dialectical, the other not; one where negativity is the task, the other where the neutral remains apart, cut off both from being and from not-being' (*WD* 20). The hypothesis that the words of *Worstward Ho* are words signifying nothing and yet continuing to be spoken by an 'it' that signifies no one is surely not a satisfactory answer to the question 'whose words?', but because there is little denying the absence of any figure resembling the voice of a speaking subjectivity in *Worstward Ho*, the best (worse) answer to this question must reflect, as Blanchot puts it, 'that not to answer is the rule – or not to receive an answer' (*WD* 31). Unfortunately for the prospects that *Worstward Ho* might cease its inquiry and stop asking the question – 'whose words?' – to which there can be no satisfactory answer, the withholding of an answer, or the answer that there can be no answer, 'does not suffice to stop questions' (*WD* 31); on the contrary, 'when the answer is the absence of any answer, then the question in turn becomes the absence of any question (the mortified answer). Words pass, return to a past which has never spoken, the past of all speech. It is thus that the disaster, although named, does not figure in language' (*WD* 31). This is why language is powerless to rescue figures sentenced to passivity, for language is constitutively symptomatic of precisely this powerlessness in the face of passivity. Its point of departure is always, *Worstward Ho* is saying from its very beginning, the folding of the present instance of speech around the unspeakable place of passivity where all speech, and at every instant, begins:

> On. Say on. Be said on. Somehow on. Till nohow on. Said nohow on.
>
> Say for be said. Missaid. From now say for be missaid.
>
> Say a body. Where none. No mind. Where none. That at least. A place. Where none. For the body. To be in. Move in. Out of. Back into. No. No out. No back. Only in. Stay in. On in. Still. (*NO* 89)

Language is powerless to restrict the secretion of words out of this place of passivity, and it is because of language's powerlessness to foreclose this place of passivity and to silence the 'worsening words whose unknown' which passivity speaks, that language is rendered responsible for prolonging the ordeal of passivity (*NO* 104). Figures of passivity are present *in* language without being present *to* language. They are 'at all costs unknown' because they are figures *par excellence* of the disintegration *of* language (and knowledge, memory and history): 'worsening words whose unknown. Whence unknown. At all costs unknown' (*NO* 104).

The 'unknown' figure in possession of all these 'worsening words' enters *Worstward Ho* by order of the imperative that it be subjected *through* these words to the question of its representability. Importantly, however, this is not a question that *Worstward Ho* poses in view of such a figure having materialised independently of either a voice or an eye that subsequently circumscribes its textual appearance. A voice does not come here in *Worstward Ho* to one *already* on his back in the dark, nor is it drawn into narrative focus by a figure who is suddenly, irrevocably *there* when and where the narrative eye opens. The uncertain progeny of words in *Worstward Ho* entraps a voice into responsibility for the encounter of words with passivity. Enlisting a voice in service of separating words from their origin in passivity is the first step to expediting a genealogical account of the irrepressible textual excrescence of the ever worsening words of *Worstward Ho*. The voice that is compelled to speak in *Worstward Ho* (to speak as the voice of *Worstward Ho*) is as if powerless to sit idly by in view of words without voices parading in places without grounds. This is its obligation, its contract with *Worstward Ho*, and one of the effects of the voice answering the call of this obligation is that its only recourse moving forward is to say by axiomatic fiat that the unknown figure has a body and that it is a figure embodied in a place stable enough for grounding its appearance. That there is no other recourse to speaking on behalf of these words is what invests the voice's figural creations – woman, old man and child – with the 'meremost minimum' of ontological credibility necessary for manipulating their bodily presence. Even as we know there is no body where the voice says there is a body, or a place where the voice says there is a place, 'it stands' nevertheless (*NO* 90): 'What? Yes. Say it stands. Had to up in the end and stand. Say bones. No bones but say bones. Say ground. No ground but say ground. So as to say pain. No mind and pain? Say yes that the bones may pain till no choice but stand' (*NO* 90). Manufacturing a body and a place for the 'unknown figure' so as to command its newly imagined textual surrogate to 'somehow stand. That or groan' (*NO* 91), to appear 'head sunk on crippled hands. Vertex vertical. Eyes clenched. Seat of all. Germ of all' (*NO* 91), is for the voice to be guilty of an ontological crime no more transgressive than disfiguring what we are given to think was already, prior to the arrival of the voice in this disastrous time of the 'pastless now' of *Worstward Ho* (*NO* 110), an essentially disfigured figure of passivity.

Do we then blame passivity for not claiming authorship over the 'worsening words' that passivity uncontrollably excretes, and for therefore signing the invitation to being (re-)admitted 'into the hell of all. Out from the hell of all' (*NO* 114) through the fragmentary writing of *Worstward Ho*? Must the voice of *Worstward Ho* approve such a request handed to it from figures of passivity for their admission into language, which is tantamount to signing on as the perpetrator of passivity's unending disfiguration? Passivity converges with the fragmentary imperative of writing there where the representation of passivity in language and the inscription of passivity in the disfiguring ground of the image come to one and the same as acts of the terror of literature:

> If, in the patience of passivity, my self takes leave of me in such a way that in this outside – where being lacks without giving place to not-being – the time of patience (time of time's absence, or time returning never present, the time of dying) has no more support, no longer finding anyone to sustain it, then by what language other than fragmentary – other than the language of shattering, of infinite dispersal – can time be marked, without this mark's making it present and pointing it out to the authority which assigns names? (WD 19)

This does not mean that through the syntactical twists and turns, the sudden backs and sudden forwards, the repetitions and the reversals of fragmentary writing we are somehow granted access to the neutered presence of passivity without it being disfigured by the negativity of language, for like passivity, Blanchot is quick to explain, 'the fragmentary, of which there is no experience, also escapes us' (WD 19). Blanchot reads the fragmentary imperative of writing as an imperative without content or concept. Failing to read it in this way would re-open the protocols of fragmentary writing to the Romantic illusion that they can be systematised and therefore programmatically deployed in the space of literature. It is less the case that the power of negativity inherent to concepts and words is ultimately powerless to capture fragmentary writing as a finite set of compositional protocols than it is that fragmentary writing derives its *raison d'être* from the unknowable, unspeakable, unexperienced experience of figures of passivity exiled from the world of knowledge, language and memory. Passivity, accordingly, is not simply an abstraction from existence, but rather points to an ontological positivity (a body and a place) that structures, through the traces, echoes and shadows of its radical unbelonging to regimes of recognisability, i.e. that which is knowable, speakable and experiential.

Reading *Worstward Ho* from these two analytical perspectives simultaneously – its fragmentary protocols of writing and its inexpressive figuration of passivity – exposes it to the first step of terror where there is no knowing if its commitment to the representation of an existence sentenced to passivity is not a commitment to the repetition of passivity. When writing is plunged into the indecision between antithetical commitments such as this as wholeheartedly

The Terror of Passivity 231

as is the writing of *Worstward Ho*, it should come as no surprise that adherence to the imperative of saying, the imperative of the 'on', which transfigures the 'unknown figure' (of passivity) variously as a woman, old man and child, is indistinguishable from the imperative, borne out of the epistemological anxiety of fragmentary indecision, of unsaying its figures and its words. Because *Worstward Ho* does not have access to a figure that is manifestly there from the very beginning as the subject or object of narrative visibility or speech, it turns the fragmentary fury that arises out of this absence against what is there, ready to be initiated into the violence of unsaying the said: 'the words too whosesoever' (*NO* 99). Like the body of Pim stumbled upon by the narrator of *How It Is* in the murky dark of the mud, words too cannot be reduced to corpse-words in the act of making them say and be what they are not inclined to say and to be. Words can never be worsened or destroyed past the point of the 'unlessenable least best worse' (*NO* 106). They can 'never', in other words, 'to naught be brought' (*NO* 106):

> Worse less. By no stretch more. Worse for want of better less. Less best. No. Naught best. Best worse. No. Not best worse. Naught not best worse. Less best worse. No. Least. Least best worse. Least never to be naught. Never to naught be brought. Never by naught be nulled. Unnullable least. Say that best worse. With leastening words say least best worse. For want of worser worst. Unlessenable least best worse. (*NO* 106)

The violence of writing here becomes the writing of violence, and it is in its internalisation of the violence of writing being turned into the writing of violence *against writing itself* in the absence of a visible figure of vulnerability, that *Worstward Ho* is positioned as exemplary of the terror of literature. It becomes this precisely because it has been preceded by Beckett's unwavering attempt to square the ethical-aesthetic circle of representation between the fragmentary imperative of writing and the constitutive unrepresentability or voicelessness of passivity.

The unnullable worseness of words is proof-positive of the impossibility of an *absolute* experience of terror that would somehow be invulnerable to the aleatory, disintegrative pressures of the fragmentary imperative, of the language of infinite repetition and dispersal. The place in language that safeguards words from total nullification – 'How almost true they sometimes almost ring! How wanting in inanity!' (*NO* 99) – is coterminous with the place outside of language where figures of passivity never cease clamouring, or 'gnawing' (*NO* 112) from out of the void and behind the walls, borders or frames that circumscribe their condemnation to invisibility and silence. Through Blanchot's reflections on passivity and the fragmentary protocols of repetition, interruption and subtraction necessary for perceiving passivity's spectral presence outside language (and of therefore catalysing the fragmentary imperative of writing), we can begin to gauge the ethical, political and philosophical complexities of so minimal a text like *Worstward Ho*. Because 'the referent' of *Worstward Ho* 'comes to coincide precisely with anything that cannot enter language explicitly, and yet can be perceived because it resists incorporation into it' (Locatelli 1990: 261–2), Locatelli rearticulates, so too does Beckett's writing of *Worstward Ho* come to coincide with the deadly (destructive without destruction) act of disappearing (as verb) figures and words to inexistence and inexpression, i.e. to 'blanks for nohow on' (*NO* 105):

> That said on back to try worse say the plodding twain. Preying since last worse said on foresaid remains. But what not on them preying? What seen? What said? What of all seen and said not on them preying? True. True! And yet say worst perhaps worst of all the old man and child. That shade as last worse seen. Left right left right barefoot unreceding on. They then the words. Back to them now for want of better on and better fail. Worser fail that perhaps of all the least. Least worse failed of all the worse failed shades. Less worse than the bowed back alone. The skull and lidless stare. Though they too for worse. But what not for worse. True. True! And yet say first the worst perhaps worst of all the old man and child. Worst in need of worse. Worse in –. (*NO* 105)

Here we witness the enactment of the substitutability of figures into words and words into figures – 'they then the words. Back to them now for want of better on and better fail' (*NO* 105) – where the one is as vulnerable as the other to the disfiguring modalities of the missaid saying of *Worstward Ho*. The common denominator in this passage back and forth between the appearance and disappearance, convergence and divergence, of figures and words, is language, but language only in so far as it is opened up, worked upon and continuously reconfigured in accordance with the fragmentary imperative of writing.

The tearing apart of the word surface of language, as Beckett puts it, is a *fait accompli* of writing assuming its responsibility for expressing the voicelessness of figural forms of subjectivities dwelling outside language in places and times saturated by disaster and distress. Writing does not choose the fragmentary route of expression as if it were presented as an optional (axiomatic) point of commencement and continuity; writing is fragmentary because writing deals with distress, and it deals with distress because it is fragmentary. It is this chiastic relation between *how* writing writes and *what* writing writes about that precipitates the terror constitutive of literature. That literature is not empowered in any celebratory way by this chiastic overdetermination of its expressive responsibilities is signalled by Beckett in the closing fragments of *Worstward Ho*, where the act of representing its three textual figures comes up against the threshold of incommensurability separating the imperative of saying what cannot be said (seeing what cannot be seen) from the knowledge that what will be said in accordance with the fragmentary imperative of the Beckettian aesthetic will only be said in the disfiguring language of saying-ill if said at all:

> nothing to show a child and yet a child. A man and yet a man. Old and yet old. Nothing but ooze how nothing and yet. One bowed back yet an old man's. The other yet a child's. A small child's.
>
> Somehow again and all in stare again. All at once as once. Better worse all. The three bowed down. The stare. The whole narrow void. No blurs. All clear. Dim clear. Black hole agape on all. Inletting all. Outletting all.
>
> Nothing and yet a woman. Old and yet old. On unseen knees. Stooped as loving memory some old gravestones stoop. In that old graveyard. Names gone and when to when. Stoop mute over the graves of none. (*NO* 115)

Beckett approaches these figures there where they cannot be figured (*nothing to show a child* . . .), and yet they are there, vulnerable as never before to the disfiguring violence of figuration (. . . *and yet a child*). Beckett submits these figures to the disfiguring machinery of writing because there is quite simply nowhere else for their figuration *qua* figures of passivity to occur. That Beckett's writing never extricates itself from the incommensurable instant of separation between the imperative and the incapacity of figuring passivity is what binds his writing to the imperative specifically of fragmentary writing. Its being bound so inextricably to the fragmentary imperative in this way is what impels us to predicate of Beckett's writing the terror of being always subject, aesthetically, to perpetrating the violence of disfiguration that its rhetorical protocols are otherwise called upon, ethically, to preclude from taking place in the space of literature (if nowhere else outside of literature).

Beckett's zeroing in on the elliptical interstice separating figure and figuration in the fragmentary detours of language is manifestly expressive of what Timothy Bewes provocatively isolates as the *shame* of (post-Auschwitz) literature, whereby 'writing is *defined* by its inadequacy; that is to say, by its profound ethical complicity' (2011: 21; italics in original). Without a protocol of representation adequate for the expression of figures sentenced to passivity, there will be no redemption of passivity. Bewes calls this the shame of literature, but coming back to Beckett (and Blanchot) via Badiou, we can also predicate the inadequacies of literature as essential to its autonomy of artistic expression: 'if there is no adequation, if the saying is not prescribed by "what is said," but governed only by saying, then ill saying is the free essence of saying or the affirmation of the prescriptive autonomy of saying. One says in order to ill say' (Badiou 2005a: 100). Blanchot says something similar in *The Writing of the Disaster* about the uncertain ethical and political valences of writing where he writes that 'writing, since it persists in a relation of irregularity with itself – and thus with the utterly other – does not know what will become of it politically: this is its intransitivity, its necessarily indirect relation to the political' (*WD* 78). The question of literature's essential, fragmentary inadequacies, it would seem, can only be answered on the side of the shame of literature or the autonomy of literature, but not on the side of one transposed onto the side of the other. Perhaps.

What this book has been calling the terror of literature is a strong conceptual candidate for understanding that literature *is* this incommensurable commitment to (aesthetic) autonomy and (ethical) shame, power and impotence, and violence and sacrifice. It is because of the ambivalent persistence of figural forms of passivity screaming out from their places of voicelessness in literary works like *Worstward Ho* that we are reminded of why we do not celebrate literature's fragmentary autonomy prematurely nor impatiently bemoan the act of writing where it submits its protocols of representation most unreservedly to the dangerous imperative of fragmentation (i.e. of what is responsible for literature's shameful inexpressiveness); rather, we are compelled to accept that literature engenders constitutively the terror that circulates the space of writing where the violence that writing visits upon itself (its figures and its words) doubles as the measure of the violence visited upon languages and existences disappeared outside of history. Knowing this is what binds literature to terror and what commands, we read through a fragment of Blanchot's from *The Writing of the Disaster*, that literature *'learn to think with pain'* (*WD* 145; italics in original). This too is the lesson of reading Beckett. It is the lesson of thinking compassionately with the suffering of Beckett's textual figures, but also therefore of accepting that writing will always, at its most compassionate, be complicit in the interminable fragmentation of language through which figures suffering so radically in passivity will continue to do so as figures of the disaster of writing itself, of the disaster of the life of what life looks like beyond life, voicelessly and facelessly, excerpted from economies of comprehension and disappeared from narratives of salvation.

Notes

1. Michael Rothberg is convinced that 'if the ethico-political call to arms after Auschwitz derives from the necessity of preventing its recurrence, then the pedagogical moment that sometimes surfaces in Adorno's writings and, especially, speeches and radio talks ought to be kept in mind. In those more obviously conjunctural interventions, Adorno stresses the concept of education to maturity, *Erziehung zur Mündigkeit*. In sketching this notion of "democratic" or "mature political pedagogy", Adorno not only leaves the autonomy of the aesthetic realm but suggests a project of "public enlightenment" whose formulation and actualisation remain today as critical as they do unfinished. Ultimately, this relocation of the confrontation with Auschwitz in the public sphere of democratic education may be as great a contribution to the process of coming to terms with the past as the more famous reflections on representation' (2000: 58).
2. Shira Wolosky positions Celan in the ambivalent space of

sociohistorical responsiveness and aesthetic autonomy where Beckett also belongs, noting along the way Adorno's insufficiency to maintain the requisite balance of theoretical attentiveness to each of these poles of responsibility simultaneously. She writes of Celan: 'In this ambivalence between history and theory, reference and self-consciousness, the case of Paul Celan emerges as pivotal exactly because his poetry is extreme and is so in both apparently opposed directions. For history-minded critics Celan is above all a Holocaust poet. But for lyric theorists his texts are par excellence autonomous, self-referential language-structures, abnegating a relation to any world outside them. This tendency appears in grotesque form in once-existing classroom instructions to teachers to prevent discussion of Celan's most famous poem, '*Todesfuge*', from digressing from formal considerations into discussions of concentration camps. But it persists in various ways through much writing on Celan. Adorno serves here as both paradigm and source' (2001: 653–4).
3. It is for this reason too that Adorno feels compelled to defend Beckett in *Negative Dialectics* against the misguided criticism that Adorno had supposedly heard from 'a man whose admirable strength enabled him to survive Auschwitz and other camps' (2005b: 367). The criticism levelled against Beckett is 'that if Beckett had been in Auschwitz he would be writing differently, more positively, with the front-line creed of the escapee. The escapee is right in a fashion', Adorno concedes, but not in the way that 'he thinks. Beckett, and whoever else remained in control of himself, would have been broken in Auschwitz and probably forced to confess that front-line creed which the escapee clothed in the words "trying to give men courage" – as if this were up to any structure of the mind; as if the intent to address men, to adjust to them, did not rob them of what is their due even if they believe the contrary' (2005b: 367–8).
4. Foucault is responding in this essay primarily to Blanchot's fiction, and specifically in this section to *Le Très-Haut* (1948), *Celui qui ne m'accompagnait pas* (1953), and *Le Dernier Homme* (1957). He is addressing Blanchot's notion of the 'outside', however, through Blanchot's reflections on it in *L'Espace littéraire* (1955).
5. For critics such as Gary Adelman and Graham Fraser, the alliance is not so secretive after all in Beckett's work, particularly after *How It Is*. 'Through violence and pain', Fraser writes, 'Beckett depicts the origins of Pim's expression as brutally limited to the reactions of his tormented body' (2009: 62), and as such Beckett has updated the relation between writing and torture on which Kafka, according

to Adelman, had elaborated so disturbingly in 'In the Penal Colony' (see Adelman 2004: 87–169).
6. In his reflections on Francis Bacon collected in *Portraits*, John Berger argues that Bacon's painting 'has nothing in common' with the 'work of an artist like Samuel Beckett. Beckett approaches despair as a result of questioning, as a result of trying to unravel the language of the conventionally given answers. Bacon questions nothing, unravels nothing. He accepts the worst has happened' (2015: 347). What Berger takes issue with in Bacon's representation of violence and the suffering that violence produces, however, is not in the mere fact that violence is everywhere in Bacon's painting or that its worldview is too pessimistic. Berger charges that what ultimately stands firmly in the way of Bacon being an 'original visual artist', what makes him a 'very remarkable but not finally important painter', is 'that Bacon's interpretation' of 'suffering and disintegration is too egocentric, that he describes horror with connivance – that his descriptions lack not only the huge perspective of compassion but even the smaller perspective of indignation. I feel myself that the Pope screams not because of the state of his conscience or the state of the world but, puppet-like, because he has been put into Bacon's glass case' (2015: 342). Here Berger is grounding a moral indictment of Bacon's painting on the supposedly non-moral basis of its aesthetic failure to reconfigure in any significantly inventive way the subject-matter of the figurations that it stages. The accusation that there is connivance in Bacon's approach to alienating the figures of his painting from the context of their mutilations is a serious one, for it bars Bacon's paintings from expressing compassion for the suffering figures exhibited on its canvases. Bacon captures suffering, violence and despair in an aesthetic order of colour and paint that basks too self-congratulatory in the shocks and unease of its juxtapositions, and because it is void of any measure of compassion that Berger believes is necessary for protecting it against the aesthetic misstep of narcissistic insulation, it makes no significant contribution to the art historical progress of painting.
7. Charles Juliet recalls Beckett explaining the 'diabolically difficult' situation of *Company* accordingly: '"you must stand here",' Beckett says to Juliet, 'pointing towards the table, "and also," pointing his index finger upward, "millions of light years away. All at the same time. [. . .] One must stand where there is no pronoun, no solution, no reaction, no tenable position"' (cited in Juliet 2009: 36).
8. Although James Knowlson notes in *Damned to Fame* (1996: 651–3)

that Beckett draws extensively on his own autobiographical past for the content of the memories imposed on the hearer by the voice, we nevertheless gain far more interpretive mileage by focusing on the link these memories establish between the imaginative world of the hearer and the outside world that Beckett, as author, inhabits. It is the relation between these two worlds that is of interest in my reading here, and not the autobiographical or sociohistorical specifics of each and every memory upon which Beckett draws for much of the content of *Company*.

9. Jonathan Boulter wonders in passing whether or not Beckett is presenting us in *Company*, through its 'meditation on the process of *losing* one's memory, [. . . with] an exploration of the disordered logic of an Alzheimer's sufferer' (2008: 139; italics in original). Although Boulter is not inclined to take up this line of inquiry, particularly as his primary objective in *Beckett: A Guide for the Perplexed* is to read the Beckettian oeuvre as an extended meditation on a more philosophically grounded reflection on posthuman subjectivity, there is a growing interest in Beckett studies towards such cognitive scientific modes of investigation into the Beckett subject.

10. H. Porter Abbott reminds us of how 'tyranny is rooted in the imagination. The creating of art, like the making of worlds, is a matter of cramming, jamming, wedging, bending, and poking' (1996: 141). Reading Beckett must therefore work through the recurring problematic, Abbott goes on to say, 'not simply [of] the imagery of tyrannical containment', but also of the 'complexities of their enactment' (1996: 142).

11. Llewellyn Brown draws on Lacan in order to flesh out the objectifying violence of the second person accusative pronoun, explaining that the ontological perniciousness of 'the *you*' inheres in the fact that 'the *you*, in its primal force, reduces the other to a thing extracted from any exchange' (2011: 186).

12. Stanley Gontarski notes in his introductory remarks to the Grove Press edition of *Nohow On* that starting 'in the mid-1960s, Samuel Beckett's fiction took a dramatic turn, away from stories featuring the compulsion to (and so solace in) motion, toward stories featuring stillness or some barely perceptible movement' (1996: vii). Such 'closed space' narratives, particularly in 'the three novels of *Nohow On* [. . .], seem to have more in common with the spatiality of painting than the chronicity of traditional storytelling' (1996: xiv). Thus it is that 'with the "closed space" novels Beckett did something new not only with his own fiction but with fiction in general – a reduc-

tion of narrative time to points of space' (1996: xxvi). Beckett's reconfiguration of narrative temporality into narrative spatiality did not happen overnight, but was something that had been germinating in his reflections on writing as early as 1949. Beckett comments in a letter to Georges Duthuit dated 2 March 1949 on how 'odd' it is that 'I always see things in terms of boxes' (*Letters II* 129). Beckett's 'odd' predilection to think and see through the lens of 'boxes' looks all too commonplace from the perspective of such late diagrammatic works of encasement and containment as *All Strange Away*, *Imagination Dead Imagine*, *The Lost Ones*, *Company*, and *Ill Seen Ill Said*.

13. Adam Piette makes a similar point in his reading of *Ill Seen Ill Said*, arguing that what distinguishes *Ill Seen Ill Said* from 'other modernist and postmodernist texts is the radical nature of confusion between reader figures, author substitutes and subjects of perception. The eye, the twelve guardians, the scribe are implied authors as well as being reader interpreters' (2014: 322). Piette goes on to observe that through these 'discrete tropological' figures, we begin to see that 'the plural narrators' gaze is outrageously ambivalent, stretched across a range from murderous and sneering violence to plangent sentimentality. It is a gaze that crosses an authorial notebook with the quasi-sociological journal of a prison visitor' (2014: 322).

14. Timothy Bewes argues that one of the defining characteristics of twentieth-century literature, particularly in its sensitivity to colonial and postcolonial experiences of violence, is its coterminous relation to shame. Bewes draws explicitly on Deleuze's remark in *Essays Critical and Clinical* that the best reason to write is simply the 'shame of being a man' (Deleuze 1997: 1). 'If one is a writer', Bewes goes on to explain, 'it is insofar as one writes that one experiences shame – shame, that is, at the inadequacy of writing' (2011: 23). Following Deleuze, Bewes adds that 'what is shameful is not just the world in which we happen to find ourselves, but the very regime of what exists, the logic of ontology and of everything that attends it: expression, identity, subjectivity, volition' (2011: 28). In so far as 'shame in Deleuze is shame for what exists, for the "shameful compromises" with "our time" that we undergo', it just might be possible to write and think from the perspective of shame as 'the basis for a kind of writing and thought that could take place in the name of the powerless' (2011: 28).

Coda: Literature at the Turning Point of Terror

As life grows more terrible, its literature grows more terrible.
(Wallace Stevens)

Blanchot begins one of the fragments of *The Writing of the Disaster* with these words: 'Last witness, end of history, close of a period, turning point, crisis – or, end of (metaphysical) philosophy' (*WD* 101). He then asks, two paragraphs later, in response to these eschatological words, 'why does writing – when we understand this movement as the change from one era to a different one, and when we think of it as the experience (the inexperience) of the disaster – always imply the words inscribed at the beginning of this "fragment," which, however, it revokes? It revokes them even if what they announce is announced as something new which has always already taken place, a *radical change* from which the present tense is excluded' (*WD* 102; italics in original). With its emphasis on the power of writing to accelerate, overturn or reboot the time of crisis, to announce the beginning of history by experiencing the disaster of history's end (the disaster of the impossibility of experience), this fragment reads as a microcosm into how the fragmentary aesthetic of literary modernity is supposed by Blanchot to (un)work (*désoeuvrement*). The movement of writing doubles, according to the disaster, as the movement of closure, the movement of interruption, but also the movement of openness, the movement that responds only to the law of the refusal of closure, the law pronouncing that every fragment, every narrative and every epoch will never be the last. Writing's responsibility before this double imperative of closure and openness is also, however, a responsibility for the traversal of the disaster precisely in so far as it compels writing to continue on with its passage through the history and the future of language,

Coda: Literature at the Turning Point of Terror 241

memory and thought without any sacred horizons guiding the way.

The disaster proper to writing is that writing inherits the terrifying responsibility for supplementing the loss of the sacred armed only with the power of producing fictions, fragments, images and narratives of what the sacred has now become. The loss of the sacred, which is lost whether we acquiesce to its disappearance or not, Blanchot believes (writing after the Second World War, after Auschwitz), is not therefore the loss of the *demand* for the sacred. It is through the infinite demand for the sacred outliving the disappearance of the sacred in the maelstroms of historical catastrophe that Beckett and Blanchot most conspicuously meet, but this is not a place of convergence that will permit either Beckett or Blanchot to formulate a blueprint for the way forward. If Beckett and Blanchot do in fact converge at the site of disaster, then they do so, in Blanchot's words, always 'without agreement. Without agreement but without discord' (*WD* 91). As Blanchot writes in *The Infinite Conversation*, 'the fact of our belonging to this moment at which a change of epoch, if there is one, is being accomplished, also takes hold of the certain knowledge that would want to determine it, making both certainty and uncertainty inappropriate. Never are we less able to get around ourselves than at such a moment, and the discrete force of the turning point lies first in this' (*IC* 264). Blanchot's thinking cannot be made to prescribe the performance of Beckett's writing, just as Beckett's writing cannot be made to encapsulate completely the fragmentary performance of writing as it is prescribed by what Blanchot names the disaster.

The decision of this book to read Beckett with Blanchot through the lens of terror was made in recognition of how the only way to responsibly set Beckett and Blanchot into dialogue is by staging Beckett's writing and Blanchot's thinking on a particular conceptual terrain that neither of them are overly regarded for inhabiting. Nevertheless, we cannot deny that Beckett registers the disaster of writing with the clarity of purpose and the courage of sacrifice required for accepting the consequences of the disaster on the work that literature, in Blanchot's estimation, is now compelled to do. We cannot conclude this dialogue with the announcement that Beckett's writing begins (always again) from the standpoint of the fragmentary imperative, the infinitely disintegrative-regenerative turning point of writing, which Blanchot links (without etiological priority) to the disaster; rather, we need to push the

Beckett-Blanchot dialogue, or relation, further and demonstrate *how it is* that Beckett's writing unfolds according to this imperative, *how it is* that Beckett's figural forms experience the passage through the labyrinth of fragmentary turning points in Beckett's writing. If the disaster is the law of writing, the writing of the law of the disaster, then terror represents the imperative but also the experience of surviving (the ordeals of radical dispossession, traumatisation and exile) under the order of this law. Terror is the experience of the figures, voices and protagonists tasked with implementing, as purveyors of disaster, and adhering to, as survivors surviving endlessly the event of disaster, the letter of its law in the space of literature.

One of the wagers of this book has been that what Blanchot articulates as the 'discrete force of the turning point' consequent of the disaster has been turned against the voices, figures and protagonists that occupy the space of Beckett's writing in such a way that the experience of their existence in Beckett's writing is the experience *par excellence* of terror. These voices, figures and protagonists are precluded through the sentence of this occupation from deciphering, for instance, friendship from exploitation, harmony (peace) from violence (war), justice from injustice, and invitations to dialogue from extortions of (true) speech. Theirs is the experience of terror having infiltrated the economy of literature and writing with the uncertainty of whether administering to the imperative to suspend violence, alleviate suffering and facilitate community through language (and *in the place* of language) is not to administer the perpetuation of violence, the intensification of suffering and the establishment of a community predicated on coercion and brutality. Beckett's is a literature of terror in accordance with the prerogative of this double imperative over the movement of writing: the imperative of disabling terror in (and outside) literature and the imperative of reproducing the experience of terror in literature precisely in the name and with the means of its disablement.

There is perhaps nothing more characteristic of Beckett than this commitment to the terror of always administering to the ethical and to the unethical potentialities of language and writing in order that the future *qua* unmastered because unmasterable possibility never be foreclosed, that the voices speaking the language of the pain that inflicts them by dwelling in the space of literature (and outside it) never be silenced. Literature must be an expression of terror, it would seem, in order that terror will have need of expression nowhere other than in literature. What we have gained by reading Beckett through the lens of terror is insight into the ethical and ontological costs that Beckett's writing, and above all its figural forms, had to pay, the ethical risks it (they) had to take, and the ontological violences it was (they were) compelled to commit so that the worsening repetitively again of the worst, to speak now with the wounded, wounding words of *Worstward Ho*, somehow always be turned against the prophetic, totalitarian commandment that we have witnessed the last of the worst, that the crisis of the worst is over, that the end of the worst is now, that the worst 'is never to come again' (*NO* 111). Beckett's writing turns and turns again with its worsening words always towards the future. The terror that *perhaps* awaits us in the future, the terror that *perhaps* directs the fragmentary movements of Beckett's writing towards the future, is *perhaps* therefore the terror still always again, *pace* Blanchot, of the very soul of literature.

References

Abbott, Porter H. (1994), 'Beginning Again: the Post-Narrative Art of *Texts for Nothing* and *How It Is*', *The Cambridge Companion to Beckett*, ed. John Pilling, New York: Cambridge University Press, 106–24.

Abbott, Porter H. (1996), *Beckett Writing Beckett: The Author in the Autograph*, Ithaca: Cornell University Press.

Adelman, Gary (2004), *Naming Beckett's Unnamable*, Lewisburg: Bucknell University Press.

Adorno, Theodor (2003), 'Trying to Understand *Endgame*', *Can One Live After Auschwitz? A Philosophical Reader*, ed. Rolf Tiedemann, trans. Rodney Livingstone et al., Stanford: Stanford University Press, 259–94.

Adorno, Theodor (2005a), *Minima Moralia: Reflections from Damaged Life*, trans. E .F. N. Jephcott, New York: Verso.

Adorno, Theodor (2005b), *Negative Dialectics*, trans. E. B. Ashton, New York: Continuum.

Agamben, Giorgio (2002), *Remnants of Auschwitz: The Witness and the Archive*, trans. Daniel Heller-Roazen, New York: Zone Books.

Allen, William S. (2016), *Aesthetics of Negativity: Blanchot, Adorno, and Autonomy*, New York: Fordham University Press.

Andress, David (2005), *The Terror: Civil War in the French Revolution*, London: Little & Brown.

Antelme, Robert (1998), *The Human Race*, trans. Jeffrey Haight and Annie Mahler, Evanston: Marlboro Press.

Arendt, Hannah (2001), *On Violence*, New York: Mariner Books.

Baczko, Bronisław (1994), 'The Terror Before the Terror? Conditions of Possibility, Logic of Realization', *The French Revolution and the Creation of Modern Political Culture: Volume 4*, ed. Keith Michael Baker, New York: Pergamon Press, 19–39.

Badiou, Alain (1999), *Manifesto for Philosophy*, ed. and trans. Norman Madarasz, Albany: SUNY Press.
Badiou, Alain (2001), *Ethics*, trans. Peter Hallward, London: Verso.
Badiou, Alain (2005a), *Handbook of Inaesthetics*, trans. Alberto Toscano, Stanford: Stanford University Press.
Badiou, Alain (2005b), *Metapolitics*, trans. Jason Barker, London: Verso.
Badiou, Alain (2007), *The Century*, trans. Alberto Toscano, Cambridge: Polity Press.
Badiou, Alain (2008), *Conditions*, trans. Steven Corcoran, London: Continuum.
Baraka, Amiri (1973), 'Names and Bodies', *The Floating Bear: A Newsletter: Numbers 1–37*, ed. Amiri Baraka and Diane de Prima, La Jolla: Laurence McGilvery.
Beckett, Samuel (1964), *How It Is*, New York: Grove Press.
Beckett, Samuel (1984), *Collected Shorter Plays*, New York: Grove Press.
Beckett, Samuel (1984), *Disjecta*, ed. Ruby Cohn, New York: Grove Press.
Beckett, Samuel (1995), *The Complete Short Prose: 1929–1989*, ed. S. E. Gontarski, New York: Grove Press.
Beckett, Samuel (1996), *Nohow On: Company, Ill Seen, Ill Said, Worstward Ho*, New York: Grove Press.
Beckett, Samuel (2009), *Three Novels: Molloy, Malone Dies, The Unnamable*, New York: Grove Press.
Beckett, Samuel (2011), *The Letters of Samuel Beckett: 1941–1956*, ed. Lois More Overbeck et al., Cambridge: Cambridge University Press.
Beckett, Samuel (2014), *The Letters of Samuel Beckett: 1957–1965*, ed. Lois More Overbeck et al., Cambridge: Cambridge University Press.
Begam, Richard (1992), 'Splitting the Différance: Beckett, Derrida and the Unnamable', *Modern Fiction Studies*, 38:4, 873–93.
Begam, Richard (1996), *Samuel Beckett and the End of Modernity*, Stanford: Stanford University Press.
Benjamin, Walter (2003), 'The Work of Art in the Age of Its Technological Reproducibility: Third Version', *Selected Writings, Vol. 4: 1938–1940*, ed. Howard Eiland and Michael W. Jennings, trans. Edmund Jephcott et al., Cambridge: Harvard University Press, 251–84.
Berger, John (2015), 'Francis Bacon', *Portraits*, ed. Tom Overton, London: Verso, 341–53.
Bernini, Marco (2015), 'Crawling Creating Creatures: On Beckett's Liminal Minds', *European Journal of English Studies*, 19:1, 39–54.
Bewes, Timothy (2011), *The Event of Postcolonial Shame*, Princeton: Princeton University Press.

Blanchot, Maurice (1981), 'Literature and the Right to Death', *The Gaze of Orpheus and Other Literary Essays*, ed. P. Adams Sitney, trans. Lydia Davis, Barrytown: Station Hill Press, 21–63.
Blanchot, Maurice (1986), *The Writing of the Disaster*, trans. Ann Smock, Lincoln: University of Nebraska Press.
Blanchot, Maurice (1992), *The Step/Not Beyond*, trans. Lycette Nelson, Albany: SUNY Press.
Blanchot, Maurice (1993), *The Infinite Conversation*, trans. Susan Hanson, Minneapolis: University of Minnesota Press.
Blanchot, Maurice (1997), *Friendship*, trans. Elizabeth Rottenberg, Stanford: Stanford University Press.
Blanchot, Maurice (2001), *Faux Pas*, trans. Charlotte Mandell, Stanford: Stanford University Press.
Blanchot, Maurice (2003), *The Book to Come*, trans. Charlotte Mandell, Stanford: Stanford University Press.
Blanchot, Maurice (2007), 'Responses and Interventions (1946–98)', trans. Michael Holland, *Paragraph*, 30:3, 5–45.
Blanchot, Maurice (2014) *Into Disaster: Chronicles of Intellectual Life, 1941*, trans. Michael Holland, New York: Fordham University Press.
Boulter, Jonathan (2001), *Interpreting Narrative in the Novels of Samuel Beckett*, Gainesville: University Press of Florida.
Boulter, Jonathan (2002), '"Wordshit, bury me": The Waste of Narrative in Samuel Beckett's *Texts for Nothing*', *Journal of Beckett Studies*, 11:2, 1–20.
Boulter, Jonathan (2004), 'Does Mourning Require a Subject? Samuel Beckett's *Texts for Nothing*', *Modern Fiction Studies*, 50:2, 332–50.
Boulter, Jonathan (2008), *Beckett: A Guide for the Perplexed*. New York: Continuum.
Boulter, Jonathan (2012), '"We have our being in justice": Samuel Beckett's *How It Is*', *Samuel Beckett and Pain*, ed. Mariko Hori Tanaka et al., New York: Rodopi, 173–200.
Brown, Llewellyn (2011), 'Voice and Pronouns in Samuel Beckett's *The Unnamable*', *Journal of Beckett Studies*, 20:2, 172–96.
Bruns, Gerald L. (1997), *Maurice Blanchot: The Refusal of Philosophy*, Baltimore: Johns Hopkins University Press.
Bruns, Gerald L. (2015), 'The Impossible Experience of Words: Blanchot, Beckett, and the Materiality of Language', *MLQ: Modern Language Quarterly*, 76:1, 76–95.
Bryden, Mary (2012), '"That or Groan": Paining and De-paining in Beckett', *Samuel Beckett and Pain*, ed. Mariko Hori Tanaka et al., New York: Rodopi, 201–17.

Buch, Robert (2010), *The Pathos of the Real: On the Aesthetics of Violence in the Twentieth Century*, Baltimore: Johns Hopkins University Press.
Butler, Judith (2009), *Frames of War: When is Life Grievable?* London: Verso.
Casanova, Pascale (2006), *Samuel Beckett: Anatomy of a Literary Revolution*, New York: Verso Press.
Celan, Paul (1990), *Collected Prose*, trans. Rosemarie Waldrop, New York: Sheep-Meadow Press.
Clément, Bruno (2006), 'What the Philosophers do with Samuel Beckett', *Beckett after Beckett*, trans. Anthony Uhlmann, ed. S. E. Gontarski and Anthony Uhlmann, Tallahassee: University Press of Florida, 116–41.
Comay, Rebecca (2011), *Mourning Sickness: Hegel and the French Revolution*, Stanford: Stanford University Press.
Cronin, Anthony (1997), *Samuel Beckett: The Last Modernist*, London: Flamingo.
Deleuze, Gilles (1994), *Difference and Repetition*, trans. Paul Patton, New York: Columbia University Press.
Deleuze, Gilles (1997), *Essays Critical and Clinical*, trans. Daniel W. Smith and Michael A. Greco, Minneapolis: University of Minnesota Press.
Deleuze, Gilles and Félix Guattari (1986), *Kafka: Toward a Minor Literature*, trans. Dana Polan, Minneapolis: University of Minnesota Press.
Deleuze, Gilles and Félix Guattari (1994), *What is Philosophy?* trans. Hugh Tomlinson and Graham Burchell, New York: Columbia University Press.
Dennis, Amanda (2015), 'Radical Indecision: Aporia as Metamorphosis in *The Unnamable*', *Journal of Beckett Studies*, 24:2, 180–97.
Dostoevsky, Fyodor (1993), *Notes from Underground*, trans. Richard Pevear and Larissa Volokhonsky, New York: Vintage Books.
Dowd, Garin (2012), 'Beckettian Pain, In the Flesh: Singularity, Community and "the Work"', *Samuel Beckett and Pain*, ed. Mariko Hori Tanaka et al., New York: Rodopi, 67–93.
Driver, Tom (1979), 'Tom Driver in "Columbia University Forum", 1961', *Samuel Beckett: The Critical Heritage*, ed. L. Graver and R. Federman, London: Routledge, 217–24.
Eagleton, Terry (2005), *Holy Terror*, New York: Oxford University Press.
Eagleton, Terry (2006a), 'Introduction', *Samuel Beckett: Anatomy of a Literary Revolution*, New York: Verso Press.

Eagleton, Terry (2006b), 'Political Beckett?' *New Left Review*, 40, 67–76.
Fifield, Peter (2013), *Late Modernist Style in Samuel Beckett and Emmanuel Levinas*, New York: Palgrave Macmillan.
Fort, Jeff (2014), *The Imperative to Write: Destitutions of the Sublime in Kafka, Blanchot, and Beckett*, New York: Fordham University Press.
Foucault, Michel (1977), 'Language to Infinity', *Language, Counter-Memory, Practice: Selected Essays and Interviews*, ed. Donald F. Bouchard, trans. Donald F. Bouchard and Sherry Simon, Ithaca: Cornell University Press, 53–67.
Foucault, Michel (1987), 'Maurice Blanchot: The Thought from Outside', *Foucault/Blanchot*, trans. Jeffrey Mehlman and Brian Massumi, New York: Zone Books, 7–61.
Fraser, Graham (2009), 'The Calligraphy of Desire: Barthes, Sade, and Beckett's *How It Is*', *Twentieth-Century Literature*, 55:1, 58–79.
Furet, François (1981), *Interpreting the French Revolution*, trans. Elborg Forster, New York: Cambridge University Press.
Fynsk, Christopher (1996a), 'Crossing the Threshold: on "Literature and the Right to Death"', *Maurice Blanchot: The Demand of Writing*, ed. Carolyn Bailey Gill, New York: Routledge.
Fynsk, Christopher (1996b), *Language and Relation: . . . that there is language*. Stanford: Stanford University Press.
Fynsk, Christopher (2013), *Last Steps: Maurice Blanchot's Exilic Writing*, New York: Fordham University Press.
Garrison, Alysia E. (2009), '"Faintly Struggling Things": Trauma, Testimony, and Inscrutable Life in Beckett's *The Unnamable*', *Samuel Beckett: History, Memory, Trauma*, ed. Séan Kennedy and Katherine Weiss, New York: Palgrave Macmillan, 89–111.
Gasché, Rodolphe (1999), *Of Minimal Things: Studies on the Notion of Relation*, Stanford: Stanford University Press.
Gasché, Rodolphe (2007), *The Honor of Thinking: Critique, Theory, Philosophy*, Stanford: Stanford University Press.
Gibson, Andrew (1999), *Postmodernity, Ethics, and the Novel: From Leavis to Levinas*, New York: Routledge.
Gibson, Andrew (2006), *Beckett and Badiou: The Pathos of Intermittency*, Oxford: Oxford University Press.
Gibson, Andrew (2010a), 'Beckett, de Gaulle and the Fourth Republic 1944–49: *L'Innommable* and *En attendant Godot*', *Limit(e) Beckett*, 1, 1–26.
Gibson, Andrew (2010b), *Samuel Beckett*, London: Reaktion.

Gontarski, S. E. (1995), 'Introduction: *From Unabandoned Works: Samuel Beckett's Short Prose*', *The Complete Short Prose: 1929–1989*, ed. S. E. Gontarski, New York: Grove Press.
Gontarski, S. E. (1996), 'Introduction: The Conjuring of Something Out of Nothing: Samuel Beckett's "Closed Space" Novels', in Samuel Beckett, *Nohow On: Company, Ill Seen Ill Said, Worstward Ho*, New York: Grove Press.
Habermas, Jürgen (1987), *The Philosophical Discourse of Modernity: Twelve Lectures*, trans. Frederick, G. Lawrence, Cambridge, MA: MIT Press.
Hägglund, Martin (2008), *Radical Atheism: Derrida and the Time of Life*, Stanford: Stanford University Press.
Hart, Kevin (2004), *The Dark Gaze: Maurice Blanchot and the Sacred*, Chicago: University of Chicago Press.
Hegel, G. W. F. (1977), *Phenomenology of Spirit*, trans. A. V. Miller, Oxford: Oxford University Press.
Hill, Leslie (1997), *Blanchot: Extreme Contemporary*, New York: Routledge.
Hill, Leslie (2010), *Radical Indecision: Barthes, Blanchot, Derrida, and the Future of Criticism*, Notre Dame: University of Notre Dame Press.
Hill, Leslie (2012), *Maurice Blanchot and Fragmentary Writing: A Change of Epoch*, New York: Continuum.
Holland, Michael (2014), 'Introduction', in Maurice Blanchot, *Desperate Clarity: Chronicles of Intellectual Life, 1942*, trans. Michael Holland, New York: Fordham University Press.
Hulle, Dirk Van and Shane Weller (2014), *The Making of Samuel Beckett's L'Innommable/The Unnamable*, New York and London: Bloomsbury.
Iser, Wolfgang (1980), *The Act of Reading: A Theory of Aesthetic Response*, Baltimore: Johns Hopkins University Press.
Israel, Nico (2015), *Spirals: The Whirled Image in Twentieth-Century Literature and Art*, New York: Columbia University Press.
Jameson, Fredric (2002), *A Singular Modernity: Essay on the Ontology of the Present*, London: Verso.
Jones, David Houston (2011), *Samuel Beckett and Testimony*, New York: Palgrave Macmillan.
Juliet, Charles (2009), *Conversations with Samuel Beckett and Bram van Velde*, trans. Tracy Cooke et al., Champaign: Dalkey Archive Press.
Katz, Daniel (1999), *Saying I No More: Subjectivity and Consciousness in the Prose of Samuel Beckett*, Evanston: Northwestern University Press.

Kennedy, Séan (2009), 'Does Beckett Studies Require a Subject? Mourning Ireland in the *Texts for Nothing*', *Samuel Beckett: History, Memory, Archive*, ed. Séan Kennedy and Katherine Weiss, New York: Palgrave Macmillan, 11–31.

Kleinberg-Levin, David (2015), *Beckett's Words: The Promise of Happiness in a Time of Mourning*, New York and London: Bloomsbury.

Knowlson, James (1996), *Damned to Fame: The Life of Samuel Beckett*, New York: Simon & Schuster.

Lacoue-Labarthe, Philippe (2007), *Heidegger and the Politics of Poetry*, trans. Jeff Fort, Urbana: University of Illinois Press.

Lacoue-Labarthe, Philippe and Jean-Luc Nancy (1988), *The Literary Absolute*, trans. Philip Barnard and Cheryl Lester, Albany: SUNY Press.

Levinas, Emmanuel (1969), *Totality and Infinity: An Essay on Exteriority*, trans. Alphonso Lingis, Pittsburgh: Duquesne University Press.

Levinas, Emmanuel (1981), *Otherwise Than Being: Or, Beyond Essence*, trans. Alphonso Lingis, Boston: M. Nijhoff.

Levinas, Emmanuel (2001), *Existence and Existents*, trans. Alphonso Lingis, Pittsburgh: Duquesne University Press.

Levinas, Emmanuel (2002), *Is It Righteous To Be?: Interviews with Emmanuel Levinas*, ed. Jill Robbins, Stanford: Stanford University Press.

Locatelli, Carla (1990), *Unwording the World: Samuel Beckett's Prose Works After the Nobel Prize*, Philadelphia: University of Pennsylvania Press.

Lyotard, Jean-François (1991), *The Inhuman: Reflection on Time*, trans. Geoffrey Bennington and Rachel Bowlby, Stanford: Stanford University Press.

Marder, Michael (2008), 'Terror of the Ethical: On Levinas's *Il y a*', *Postmodern Culture*, 18:2, Project MUSE, 5 July 2016, https://muse.jhu.edu.

Miller, Steven (2014), *War after Death: On Violence and Its Limits*, New York: Fordham University Press.

Naas, Michael (2012), *Miracle and Machine: Jacques Derrida and the Two Sources of Religion, Science, and the Media*, New York: Fordham University Press.

Nancy, Jean-Luc (2005), *The Ground of the Image*, trans. Jeff Fort, New York: Fordham University Press.

Nixon, Mark (2011), *Samuel Beckett's German Diaries: 1936–1937*, New York and London: Bloomsbury.

Passaro, Vince (1991), 'Dangerous Don DeLillo', *New York Times*, 19 May, https://www.nytimes.com/books/97/03/16/lifetimes/del-v-dangerous.html.
Perloff, Marjorie (2005), 'In Love with Hiding: Samuel Beckett's War', *The Iowa Review*, 35:1, 76–103.
Piette, Adam (2014), 'Beckett's *Ill Seen Ill Said*: Reading the Subject, Subject to Reading', *The Edinburgh Companion to Samuel Beckett and the Arts*, ed. S. E. Gontarski, Edinburgh: Edinburgh University Press, 320–3.
Piette, Adam (2016), 'Torture, Text, Human Rights: Beckett's *Comment c'est/How It Is* and the Algerian War', *Around 1945: Literature, Citizenship, Rights*, ed. Allan Hepburn, Kingston: McGill-Queen's University Press, 151–74.
Pilling, John (2014), 'Beckett/Sade: Texts for Nothing', *The Edinburgh Companion to Samuel Beckett and the Arts*, ed. S. E. Gontarski, Edinburgh: Edinburgh University Press, 117–31.
Puchner, Martin (2006), *Poetry of the Revolution: Marx, Manifestos, and the Avant-Gardes*, Princeton: Princeton University Press.
Quayson, Ato (2007), *Aesthetic Nervousness: Disability and the Crisis of Representation*, New York: Columbia University Press.
Rabaté, Jean-Michel (2010), 'Philosophizing with Beckett: Adorno and Badiou', *A Companion to Samuel Beckett*, ed. S. E. Gontarski, Oxford: Wiley-Blackwell, 97–118.
Rabaté, Jean-Michel (2012), 'Bataille, Beckett, Blanchot: From the Impossible to the Unknowing', *Journal of Beckett Studies*, 21:1, 56–64.
Rabaté, Jean-Michel (2015), 'Love and Lobsters: Beckett's Meta-Ethics', *The New Cambridge Companion to Samuel Beckett*, ed. Dirk Van Hulle, Cambridge: Cambridge University Press, 158–70.
Rabaté, Jean-Michel (2016), *Think, Pig!: Beckett at the Limit of the Human*, New York: Fordham University Press.
Rilke, Rainer Maria (2009), *Duino Elegies and the Sonnets of Orpheus*, trans. and ed. Stephen Mitchell, New York: Vintage Books.
Robespierre, Maximilien (2006), *Robespierre: Virtue and Terror*, ed. Slavoj Žižek, trans. Jean Ducange and John Howe, New York: Verso.
Rorty, Richard (1989), *Contingency, Irony, and Solidarity*, Cambridge: Cambridge University Press.
Rothberg, Michael (2000), *Traumatic Realism: The Demands of Holocaust Representation*, Minneapolis: University of Minnesota Press.

Salisbury, Laura (2012), *Samuel Beckett: Laughing Matters, Comic Timing*, Edinburgh: Edinburgh University Press.

Sapiro, Gisèle (2014), *The French Writers' War: 1940–1953*, trans. Vanessa Doriott Anderson and Dorrit Cohn, Durham, NC: Duke University Press.

Sartre, Jean-Paul (1988), *What is Literature? And Other Essays*, Cambridge, MA: Harvard University Press.

Sheehan, Paul (2001), '"Nothing is More Real": Experiencing Theory in the *Texts for Nothing*', *Journal of Beckett Studies*, 10:1–2, 89–104.

Sheehan, Paul (2002), *Modernism, Narrative, and Humanism*, Cambridge: Cambridge University Press.

Shenker, Israel (1999), 'An Interview with Beckett (1956)', *Samuel Beckett: The Critical Heritage*, ed. L. Graver and R. Federman, London: Routledge, 146–50.

Slote, Sam (2014), 'Pain Degree Zero', *The Edinburgh Companion to Samuel Beckett and the Arts*, ed. S. E. Gontarski, Edinburgh: Edinburgh University Press, 54–67.

Smith, Russell (2008), 'Bearing Witness in *How It Is*', *Samuel Beckett Today/Aujourd'hui*, 19, 351–60.

Stevens, Wallace (1989), *Opus Posthumous: Poems, Plays, Prose*, ed. Milton J. Bates, New York: Vintage Books.

Stewart, Paul (2006), *Zone of Evaporation: Samuel Beckett's Disjunctions*, New York: Rodopi.

Uhlmann, Anthony (1999), *Beckett and Poststructuralism*, Cambridge: Cambridge University Press.

Wahnich, Sophie (2012), *In Defence of the Terror: Liberty or Death in the French Revolution*, trans. David Fernbach, London: Verso.

Weber, Caroline (2003), *Terror and Its Discontents: Suspect Words in Revolutionary France*, Minneapolis: University of Minnesota Press.

Weller, Shane (2006), *Beckett, Literature, and the Ethics of Alterity*, New York: Palgrave Macmillan.

Weller, Shane (2007), 'Beckett/Blanchot: Debts, Legacies, Affinities', *Beckett's Literary Legacies*, ed. Matthew Feldman and Mark Nixon, Newcastle: Cambridge Scholars Publishing, 22–40.

Weller, Shane (2010), 'Beckett and Ethics', *A Companion to Samuel Beckett*, ed. S. E. Gontarski, Oxford: Wiley-Blackwell, 118–30.

Weller, Shane (2013), 'Post-World War Two Paris', *Samuel Beckett in Context*, ed. Anthony Uhlmann, Cambridge: Cambridge University Press, 160–73.

Wolosky, Shira (2001), 'The Lyric, History, and the Avant-Garde: Theorizing Paul Celan', *Poetics Today*, 22:3, 651–68.

Young, Robert J. C. (2010), 'Terror Effects', *Terror and the Postcolonial*, ed. Elleke Boehmer and Stephen Morton, Oxford: Wiley-Blackwell.

Ziarek, Ewa Płonowska (1995), *The Rhetoric of Failure: Deconstruction of Skepticism, Reinvention of Modernism*, Albany: SUNY Press.

Index

Abbott, H. Porter, 97, 99, 135, 238
Adelman, Gary, 236–7
Adorno, Theodor, 141, 185–6, 213, 235–6
aesthetics, 2, 8, 11, 15, 22, 24, 26–9, 34, 43–4, 53, 93, 97–8, 103–5, 107–8, 136–7, 160, 164, 179, 185–6, 189–90, 192, 194, 213, 222–3, 231, 233–7, 240
Agamben, Giorgio, 79–80, 145
All Strange Away (Beckett), 239
Allen, William S., 158
alterity, 11, 14, 17, 37, 52, 54, 120–1, 127, 133, 139–40, 142–3, 145–6, 156, 161, 163–5, 168, 170–2, 175, 179, 182–3, 202
Andress, David, 137
Antelme, Robert, 33, 47–61, 67–8, 84–5, 92, 192–3
aporia, 43, 87, 133, 211
Arendt, Hannah, 34, 144, 178, 180
Artaud, Antonin, 57–9, 91
Auschwitz, 38, 234–6, 241
autrui (other), 53–5, 58, 93, 168, 170–1, 174

Bacon, Francis, 137, 237
Baczko, Bronisław, 37
Badiou, Alain, 2–11, 14, 29, 36, 98–106, 110, 118, 137, 139–41, 222–6, 234
Bataille, Georges, 23, 27, 32, 39, 135, 137, 191
Begam, Richard, 136
Béguin, Albert, 107
Benjamin, Walter, 104, 136
Berger, John, 237
Bernini, Marco, 210
Bewes, Timothy, 234, 239

Blanchot, Maurice, 2–3, 12–18, 20–34, 36–40, 42–61, 64, 67, 81, 91–3, 99, 104, 106–10, 114, 126, 133, 135, 140, 151, 155, 157–8, 160, 164–5, 167–77, 180–1, 183, 186–94, 197, 199–200, 202, 209, 211–13, 215–17, 220–2, 226–7, 230, 232, 234–6, 240–3
body, 9, 47, 133, 141, 144, 152, 159–60, 163, 167, 169, 176, 178, 182, 210, 225, 229–31, 236
The Book to Come (Blanchot), 57–8
Boulter, Jonathan, 93, 110, 135, 137–8, 238
Brown, Llewellyn, 238
Bruns, Gerald L., 194
Bryden, Mary, 65–7
Buch, Robert, 101, 137
Butler, Judith, 34, 212–13, 215, 222

'The Calmative' (Beckett), 121
Casanova, Pascale, 33, 39
Celan, Paul, 57, 150, 186, 235–6
The Century (Badiou), 100
Clément, Bruno, 32
cogito, 8–10, 50, 57, 95, 111, 139
Comay, Rebecca, 27, 114, 126
community, 14, 25, 55, 142–3, 158, 174, 192, 197, 242
Company (Beckett), 2, 20, 34, 194–210, 223, 226, 237–9
compassion, 34, 186, 188–9, 207, 235, 237
complicity, 24, 34, 144, 157, 169, 174, 186, 207, 218, 234
concept, 2–4, 7, 10–17, 21–2, 25–7, 29, 38, 46–7, 56–7, 66, 82, 93–4, 101, 108, 110, 113, 117, 121, 126–8, 133, 138, 143–5, 160,

254

164, 174, 185, 187–9, 192–4, 219, 225, 230, 235
condemnation, 34, 60, 78, 89–91, 96, 99, 111, 118, 120–1, 128, 151, 174, 177–8, 203–4, 207, 232
consciousness, 1, 12, 38, 46–7, 68, 74–5, 79, 89, 99–100, 105, 109, 112, 118, 124, 126–7, 129, 141
criticism, 3, 13, 15–16, 23, 39, 59, 89, 99, 104, 185, 236
Cronin, Anthony, 18–19

death, 4, 7, 19–20, 25, 27–8, 43, 49, 64–5, 69–70, 73, 75–6, 80, 82, 84, 102, 109–11, 113–14, 117, 124, 129–32, 137–8, 164, 167, 170, 172–3, 193, 218–19, 225
deconstruction, 127, 183, 222
Deleuze, Gilles, 12, 36, 39, 44, 60, 93–4, 122
DeLillo, Don, 1–2, 34
Dennis, Amanda, 43
Derrida, Jacques, 92, 141
Deschevaux-Dumesnil, Suzanne, 18, 38
desire, 28, 30, 74, 85–6, 88, 98, 105, 117, 121, 125, 129, 131, 136, 141, 146, 151–3, 156, 161, 164–5, 167, 174–5, 180, 182, 191, 207, 209, 212, 215, 217, 219
destruction, 2, 5, 7, 10, 23, 25, 27, 47–8, 52, 56, 60, 62, 74, 100, 104, 106, 115, 121, 135, 137, 150, 199, 212–13, 215, 222, 227, 232
dialectics, 31, 47, 52, 57, 60, 65, 70, 80, 82, 98, 100, 118, 126, 142, 144–6, 153, 162–3, 168, 172–3, 185, 197, 227
dialogue, 12, 31, 33–4, 108, 142, 144–5, 158–9, 164, 167–8, 175–6, 178–80, 190, 201, 241–2
différance, 92
disaster, 3, 6–8, 10, 24–5, 46–7, 58, 62, 78, 132, 146, 177, 192, 199, 212, 227–8, 233, 235, 240, 242
Dowd, Garin, 66
dread, 20, 116, 181, 205
Drieu La Rochelle, Pierre, 19, 24
Driver, Tom, 184
Duthuit, Georges, 32, 239

Eagleton, Terry, 34, 39, 186
encounter, 8, 11, 15, 17, 25, 41–2, 44, 47–8, 55, 57–60, 62, 70, 75, 78–80, 82, 87, 89, 99, 112, 123, 139–41, 161–3, 167–9, 171–2, 178–81, 200, 210, 213, 225, 229
Endgame (Beckett), 139
enlightenment, 60, 235
eternal return, 10, 12, 61, 140, 143, 146, 160, 165
ethics, 14–17, 33, 37, 44, 140–1, 143, 145, 160–9, 183, 191
event, 3, 7, 9, 11, 13, 17, 23, 25, 37–8, 42, 44–5, 48, 60–1, 76, 78–9, 87, 89, 108, 111, 113, 118, 124, 130, 137, 140, 149, 158, 161–3, 168, 171, 187, 191, 194, 199–200, 204, 214, 222–4, 226, 242
exile, 18, 52–3, 60, 84, 109, 123, 126, 187–9, 192–3, 199, 203–4, 210, 215, 223, 230, 242

failure, 3, 10, 14–16, 45, 60, 75, 80–2, 84–5, 87, 96, 100, 107, 110–11, 117–18, 124, 135, 142, 148, 151–3, 203, 219, 221, 225, 232, 237
Faux Pas (Blanchot), 13, 21, 30
fiction, 1–2, 9–12, 33–4, 41, 47–8, 56, 58, 65, 69, 71, 73–7, 86–8, 97, 100–6, 109, 111, 118, 126–7, 129–31, 134–5, 139–40, 148, 158, 194, 197, 202, 204–6, 210–11, 217, 219, 222–3, 236, 238, 241
Fifield, Peter, 143, 182
finitude, 20, 46, 49, 92, 109, 111, 114–15, 117–18, 130–1, 159, 183
First World War, 100
Fort, Jeff, 13–16, 79, 210
Foucault, Michel, 27, 39, 184, 186–7, 236
fragmentary imperative, 15, 21, 25, 27, 31, 58, 61, 83, 106, 120, 132, 135, 187–8, 191, 194, 210–11, 213, 216, 218, 222, 226, 229–34, 241
Fraser, Graham, 236
French Resistance, 18, 38, 50, 103
French Revolution, 4–5, 22, 35, 108

future, 22, 30, 54, 60–1, 68, 80, 101, 105, 109, 126, 136, 147, 155, 197, 199, 201, 203, 208, 220, 223, 240, 242–3
Fynsk, Christopher, 22, 92–3, 226

Garrison, Alysia E., 135
Gasché, Rodolphe, 21, 93–4
Gibson, Andrew, 20, 35, 104–5, 137
Gontarski, S. E., 97, 99, 238
Guattari, Felix, 12, 93–4
guilt, 21, 65, 124–5, 127–8, 229

Hägglund, Martin, 92, 182
Happy Days (Beckett), 139
Hart, Kevin, 171
Hegel, G. W. F., 21–2, 102, 106–7, 111, 164–5
Heidegger, Martin, 6, 164–5
hermeneutics, 8, 15, 41–2, 45, 49, 59, 80, 89, 93, 99, 113, 128, 129, 140
Hill, Leslie, 22, 25, 59, 188
Hitler, Adolf, 5, 7, 18, 158
Holland, Michael, 24, 38
horror, 16–17, 23–4, 38–9, 45, 46, 55, 77, 88, 101, 114, 130, 137, 146, 211, 213–14, 237
hospitality, 14, 161
How It Is (Beckett), 97, 139–47, 149–51, 153, 155–60, 165–7, 169, 174–7, 179, 181–3, 194, 204, 231, 236
Hulle, Dirk Van, 39
human relation, 17, 34, 54, 140, 159–60, 165, 168–73, 175–6, 180, 183, 191
humanity, 19, 47–8, 51, 56, 64, 68, 70, 76–8, 84, 87, 89, 131, 164, 166, 169, 175, 188–9, 197, 227

Il y a ('there is'), 16–17, 21, 37–8, 82, 114, 146, 182
Ill Seen Ill Said (Beckett), 2, 20, 34, 194, 213–23, 226–7, 239
image, 44, 60–1, 63, 67, 72, 78–9, 85, 88, 93–4, 110, 115–16, 118, 124, 131, 133–4, 136, 147–8, 151–5, 160–1, 163, 173, 187, 214, 216–18, 221, 230
imagination, 23, 62, 70, 74, 83–4, 87, 103, 110, 123, 148, 203, 217, 238

Imagination Dead Imagine (Beckett), 239
immanence, 8, 10, 12–13, 36, 114, 116–17, 121, 123, 146, 154
imperative, 3, 6, 8, 10–11, 13–17, 25, 29–30, 33–4, 36–7, 46, 52–3, 59–60, 62, 69, 73, 79–80, 82, 91, 102–3, 105, 107–8, 111, 139, 141, 155, 159, 179, 181, 185, 190, 193, 211–12, 218–21, 224–6, 228, 230–1, 233–5, 240, 242
impossibility, 25, 30, 45, 49, 56–7, 61, 79–80, 102, 105, 110, 117, 120–1, 130, 136, 163, 167, 191, 193, 219, 223–4, 231, 240
infinite, 20, 47–8, 52, 54, 67, 70, 121, 131, 146, 150, 155, 161, 163, 170–2, 174, 180, 203, 208, 227, 230–1, 241
The Infinite Conversation (Blanchot), 20, 29, 33, 45, 47, 53, 55, 58, 61, 92, 106–7, 151, 155, 158, 172, 174, 187–90, 192, 202, 216, 222, 241
inhuman, 9, 27, 49–52, 65, 80, 120–2, 124–5, 131, 189, 197
injustice, 157, 169, 242
interrogation, 12, 31, 119, 128, 183, 189–90, 192, 200, 202, 218, 220
interruption, 3, 10, 22–3, 29, 121, 129, 140, 158–9, 166, 197, 199–200, 203, 213, 224–5, 232, 240
Iser, Wolfgang, 89
Israel, Nico, 94

Jones, David Houston, 78–80
Joyce, James, 105, 155
Juliet, Charles, 237
justice, 55, 141, 144–5, 147, 156, 161, 163–6, 168, 183, 242

Kafka, Franz, 13–14, 16–17, 57, 137, 236
Katz, Daniel, 91–2, 99
Kaun, Axel, 98, 104
Kennedy, Séan, 137–8
Kleinberg-Levin, David, 36, 141
knowledge, 9, 27, 46, 55–7, 60–1, 65, 69, 103, 109, 112, 115, 117, 131, 143, 150, 158, 162, 188,

193, 196–7, 202, 221–2, 225–6, 228, 230, 233, 241
Knowlson, James, 237
Krapp's Last Tape (Beckett), 139

Lacan, Jacques, 27, 101, 238
Lacoue-Labarthe, Philippe, 13, 36, 104, 107
language, 1–3, 9, 12, 15, 17, 21, 25–8, 33–4, 38–9, 42–3, 47–8, 52, 61, 64–6, 89–90, 92, 94, 98, 105–6, 108–14, 117–22, 126–8, 131, 133, 138, 141–2, 144–6, 150–1, 155–61, 163–6, 169–77, 179–82, 184–5, 187–94, 197, 210–11, 215, 217, 221–2, 225–37, 240, 242
law, 14, 29–30, 35, 47–8, 60–1, 105, 108, 118–19, 134–6, 149, 152–4, 170, 188, 190–1, 223, 240, 242
Lefebvre, Henri, 107
Levi, Primo, 145
Levinas, Immanuel, 16–17, 33, 37–8, 53, 93, 118, 130, 141, 160–70, 182–3, 190
literature, 1–3, 7–18, 20–32, 34, 36–9, 42–3, 45–7, 49, 60–2, 65–7, 89, 91, 93–4, 97–8, 100, 103–11, 119, 126–7, 131–4, 136, 140–1, 144–5, 155–6, 164–5, 169, 174–5, 181–2, 185–8, 192, 194, 197, 207–8, 210–11, 213, 219, 222, 225–6, 230–1, 233–5, 239, 241–3
'Literature and the Right to Death' (Blanchot), 21–2, 25, 67, 109, 126
Locatelli, Carla, 143, 211, 232
The Lost Ones (Beckett), 80, 239
Lottman, Herbert, 20
love, 77, 156, 159
Lukács, Georg, 107
Lyotard, Jean-François, 138

MacGreevy, Thomas, 19–20
Mallarmé, Stéphane, 11, 57, 104, 225
Mallet, Robert, 32–3
Manifesto for Philosophy (Badiou), 5, 36
Marder, Michael, 182
metaphysics, 61, 65, 69
Metapolitics (Badiou), 4

modernism, 97, 186
modernity, 4, 12, 22, 31, 35–6, 102, 106, 108, 136, 165, 186, 197, 240
Molloy (Beckett), 32, 39
mourning, 19, 75–6, 138, 215

Naas, Michael, 34
Nadeau, Maurice, 23, 32
Nancy, Jean-Luc, 104, 107, 143–4, 149, 152–3
narrative, 1–2, 9–10, 12, 33, 35, 41–53, 55, 58–76, 78–80, 82, 85–90, 94, 96–100, 106, 109, 111–28, 130–4, 139–45, 149–51, 153, 155, 157–9, 166, 168–9, 175–7, 179, 181–2, 192, 195, 198–200, 202–6, 208–11, 214–20, 224–5, 228, 231, 235, 238–41
narrative voice, 8, 16, 33, 41–4, 49, 53, 59–62, 64–7, 71, 88–9, 92, 99, 106, 110–11, 113–14, 117–18, 120, 130, 132, 140, 158, 165, 178, 202
Nazism, 18–20, 23–4, 38, 50, 55, 78, 103–4, 107
need, 53–5, 85–6, 165, 193
Negative Dialectics (Adorno), 52, 185
negativity, 7, 13, 15, 27, 47, 49, 57, 65, 89, 98, 109, 118–20, 122, 124, 132, 172, 185–6, 227, 230
neuter, 39, 42
neutral/neutered speech, 31, 42, 48–9, 106, 173, 227
Nietzsche, Friedrich, 6, 56
nihilism, 2, 5, 7, 10, 37, 56–8, 98–9, 104, 106, 185–6, 223–4
Nixon, Mark, 103
nothingness, 7, 13–14, 27, 37, 42, 84, 98–9, 105, 109, 118, 125, 133–5, 203, 211, 227, 237

obligation, 13, 46, 53–5, 105, 124–5, 177, 183, 191, 229
ontology, 78, 116, 128, 130, 161, 168, 212, 223, 239

pain, 34, 57, 64–7, 85, 140, 225, 229, 235, 242
parataxis, 141–3, 145–6, 152–8, 167, 173–5, 178–83, 211

passivity, 34, 84, 189–201, 203, 207–13, 215–19, 221–3, 225–32, 234–5
Paulhan, Jean, 21–2, 25–7
pedagogy, 77, 142, 177, 185, 235
Perloff, Marjorie, 18
Péron, Alfred, 18–19
phenomenology, 46, 183
philosophy, 3–4, 6–8, 12, 14–15, 17, 22, 36, 46–7, 53–4, 56–7, 59, 61, 64, 80, 93–4, 98, 100, 105, 122, 127, 133, 151, 160–1, 163–6, 182, 185, 187, 222–3, 232, 238, 240
Piette, Adam, 183, 239
Pilling, John, 135
poetics, 2–3, 11, 59, 97, 107, 111, 121–2, 136, 140, 182, 224
poetry, 225, 236
politics, 3–8, 11–13, 19, 21–4, 27–9, 33, 35–9, 100–1, 103, 105–9, 133, 136–8, 144, 163, 165, 168–9, 185, 187, 232, 234–5
postmodernism, 97, 136
presence, 6, 16, 42, 51–6, 74–5, 79, 85, 87, 91, 103, 106, 111–13, 119, 121–3, 127, 129, 133, 140, 143, 147, 153–4, 158–60, 162, 164, 168–74, 177, 179, 181–2, 185, 193, 195–9, 201–2, 205, 214–27, 229–30, 232
Puchner, Martin, 136

Quayson, Ato, 67

Rabaté, Jean-Michel, 39, 141, 186
reality, 4, 26, 36, 47, 65, 101–2, 110–11, 113, 115, 121, 149–50, 163, 175, 219
redemption, 2, 13, 36, 46, 56, 66, 69, 110, 122, 125, 151, 181, 185, 210, 234
repetition, 3, 96, 147
resistance, 23, 25, 47, 49, 59, 119, 142–6, 148, 160–3, 165, 181, 186
responsibility, 3, 13–14, 17, 23, 28, 43, 45, 55, 80, 88–9, 124–5, 129, 152, 156–8, 164, 168, 185, 188–91, 197, 206–10, 213, 219, 229, 233, 236, 240–1
Robespierre, Maximilien, 4–5, 7, 19, 23, 29, 36–7, 108, 137

romanticism, 22, 29, 104, 107–8
Rosset, Barney, 3, 96, 147
Rothberg, Michael, 185, 235
ruins, 19, 62, 101, 103, 135, 150, 219

sacred, 2, 6–7, 34, 36, 171–2, 192, 241
sacrifice, 5, 25, 57, 105, 109, 157, 213, 234, 241
Sade, Marquis de, 21–2, 27–32, 37, 57, 107–8, 135
Sapiro, Gisèle, 23
Sartre, Jean-Paul, 27, 37–8
Second World War, 18, 20–1, 24–5, 38, 48, 103, 141, 185, 241
shame, 37, 79–80, 217, 227, 234–5, 239
Sheehan, Paul, 66, 97–9
Shenker, Israel, 3, 20, 96
silence, 8–10, 17, 25, 38, 43, 53, 64–6, 84, 88–9, 91, 97–8, 118, 128, 131, 133–4, 138, 140, 147, 150, 154–5, 157–9, 174, 177, 179–80, 188–90, 192, 198, 200, 203, 206–7, 211, 213–14, 224, 226, 228, 232, 242
Slote, Sam, 66
Smith, Russell, 145, 179
Socrates, 64–5
solipsism, 8, 10–12, 16, 122, 139–41, 148, 169, 177
solitude, 69, 73, 76, 121, 138, 147–8, 154
sovereignty, 4, 14–16, 35, 91, 98, 109–10, 131, 152, 156, 158, 162, 164, 176–7, 187, 193
space (of literature), 2, 7–8, 12–14, 16, 25, 29, 60–2, 65–6, 108, 127, 145, 169, 185, 188, 192, 211, 219, 222, 230, 234, 242
Stalinism, 6
Stein, Gertrude, 105
The Step/Not Beyond (Blanchot), 135, 187
Stewart, Paul, 81
subject, 8–10, 12, 16, 31, 38, 43, 46–8, 50, 53–5, 61, 67–9, 74–6, 84, 96, 109–10, 113, 116, 118–19, 122–7, 130–1, 133, 137–9, 142, 146, 149, 154, 158, 161, 166, 168–9, 178–80, 185, 191–4, 201, 207–9, 212, 223–4, 231, 238–9

subjectivity, 8, 20, 33, 38, 42–3, 45–50, 52–5, 57, 59, 61–2, 64, 68–9, 71–2, 74–6, 79–80, 82, 84, 87–8, 92, 96, 98–9, 109–10, 112–14, 116–19, 121–4, 126–8, 130–4, 158, 160–1, 169, 189, 192–4, 197, 202, 205, 207–8, 212–13, 226–7, 238–9
subtraction, 5, 16, 46, 72, 106, 118, 223, 225, 232
suffering, 19, 28, 33–4, 43–76, 78, 80–91, 93–4, 117, 128, 137, 145, 181, 185–6, 188, 191–4, 197–8, 203, 207–8, 213, 235, 237, 242

temporality, 46, 61, 64, 68–9, 92, 113–15, 117, 126–7, 176, 181–2, 239
testimony, 34, 62, 73, 75, 78–80
Texts for Nothing (Beckett), 2–3, 8, 10–11, 16–17, 20, 33, 71, 96–100, 106–7, 109–23, 125–35, 137, 139–41, 157, 207
Thermidor(ian), 4–5, 7, 10, 35, 37, 108, 137
thinking, 2–8, 10, 17, 21, 24, 32–3, 44, 46–7, 56–62, 66, 74–5, 80, 82–4, 88–91, 93–6, 99, 103, 105, 109, 122–3, 126, 128–9, 133, 151, 155, 165, 185–7, 217, 225, 235, 241
'Three Dialogues with Georges Duthuit' (Beckett), 53
torture, 8, 12, 28, 43, 48, 52–4, 65, 71, 140, 142, 145, 156, 177–8, 183, 189–90, 192, 198, 200, 203, 205–6, 210, 212, 236
transcendence, 10, 12–13, 15, 56–7, 82, 118, 130, 136, 146, 160–4, 166, 168, 170–1, 173
transgression, 2, 25, 80, 99, 136, 188, 192, 208

trauma, 11, 13, 43–4, 62, 72, 76–7, 79, 109, 111, 118, 126–7, 138, 141, 149, 211–12, 215, 242

Uhlmann, Anthony, 87
The Unnamable (Beckett), 2–3, 8–12, 16–17, 20, 32–3, 39, 41–5, 49, 52–3, 59–67, 72, 78–81, 85, 87–9, 91–100, 110–11, 117, 129, 133, 135–6, 139–41, 157, 194, 198, 208

violence, 2, 4, 6, 8, 13, 19–20, 22, 28–9, 33–5, 44, 48, 50–2, 54, 61, 64–5, 74, 83–4, 91, 100, 106–8, 126, 133, 137, 140, 142–6, 149–55, 158–76, 178–81, 186, 188–92, 198, 203–8, 210–13, 231, 233–9, 242–3
voice, 8–10, 16–17, 20, 39, 41–3, 52–3, 64–5, 67, 70, 74, 83, 85, 91, 96–7, 109–35, 141, 148–60, 166–7, 175–83, 185, 187–9, 192

Wahnich, Sophie, 35
Weber, Caroline, 28
Weller, Shane, 16–17, 19, 37, 39
What Where (Beckett), 203
witness, 41, 75, 79–80, 93, 145, 199, 240
Wolosky, Shira, 235
Worstward Ho (Beckett), 2, 20, 34, 194, 197, 222–3, 235, 243
The Writing of the Disaster (Blanchot), 30, 47, 57, 67, 187–90, 192–4, 200, 212, 222, 226, 234–5, 240

Young, Robert J. C., 11–12, 21

Ziarek, Ewa, 141–3, 145, 179

EU representative:
Easy Access System Europe
Mustamäe tee 50, 10621 Tallinn, Estonia
Gpsr.requests@easproject.com

www.ingramcontent.com/pod-product-compliance
Lightning Source LLC
Chambersburg PA
CBHW062126300426
44115CB00012BA/1833